"Written by a young mother herself, Leigh's book will help families newly grappling with the diagnosis of autism with wise, honest, and helpful advice."

—Susan Senator, author of *Autism Adulthood: Insights and Creative Strategies for a Fulfilling Life*

"*The Scenic Route* is a must-read guide for families who have a child with autism who remains nonverbal with severe behavior problems. Lots of good practical and down-to-earth advice."

—Temple Grandin, author of *Thinking in Pictures*

" 'A sense of humor and a sense of wonder can get you far,' says Leigh Merryday Porch, in her moving and beautifully written book *The Scenic Route*. Warm, reassuring, and candid about her own wrong turns and detours, Porch is a gifted storyteller. She deftly weaves personal narrative with practical guidance in this realistic yet often humorous road map to navigating the struggles and joys of raising an autistic child. Eloquent and instructive, *The Scenic Route* is must-reading for every parent and professional working with autistic children."

—Liane Kupferberg Carter, author of *Ketchup Is My Favorite Vegetable: A Family Grows Up with Autism*

"The book is such a beautiful expression of the author's love for her kids—and an unflinching depiction of every aspect of the experience. So much vital information and advice along with so much heart. Its narrative voice is perfect—reading it feels like sitting down for a long cup of coffee (or wine) with a good friend you turn to for advice, hugs, pep talks, tough love, and shared laughter and tears. A must-read for any parent starting out on the journey; for moms like me who have been on this road for almost twenty years; and for the families, friends, and teachers who touch our kids' lives along the way."

—Nancy Burrows, coauthor of *Chicken Soup for the Soul: Raising Kids on the Spectrum*

"If you have a child with autism, *The Scenic Route* is like a sit-down with an utterly pragmatic and empathetic fellow parent who's already been there and faced all the same bewildering questions. It's candid, thoughtful, and truly helpful."

—Paul Collins, author of *Not Even Wrong: Adventures in Autism*

"It's no surprise that a former librarian has written *What to Expect When You're Expecting: The Autism Version*. Leigh's insights are poignant and thoughtful, her focus on preparing the child for the village, as well as the village for the child. A must-read for anyone interested in advocacy."

—Jeni Decker, author of *I Wish I Were Engulfed in Flames*

"Leigh has a talent for sharing her experiences both as a mother of a child with autism and as a professional in the field with a perfect balance of vulnerability and wisdom. *The Scenic Route* is compelling and relatable as a memoir but also as a guide to less obvious dynamics, issues, and culture of raising a child on the autism spectrum within family and community systems. A wonderful read regardless of where you might be with your child's diagnosis."

—Jodi Collins, LCSW, presenter, two-time TEDx speaker on autism (and autism parent)

The Scenic Route

*Embracing the Detours,
Roadblocks, and Unexpected Joys
of Raising an Autistic Child*

Leigh Merryday Porch

A TarcherPerigee Book

tarcherperigee

an imprint of Penguin Random House LLC
penguinrandomhouse.com

Most TarcherPerigee books are available at special quantity discounts for bulk
purchase for sales promotions, premiums, fund-raising, and educational needs.
Special books or book excerpts also can be created to fit specific needs.
For details, write: SpecialMarkets@penguinrandomhouse.com.

Hardcover ISBN: 9780593328729
Ebook ISBN: 9780593328736

Printed in the United States of America
10 9 8 7 6 5 4 3 2 1

Book design by Laura K. Corless

For Bronwyn and Callum:

I once had dreams of you both, and you've surpassed them all.
I hope I found the right words, my punkins.

And for Daddy:

The standard by which I've judged all men.

Contents

Off-Roading

Other Passengers

Recalibrating

On the Unreliability of Navigational Tools

One of the Four Great Inventions of ancient China, the compass, operates on a simple principle—its needle aligns with the earth's magnetic field and points to magnetic north. Once we know where north is, we can calculate the other directions and navigate to our desired destinations.

But it's all based on the premise that we've already established where we're going.

RAISING a child to adulthood is a little like this.

Whether new parents think about it or not, we, regardless of our culture or walk of life, have a magnetic north established from go. Rich, poor, religious or not, liberal or conservative, in ancient times or modern, parental north is always the same. Always. When we're finished raising them, we want them to be able to fend for themselves when we're gone.

Parents may envision different dreams for their children. Some may impose their own dreams—pushing their offspring toward medicine, entertainment, or the trades of their parents. But even for a mother who wants her son to become a priest and he doesn't, the priesthood is not his mother's true parental north. Self-sufficiency is.

If they lack shelter, food, or community, their lives will be reduced to little more than survival. And those merely surviving will never have what life is really all about: meaning and satisfaction.

So, we teach them how to live without us. For almost every mammal whose young are born helpless, that's north. That's the destination.

But what happens when you have a child whose ability to fend for themselves is in question? What's a parent to do if their parental compass doesn't point north? What's the new destination? Where is the detour taking us? And without a functioning compass, how do we get back on the highway to join the others?

THERE'S something about magnetic north and the invention of the compass that's unknown to most. Yes, the ancient Chinese invented it, but its original purpose wasn't navigation—it was *divination*. Divination is the human attempt to derive applicable meaning from seemingly unrelated aspects of life. Their compasses weren't expected to point toward a destination. They were designed to guide them in decisions based on their current circumstances—with the intent of providing happier and more meaningful lives.

And, if you really think about it, that's what every parent ultimately wants for their child. Happiness. Meaning. Because in the end, it's not about how great our lives were, but whether or not we loved living them. It's cliché, but life really is all about the journey, not the destination.

LIKE most parents, I began my journey guided by the standard magnetic north: to teach my child how to live after I was gone. So I pulled onto the interstate, mindful of the rules, the signs, and intent on reaching my instinctual destination. But shortly after loading up the car and taking off, the itinerary changed—*dramatically*. Our son, now twelve, was born with high-needs autism *and* is profoundly intellectually disabled, so he wasn't meeting expected milestones. Our compass, suddenly, didn't point north anymore, and our GPS directed us off the highway.

We found ourselves on the scenic route—traveling unfamiliar roads, taking questionable detours, getting lost, arguing about where to turn, and meeting interesting characters.

HERE'S the thing about scenic routes: They take longer. They involve a lot of planning. They require a lot of patience when those plans go awry. They can be costly. The roads are bumpier, and everyone you meet has a different suggestion for where you should go and how you should get there.

And here's the other thing about the scenic route: it's not a lesser journey.

It's merely a different one. It's one where you learn to appreciate the view more than the map and to savor where you *are* more than where you were hoping to be by now. Of course, it will involve frustrations, but a sense of humor and a sense of wonder can get you far.

AT some point in your parenting of a disabled child, you will likely read "Welcome to Holland," a famous essay by Emily Perl Kingsley, the mother of a child with Down syndrome. It compares parenting a disabled child to buying a ticket for Italy and landing in Holland instead. While the mother didn't get to see the antiquities and art of Italy as she'd dreamed, she learned to appreciate the tulips and windmills of Holland. The essay is written out of love for her child, and it has been shared with parents of children with many disabilities all across the world.

But for me, the metaphor is problematic. Because children with disabilities don't live in another world where everything is equally lovely. They live in *this* world—a world not designed for or terribly accommodating to them. In other words, the world is not all tulips and windmills. There are genuine challenges to overcome and needs to be understood, accepted, and accommodated. Also, it's not healthy for a parent to forever mourn *a living child* while wistfully missing the one who never existed.

The problem in inspirational essays like this is the onus they place on the disabled person to enlighten and make able-bodied people better, as though doing so is their sole purpose for living.

It's not. A disabled person's purpose for living is the same as for all people: to laugh, play, love, learn, create, give, and grow. As parents, our job is to make opportunities for those as accessible for our children as is possible.

That's our truest magnetic north.

Analogies aren't perfect, of course, and neither are we. But reducing the challenges of raising children with disabilities to flowery reframes is misleading. For scenic routes are rarely as efficient as interstates.

YET meandering paths do lead to unexpected gems—like the scenery you may have zipped right past otherwise and never noticed. You can stop at elevation points on the scenic route—where you can see how far you've come and look out at where you aspire to go. Scenic routes are less about making good time and more about time spent now. Learning how to pause and appreciate the beauty of what you have in the moment creates the snapshots you'll put in your album. Those are the truly important shots.

You get to meet friendly strangers getting out of their station wagons on the scenic route. Sometimes they'll offer to take your family's picture, and you can return the favor. You'll swap stories about your journeys and provide roadside diner recommendations.

It's a hell of a view from here, too.

WHETHER you're an established scenic router or just beginning your own parenting journey—or are a loved one or professional seeking to support them—this book contains everything I've learned so far about taking the scenic route when raising a profoundly autistic child. I've tried to think of all the detour notifications I wish I'd known about when I got in the car years ago.

So, roll down the windows. Turn up the music. Sing along badly. Keep an eye out for—but don't trust all—directional signs, and savor every moment with your traveling companions and *especially* your tour guide.

Safe travels.

On the Virtues of "Identity-First" Language

can't talk about anything with regard to my child or autism without talking about terminology first. (It's not a terribly exciting start, I know. But it's important in navigating this community.) The autism community is part of the greater disability community, and both are at all times cognizant of the words used to describe themselves and others.

And they're not all in agreement.

I'm going to go so far as to speculate that it would be difficult to write a single sentence about disability that wouldn't offend someone. I get it. Sometimes we humans can be too sensitive and lose our senses of humor altogether. Those of us reaching the midpoint of life or beyond sometimes get overwhelmed at keeping up with it. But when it comes to people, we should always aim to do better, even if better doesn't always come naturally. You can learn. And it will make you a more respected and valued member of the disability community if you take the time to check or respectfully ask.

I'm starting here with "autistic," although I discuss other terminology later. But this is the one most likely to alter your perspective and prevent you from embarrassing yourself. Brace yourselves (especially if you're an education- or social work–type professional).

"Autistic" is not a bad word.

This is hard, I know. You may have been trained to speak in "person-first" language. (That means you always place the person before the condition in the sentence. Hence, "child with autism" versus "autistic child.") It might even be in the employee manual at your workplace. But before you get ready to write me with a condescending explanation of how disrespectful it is to emphasize a condition before a person . . . blah blah . . . hear me out.

Autistic describes the state of being autistic. Person-first language proponents will argue saying "autistic person" somehow reduces the personhood of the individual described. Which, on the surface, seems like a terrible thing, no? It's not appropriate to say "The paralyzed man voted for _____ for Supervisor of Elections." Why? Well, it's doubtful that paralysis formed this man's opinion of the candidate, provided polling stations had accessible entrances and other accommodations. He probably doesn't feel too different about elections now than before he was hurt in an accident. Being paralyzed, though certainly a traumatic and life-changing event, didn't form his personality, values, or faith. The paralysis doesn't extend to his mind. And you'd still be you without your big toe.

Autism is not the same way at all. Autism involves atypical neurology in the brain. It's not the only filter by which a child experiences the world, but it's hella significant. It's a condition that's all about perception, thought, expression. To deny that autism shapes not just some experiences but all experiences is to deny the person that respect. It's a different way of seeing, experiencing, and interacting with the world. And autistic advocates the world over generally prefer to self-identify as "autistic," saying, "It's an inseparable part of me and my identity. I am autistic. I'm not a typical person who 'just happens' to 'have autism.'" (Reminiscent of "having lice," isn't it?)

After a decade spent in parts of the autism community, I can tell you that precisely none of them enjoy witnessing a social worker, psychologist, or school staffing specialist *correct* what an autistic person prefers to call themselves. That's a *big* no-no, a great disrespect, and . . . just don't do it. It's perfectly okay and respectful to ask their preference in terminology. It's also perfectly okay if you wish to stick with your training and use person-first language until the manual is officially changed. But it is not your job to lecture anyone else on how they refer to their autistic children or how they refer to themselves.

As a teacher, I've had that training, too. I've heard all the impassioned reasons and used it with gusto myself. But it should never trump what a person wishes to call themselves. And to what end? You've chided them, condescended to them about something they've been condescended to dozens of times, and you've shown your ignorance of the autism community itself. That's not a good start to your relationship.

A long time ago, I was made to see autism differently, and I made the conscious decision to use mostly "autistic" in my descriptions. Occasionally, for want of variety, I might say "people with autism," but it's just a word flow thing and not a statement. Officially, I'm pro-"autistic." It's deliberate. I know the arguments for person-first language. I'm also aware that the view of person-first language in the autism community isn't the view of the entire disability community. Tread carefully and ask, or do some research. Person-first isn't preferred in the self-advocate autism community, but it is in other disability communities. I don't pretend to know what to tell you if your child winds up in both, but to do the best you can respectfully.

If you're a professional, and a parent in an IEP—individualized education plan—keeps using person-first language, follow their lead. If a fifteen-year-old calls herself "an Aspie," let her. And use it yourself with them. (It's kind of an affectionate term of pride those with Asperger's sometimes call themselves. It's also fine for the people who love them.)

As for what you teach your own child, I'll always be an advocate for truth. The autism-identity argument is valid. And it's not really any kind of hassle to be considerate. Although many fully subscribe to the autism-identity reasoning, neither I nor most people are going to be offended by whichever you choose.

They just don't want the insult of those who can't possibly know disregarding the experience of those who do. And I think we'd be hard-pressed to find a time in history when doing so has turned out well.

Detours

The three things I cannot change are the past, the truth, and you.

—Anne Lamott, *Help, Thanks, Wow: The Three Essential Prayers*

Chapter 1

I Heard It Before I Saw It: On the Moment I Knew

heard it before I saw it. That seems a strange way to describe the moment I knew my son was autistic, but it's true. Callum was a baby, just a little over a year old. That year I taught middle school language arts classes in addition to being the school librarian. And I was propped up on the couch entering grades, having just graded a set of essays. Callum was sitting on the living room rug in front of me, watching *Yo Gabba Gabba!* I could just see the back of his head over my laptop screen. And that's when I heard it. The slightest whipping of air—just enough to make me look over.

There was my beautiful, sweet baby boy flapping away excitedly at the screen.

Most people probably wouldn't have thought much of it. It might have been many more months or years before the word "autism" came to mind, except that we have autists in our family. And I knew that sound. I knew that flapping. Yes, lots of babies will flap their arms excitedly for a moment or two. But autistic flapping, once you've become acquainted with it, is unmistakable.

You'll recognize it every time you see it. At the grocery store, in restaurants, at barbecues. It's one of the "red flags" that indicate autism in young children. And there in front of me, my baby was flapping away.

People will sometimes describe moments when the walls close in and they experience something through a tunnel. Tunnel vision perfectly describes what happened. I didn't hear or see anything else in the house. Instead, I had a laser focus on the baby boy in front of me, and my heart began pounding. I'm sure I was holding my breath when I called out his name. Only he didn't turn around to look.

As a blogger, advocate, and consultant, I've heard hundreds of stories of how families came to understand their children's autism diagnoses. In our own family, I'd seen diagnosis gradually unfold over a few years. Usually, that's how it goes.

According to the Centers for Disease Control, most autistic children are diagnosed after four. Parents will describe signs they came to gradually realize or had pointed out to them by professionals or family. Sometimes, they have to be made to see. Sometimes they refuse to open their eyes.

But I knew instantly. In our family, we'd seen the more severe variety more than once, and the sudden certainty of autism hit me like a truck. I didn't suspect—I *knew*. I didn't know to what degree he might be affected. I knew we wouldn't be able to make predictions for several years. But down to my bones, I knew he was autistic.

There are some moments in life etched permanently in memory. Every sound, sight, and scent. That's one I've never forgotten. And for me, life divided into two parts—before that afternoon with my baby flapping away on a rug. And after.

In the autism community, it's controversial for a parent to admit to mourning an autism diagnosis in a child. More than a decade later, I understand the reasons why. I've met intelligent, kind, witty, intuitive, and helpful autistic adults—who most definitely do *not* wish their existence to be mourned. And I've also met autistic adults requiring substantial living supports who also enjoy their lives—lives that have value.

But I'm not going to lie. That day I mourned, and I mourned hard. My father took my first call. My daddy, a lawyer, was the listening type. He respected me enough to not dismiss my concerns. But he was also familiar with autism, and he believed that Callum was "too social" to be "severe"—*if* he had it. The autism he had seen before in very young children seemed to him like the child "wasn't in the room with everyone else." And Callum, my father insisted, was "in the room with us." But, in the way Daddy always had, his words calmed me down—a little.

Unfortunately, my father's belief that autistic children weren't overly social was based on a stereotype. It can be true, but some autists love being with people. Callum was too excited that afternoon about the Gabba gang to respond to me calling his name. But he usually was a very smiley, snuggly, interactive baby. He *did* make eye contact, which my dad mistakenly took as a sign that maybe I was overreacting. (Eye contact can also be a misleading sign when evaluating a child for autism. Some autistic people have no trouble with it or can "mask." In contrast, others can handle it in a regular, limited, or atypical fashion.)

Sean, my husband, wasn't even marginally convinced. But he hadn't known anyone personally with autism. The other minor delays and differences we had laughingly chalked up to Callum being "laid back" also didn't concern him. When he looked at Callum, he saw a typical baby. Years later, Sean would admit that his own experiences with ADHD and reading problems probably made him resistant to any diagnosis for his son. He didn't *want* him to struggle, so he couldn't allow himself to consider it. I forget where he went that evening, but I remember being alone with my thoughts when I panicked. I'm not much of a crier. But I called my friend Sandy in hysterics. She's a great listener, and she just let me get it out and soothingly talked me down until I could go to bed. But my mind wasn't finished with me, and I woke in the middle of the night. And with no one there to argue with me, my instincts screamed. And I did something I had not ever *genuinely* done before—despite being a child of the Bible Belt. I got down on my knees in the dark. Sobbing hysterically, I *begged* a God I hadn't fully come to terms with. That begging was specific.

Give me anything. Any condition at all. But take this away from my son.

I knew it didn't work that way. But I don't believe I've met many avowed atheists or agnostics who wouldn't resort to prayer when terrified for a beloved child.

Years later, I'm glad that prayer wasn't answered. Because there are far worse things in this world than autism. Things like apathy, cruelty, and exclusivity. But I didn't understand that yet. Eventually, Sean woke to my crying and tried his best to convince me I was worrying about nothing. But my understanding of my son's autism was sudden and absolute.

The funny thing is, I cried it all out in one night. And I've never once cried about it again. I've gotten tearful over accomplishments and sweet moments. I've worried. But I never cried again. Crying is cathartic, but it rarely accomplishes much else. When I woke the following day, I began a list of phone calls to make, a list of therapies to arrange, a list of assessments to schedule, and a list of what I needed to learn. I stared into the mirror before school and panicked, wondering what I would say to coworkers and students. I had cried so long and hard that my eyes were as swollen as a prizefighter's. Not yet ready to "put a label on him," I wasn't prepared to discuss my fears with the world. So, I lied and told my administrators and everyone who openly stared at my face that day that I had had an allergic reaction to shellfish. I even concocted a story about going to Urgent Care for a shot of epinephrine. I smiled and listened to other severe allergy tales throughout that day and never let on what was really going on. It took three days for the swelling to go down.

But I could not forget the sight of Callum flapping on that rug. And I was haunted by the realization that my baby bird's atypical flapping meant he might never be able to fly on his own.

Chapter 2

I Wasn't Crazy:
On Finding Help and Support

My daughter Bronwyn arrived in the world screaming and kept at it for nearly an hour. She was such a terrific screamer that the nurses remarked upon it and made jokes I'd have my "hands full with her." They weren't wrong. Yes, my girl entered this life opinionated and loud—traits that both inspire and exhaust me.

Just twenty months later, Callum was born. And when the midwife handed him to me, he didn't cry at all. He just looked at me. Yes, I know newborns aren't supposed to see far and can't focus on a person's eyes, blah blah. But I have witnesses. And I'm telling you all that baby did was look back at me with my father's eyes. The nurses were concerned and started turning him over, trying to get a good cry, but he just wouldn't do more than mildly fuss at the mistreatment. He pinked right up and did all the other things he was supposed to do, including breathing. But my boy came into this world a profound observer of it, and that's that.

My father was like that, too. And because Callum was born looking just like him and had his easygoing temperament, we attributed minor delays to him being like his grandpa. We even teased my dad about it. (Interestingly, according to my grandmother, my daddy didn't talk until he was three.) But even though Callum still favors him, and I find their temperaments and mannerisms similar, it wasn't merely their shared easygoing nature.

Callum was a smiley baby. Always delighted to be with people, with gummy smiles and cooing. And he was a charmer. He loved to be snuggled, loved touching people, and made deep eye contact with anyone who spoke to him. We joked a lot about him being so mellow, he was lazy. But, of course, now that I've had formal training in autism and child development, that expression would have perked up my ears. Because *babies aren't lazy*.

Ellen DeGeneres once did an amusing bit in one of her stand-ups about how utterly delighted babies are to take their first steps. She then hilariously compared it to how annoyed adults are at having to walk across a room to get something. It's funny, but it's true. Babies *want* to explore their worlds even before they're any good at moving about safely in them. But Callum was simply content to sit in a bouncy seat or on a lap or play mat. He rolled over, but he did it a month or two later than most. Sitting up was barely within the developmental window, but Callum wasn't proficient at it. He'd topple over at times when we should have expected him to be steady. My mother-in-law remembers taking him for his first birthday pictures as a surprise for us. But she recalls having to slip her hand behind him to keep him steady while sitting up for photos.

But he was also doing something else by then that should have set off alarms. Even though he wasn't sitting up perfectly yet, he *was* getting about. *But he never crawled.*

Callum walked on his knees.

Now, *that* I noticed. But when I went to research it, I mistook what I read as indicating it was okay. For some babies *do* crawl a little differently. Some scoot, using their arms to slide themselves sitting up across the floor. Some use both arms and a leg. Some "army crawl" on their bellies. I read the descriptions of different ways babies crawled and decided it was okay. However, I failed to notice what those babies were doing that Callum wasn't.

They were using all four limbs.

That distinction turns out to be not a minor one. Because it's in using all four limbs that babies "pattern," something that impacts their strength, motor skills, and cognitive development. Callum's knee walking wasn't cute or quirky. It was an early sign his brain was wired differently, and we missed it. It wasn't until he approached fifteen months and wasn't walking that we became concerned. Not overly worried because he was still within the "normal" window for not walking, albeit reaching the end of that window. But it was one more difference on top of other differences, and we requested a physical therapy consult. We went once. The therapist made a plan, and he walked a week later before we even carried out the next appointment. So, we canceled it and thought everything would be okay—until that day on the rug when he began flapping those arms.

THE day Callum turned eighteen months old, I scheduled him for a visit based on developmental concerns. His regular doctor in the pediatric practice was on vacation, so we saw another doctor we'd visited a few times before. Their offices are bright, colorful, and encourage play. But the exam rooms themselves are relatively empty, save for a box of toys on the floor. They're really the only thing in the room to look at, which makes sense. So when the doctor entered, Callum was on the floor in front of the toy box, holding a truck. And, being his little smiley self, he turned and gave the doctor a megawatt Callum grin. So the doctor said he wasn't worried about autism.

Looking back, I can tell you the things the doctor missed. He didn't notice that Callum wasn't pushing the truck. He had it flipped over and was spinning one wheel. That's the thing about toys: well-designed ones don't require an adult to explain. Neurotypical children will know what to do with them. But a child playing with toys in ways they weren't designed is showing signs. And although he made eye contact, I can tell you that it was either fleeting or intense, and only if *he* wanted to. His eye contact *was* atypical, and a practiced eye would have spotted it.

But that doctor is a dear man, and he was a good doctor. Until he retired recently, we still saw him on occasion when our regular doctor was out. This was more than a decade ago, and I don't believe pediatricians were as well-versed then in picking up early indicators of autism. Especially in smiley toddlers who will tell you what sound a lion makes—if requested and by rote. I know the doctor thought he was fine and that I was worried about the family history of autism unnecessarily. (At that time, it was still often said that it didn't run in families.) However, he did give me a referral to Florida's Early Steps program for a free developmental assessment and sent us on our way.

The very next day, I couldn't shake off the feeling I'd walked away too easy. I called back and asked to schedule an appointment with our regular doctor. I don't believe she thought there was anything wrong, either. Still, she pulled out an M-CHAT (an early-childhood autism screening questionnaire for parents), to her credit. To qualify for a developmental pediatric referral, he had to score a 4 or more. Callum scored precisely 4, and she referred him to a developmental pediatrician at a nearby teaching hospital. It took six months to get him seen, so we pursued Early Steps in the meantime.

BY this point, we began to share our concerns with friends and family. I don't know why human beings have an instinct to deny problems exist, but we do. I remember hearing a lot of "He'll be fine; you'll see!" And "He's just taking his time. Don't worry! He'll still go to college." I heard a *lot* of stories of delayed development followed by a typical life with marriage and kids. It's all well-intentioned but not terribly helpful when you're trying to find answers. The condescension was the worst. "I know you have autism in the family. Are you sure you're just not seeing it everywhere?" That's something that was actually said to me in some form—more than once.

The Early Steps evaluation was our first official confirmation Callum had developmental delays. They spent a lot of time with him and us, mainly in a floor-based play scenario. He immediately took to the two young women evaluating him and had a ball with all the attention. At the end of the evaluation, he scored as "globally developmentally delayed" with significant communication and motor control delays, etc. They recommended early intervention services in speech, physical therapy, and occupational therapy, along with day care–based developmental therapy.

Early Steps does not diagnose. Their role is to evaluate for delays and recommend therapies and consultations. But I wanted their thoughts. So I asked them—in their judgment—if I needed to take Callum to a developmental pediatrician for an autism evaluation. I asked them point-blank if they "saw autism" in Callum. I remember them both looking at each other and back at me before not so confidently shaking their heads no. On the way out to the car, Sean was relieved. He knew there were delays, but two people he viewed as experts had said they didn't think it was autism.

But all I saw in my head was my baby flapping on that carpet. I knew. I just knew. And it wouldn't be long before everyone else saw it, too.

I took this photo on that very day in front of the television. I had been trying to get his attention, couldn't, and walked around to find him focused like this.

WE were the last appointment of the day when we took Callum for his first occupational therapy consult. The therapist's name was Robin, and I have no doubt she'd already had a long day. But we handed over the parent questionnaires and followed her to the therapy area for his evaluation. Callum wasn't interested in being evaluated and wanted to jump around and explore all the things, so eventually she placed him in a therapy chair similar to a high chair in front of her. I remember there being building blocks and other manipulatives. It was calm, and she went about the evaluative tasks with him while listening to our story and what had already transpired. She then handed him some paper, showed him a pencil, and demonstrated how to run the pencil across it to make a mark before sitting back and watching him for a moment.

That's when she adjusted his chair a bit to the side and turned her own to face me directly. And although much of the evaluation has faded in my memory, I'll never forget what she said to me.

"First, I want you to know I don't think you're crazy. I see what you see. You're not imagining it. And, yes, I think you are right to be concerned about autism and be following up with the developmental pediatrician."

She then turned and pointed out the paper on the tray and the pencil Callum was holding.

"Do you see how he's holding that pencil? Typically, when you hand a child his age a pencil and paper and demonstrate writing, they'll run the pencil back and forth on the paper. But do you see what he's doing instead?"

"He's looking at the imprint on the pencil barrel," I replied.

"Yes. He's been looking at it. And the metal that connects the eraser. And the ridges on the pencil . . . all the details. But he's not once tried to imitate what I did by running the pencil across the paper. That extreme attention to detail is a red flag for me as a therapist. So, yes. I see it. I think you're right. And I think we need to start working with him immediately regardless of what we call it now."

I didn't want to hear her words. But, oh, how I *needed* them. I'm sure gaslighting isn't the intent of most people who pooh-pooh your worries for your child. But it does a number on your head regardless. I will always appreciate her respect and honesty. It granted me permission to stop doubting myself and instead get to work helping my son.

So, at the tender age of nineteen months, all the therapies began.

Chapter 3

An Invitation to the Club:
On What Others Can't Know Until They Do

S hortly after beginning the path to diagnosis, I knew who I needed to call. It's instinctive to seek out those who understand. For information, guidance, affirmation, and all the things that come with a significant event, condition, or revelation. When women worry about children, they turn to experienced mom friends. It's just what we do, and it's exactly what I did.

I had not been in touch with Christy as much as I should have been. We spent a lot of time together up through her marriage and first child. But the arrival of her second child traumatized her in a way that forever changed her—not because of who he was, but in the circumstances and chaos of his entry. He was born with a condition more likely than not to leave her baby with a short life span and the possibility of a vegetative state. In addition to her newborn son's medical emergency, three days following his birth, two planes flew into the World Trade Center. Christy remembers when the hospital—including the NICU—was evacuated due to the nearly constant bomb and ricin threats plaguing the country as we headed toward inevitable war. She remembers pushing her three-day-old son's incubator down hallways with other terrified patients and staff. Already shaken, Christy then had to evacuate a newborn with a PICC line, internal bleeding, low oxygenation, and an enlarged liver. A baby they hadn't yet determined would live.

It was an experience I didn't understand she was going through, us having seen less of each other as adulthood took over and before the era of social media.

When he came home, their lives were consumed with global developmental delays, specialists, hearing and vision loss, speech therapy, physical therapy, and occupational therapy. I remember Christy telling me that there was only one department he'd never visited at the nearby pediatric hospital.

Her life became unknowable to me. I didn't consciously stay away. I called occasionally and met up for lunch sometimes. But I know now not nearly enough. I know now how much my insistence in learning how to help care for him in the early days would have meant the world to an exhausted and anxious mom.

But I wasn't in the club yet. I didn't know. And neither can anyone who hasn't experienced uncertainty about their child's future independence. I know I should have tried harder.

So, I reached out, and she invited me to dinner. We met one evening at Chili's, and this post followed. A decade later, there are words and phrases I'd like to remove. But that wouldn't be honest. For one, I wouldn't now describe autism as a "crisis." I'm now on board with using the word "disability" over "special needs." I'm no longer afraid of how he'll develop; I'm fearful of the world around him.

In the years that followed, I learned a lot. Mainly about the applicability of loving life and being brave *anyway*. Not solely about autism, but in all things. I learned what constitutes an actual emergency and what doesn't. I learned much about battle selection. Having suffered loss, I know life is indeed short. And if you aren't actively looking around for what's beautiful in it, you'll miss it before you reach the end.

Love Life, Be Brave

I'm learning more than I ever wanted to know these days. Lessons about isolation, humility, frustration, real fear, unconditional love, what's important, patience, gratitude, and so very much more. But what I have really learned the most about is friendship. Friendship takes on a whole different meaning when your life is affected by ASD— or any crisis or special-needs issue that affects your child. For, no matter how much your friends love you, there are some things in life that you cannot possibly understand until you have experienced them. Please understand me. I have dear friends who kept me sane throughout the last year of panic, fear, depression. There were instances of regression, moments of joy, and my personal obsession with learning more about my child's condition. (It's even worse when you are a librarian.) They've tolerated me obsessing, repeating myself, forgetting to ask about their lives and every other way I have slacked off in the friendship department over the past year. (You guys know who you are, and I love you.)

But there is a part of my heart now that even they cannot access. The part that toddles around, smiling and flapping away, still happily oblivious to the difficulties ahead. That part of me is only accessible to those who know. That kind of friendship and sisterhood/brotherhood is intimate indeed.

I have such a friend. Her name is Christy, and she is now the reason I can believe in destiny—that certain people are simply meant to find one another. I think we both endured a summer of algebraic torture in college simply because these two boys were on the way.

Christy has been on this road far longer than I. Her journey raising a disabled child began in 2001 with a CMV-affected child. And, though we were friends, I didn't truly understand her pain and isolation. It wasn't until last year that our friendship took on new meaning for us both. When I began to face that Callum was on the spectrum, I reached out to her. I sent a message apologizing for all the missed opportunities to help and support her. But she already knew more than me and wisely informed me that I couldn't possibly have known. She, with open arms, welcomed me to a club you don't imagine yourself joining.

She invited me to dinner at Chili's. After ordering, she looked me straight in the eye and announced she had some things to say that I needed to know. And then she leveled with me. Her advice was candid and unfiltered. She talked to me about growing thicker skin—that I wouldn't have it yet, that it would never be impermeable, but that it would grow and make things easier. I would learn I was stronger than I believed then. Not because of my child. But because of all the people who would now accompany him—from schools to therapists, to insurance, to specialists, to strangers commenting, to other parents of similar kids, and his own family. She also spoke the truth about friendships. She told me I would soon learn who my friends really were. She told me to learn as much as I could about IEPs and educational law. And she addressed the torture of uncertainty. You can't predict in a year or two. No matter how much googling I did, I could not find an answer to the looming question of Will he be able to care for himself? She told me straight up that I would have to learn to live without knowing, or it would eat me alive inside. That parenting a child with a disability required a day-by-day mindset.

And she gave me a gift. A gift that I explain each and every time someone asks me about it. A gift that makes me smile again just writing about it. She pulled out of her purse a small box. A silver ring was inside. It said, "Love Life," and on the inside, "Be Brave."

And then she stunned me. She told me that she had a matching ring. Years earlier, she had seen the ring and knew, simply knew, that one day she would need to give it to someone else. She didn't know who, but she had kept it for years—until I emerged as the person who needed it. I now wear that ring every day. It has become as valuable to me as my wedding band. It's my mantra on hard days and my joy on the good ones.

Over the past few days, my readers have also taught me much about friendship and destiny. To each of you who have reached out via Twitter, Facebook, email, and this blog, thank you from the very bottom of my heart. All of you have also been placed squarely on my path in this new journey. Your words and support are no accident; they are destiny. Thank you for the open arms into which you have also welcomed me into The Club. All of you have reassured me that it's gonna be okay.

Thank you to my dear friend Christy and all of my new dear friends in the blogosphere. You are all my heroes.

Love life. Be brave.

A few years later, I ordered another ring just like it. And I invited another anxious mama to dinner at Chili's. After which I welcomed her to the club, gave her a ring, and told her, too, what she needed to know.

If you're a parent and one day find an opportunity to do the same, *do*. Then we can lend wisdom, share resources, and encourage. And perhaps that might serve to help another parent navigate the unknown and their own chaotic emotions so they can settle down and get back to what they signed up for: loving and nurturing their child.

Chapter 4

A Not So United Front:
On Acceptance of a Diagnosis

I f you parent with a partner, you probably already know you don't agree on all matters related to your children. It's hard enough to decide on paint colors when sharing life. But bedtimes, junk food, messy bedrooms, grades, etc., all have a way of revealing our respective childhoods and upbringing. And those experiences, perhaps even only vaguely remembered, shape us as parents. They shape our hopes, fears, convictions, and perception of ourselves as parents. So, it isn't any wonder that the process of accepting a diagnosis of a significant developmental delay plays out differently for Mom and Dad. The most common question I'm asked by therapists, teachers, grandparents, and one-half of the couple themselves is how to talk to a parent resistant to a discussion of autism.

I wish I could outline a series of steps for leading them to that water, but I can't. I've seen instances of medical doctors who refuse to consider a diagnosis for a clearly autistic child. Parents who react angrily and believe the school is trying to say their child is dumb. Otherwise loving moms and dads who somewhat knew unofficially but sat back for years—years while their child struggled socially, emotionally, and academically without ever getting desperately needed services out of a fear of "labeling." And I've met parents with great regret that they didn't see or act because their children's stories ended tragically by suicide.

Most of the time, however, the lagging one catches up to the other.

Sometimes you'll find that parents want to soften the perception by stressing PDD-NOS (Pervasive Developmental Disorder–Not Otherwise Specified), Social-Pragmatic Communication Disorder, or Asperger's syndrome because they carry less of a stigma. I've always suspected that some of their doctors knew it and didn't mind calling it other things just so long as Mom and Dad got moving on it. It's less important in the early days what it's called than that the child is receiving therapies to communicate, move, play, and learn.

While my realization and acceptance were unusually instantaneous, my husband, Sean, wasn't quite the same. For one, he wasn't as familiar with autism. And, two, his own experiences impacted his willingness to consider it.

Sean's antics as a kid were kind of legendary. In the seventies, nobody was using the term ADHD widely, and parents and schools rarely knew what to do with it. Since it became a commonly understood condition, Sean matter-of-factly admitted to having it. But he was in his late thirties when he was finally diagnosed.

ADHD manifests for him differently now in adulthood. But as much as we affectionately tease him about squirrels and as much as he laughs about it, there's no question ADHD has had an impact in every part of his life. From learning and reading to employment, personal life, impulsivity, substance abuse, and maturity. There are ways his ADHD makes him shine; he's creative, a problem solver, energetic, and able to hyperfocus in positive ways. Combined with his fun-loving, affectionate enthusiasm and witty banter, people just love Sean. Even those who've known him long enough to want to throttle him at times will tell you he's the first person *there*. He'll help you move, change your tire, and is the first in the room to speak up when someone is being wronged. His heart and desire to make others happy make him popular with everyone, from babies to little old ladies. When I was a freshman (he was a senior), I remember *just* how popular he was with young ladies. Many of my friends had crushes on him, and I have a slew of old high school dance photos with him and various friends. (He and I didn't officially meet until many years later, in our thirties.)

But while ADHD shaped many of the parts of him that are wonderful, it also negatively impacted his life. His mother chose to hold him back in the third grade due to reading problems. (These days, he wouldn't have entered kindergarten as a late October baby anyway.) It was a wise decision. He became an excellent reader and enjoys it as a hobby to this day. But being held back contributes negatively to a child's self-esteem, and he's mentioned it often.

Rushes to judgment and action can lead to trouble—loss of temper, impatience, unwise financial decisions, etc. Friends and family don't always understand why and what is needed. They don't see this screwup or mistake for what it is; they're just disappointed. And disappointment reflected in the eyes of family hurts so far down deep, no one can ever touch it. As a result, it can take a longer time to learn life lessons others pick up quickly.

He's got it together now at fifty-two, but he laughs with a wry expression and wishes he'd had a little guidance when he was young and needed it. He wonders if it would have made a difference in career choices and formal education. And then there are the little things: the misplaced glasses, the forgotten appointment, me getting irritated because he isn't paying attention, and more. They plague him every day. The compensating can be exhausting, the fear of screwing up great.

So, even more than the average person, Sean didn't want his children to struggle through school and in life. Having started fatherhood later than all of his friends, it was all the more miraculous to him. These perfect babies, with fresh starts and two parents watching over and guiding them. To him, he'd done the first right thing in his life. He hadn't screwed something up. He was the proudest daddy you could imagine, equally involved with their care, diaper changing, and feeding.

So, when signs began emerging, and concerns were voiced, he took that defensively. Not unreasonably so, but I could hear the hurt. Sean was always willing to talk about it as a possibility. But he held out hope longer over signs of little consequence in Callum. And he was sure that the minor early symptoms of hyperactivity in Bronwyn were what "all kids do." Until one day, I pushed a little further than before, and it broke through in one anguished plea: "I just didn't want my kids to have to go through anything I went through! I thought my kids were okay! And now I'm being told my kids are screwed up, too, and I probably gave that to them!" He wasn't in denial out of shame. He was in pain at the idea of the challenges he knew they faced, respectively.

I remember him seeming just as stunned that he'd said it—finally said it out loud. We sat there quietly for a bit and talked it out. And from that moment forward—to testing, diagnosis, entry into pre-K ESE (Exceptional Student Education), etc.—he's always been on board. And you couldn't find a prouder daddy the world over. The employees at our local Publix know Sean and Callum, who come in together every Saturday and Sunday morning so Callum can do his preferred snacks shopping. The people in various departments know "the little boy with the ball" and offer him free cookies and balloons. Usually, he happily flaps his way in, full megawatt smiling, and charms anyone he can. They go to the barbershop, the auto spa, and find coffee somewhere. People love him. And Sean *beams*. Callum loves the rough horseplay, singing, loud music, and fun of Daddy. They're great buddies.

He can read Bronwyn reasonably well, too, often pointing out signs she's tuning out, becoming overwhelmed, or in dire need of movement long before I notice. I don't have a hyperactive bone in my body. (And I don't appreciate those who've known me my whole life reading that line and rolling about the floor and cackling at the very idea.) Sean and Bronwyn are wired similarly in that way—enthusiasm, impulsivity, hyperactivity, and boredom. They get that in each other and can be thick as thieves in that way. She's his number one on all roller coasters and the person he seeks to make laugh in joining and (unfortunately) performing on TikTok.

FEW of the big things in life are instantly knowable and efficiently processed. Most take time. And just because you married someone doesn't mean your processing speeds are the same. Odds are good, unless as a parent you are autistic yourself, that somebody resisted the idea a little more than the other. Lots can contribute to that.

Some people automatically equate autism with either intellectual disability or having savant qualities. They don't realize they've lived among those on the spectrum their whole lives. (They might even be on the spectrum themselves and have fewer social skills by which to judge their own evidencing of those traits.) But they immediately assume either a career in theoretical physics or a devastating future, not knowing autistic people get married, go to work, and raise families every day. It's complex, can be found combined with any IQ, and it doesn't have a "look" to it. Denial, however, comes from fear, which comes from ignorance.

I've heard there are fathers who are ashamed to have sons flap in public or not play team sports, but I've never actually met any of those men. I've only ever met dads scared about the future but insanely proud of their children's accomplishments and happy to share the good news with others. Most men unfamiliar with autism are fascinated by him, willing to ask questions, get a kick out of doing/saying something to make Callum smile, and enjoy meeting him. So, having not met any of those dads, I'm afraid I can't comment much on the truth of that claim—only tell you that loving a severely autistic child changes you. It changes the very lens through which you view the world. It did in me. I know it did the same for him.

If you are struggling with a partner about what label doctors might come up with for your child, *don't*. Instead, put your energies into having your child assessed by a neuropsychologist or developmental pediatrician, speech therapist, occupational therapist, physical therapist, and BCBA (Board Certified Behavior Analyst) to see what *needs* they have. The fundamental principles of teaching language acquisition aren't a secret. But these specialists know what they're doing—no matter what Mom and Dad are currently calling "it." Stress evaluations "just to rule out early problems." Say therapies are "to help with such and such a problem"—*but do not delay having your child assessed if your gut keeps screaming at you to do so.* Leave it to the experts to explain their findings. They're good at it. They'll have examples, and they do this every day. They'll explain the urgency of early intervention to your partner and, hopefully, you'll have a game plan.

Your partner still may not see it the same way for months or even years. But I've rarely met parents of teens who remain clueless about the nature of their atypical children. So just get them what they need now to give them functional communication and the promise of less restrictive care in the future.

You may remain unsure as to the source of a high fever. You may not delay giving your child Tylenol while you bicker about it. We've got a long way to go from here to autism acceptance and inclusion. But that's okay. As an educator, I'm more concerned with the child getting what they need. We can work on Mom or Dad later. *First things first.* Which is a phrase you'll find yourself repeating a lot over the years as you begin to process the world through the potential perspective of your child. Cut yourself some slack. We're all still works in progress.

It's going to be okay.

Having said that, I was once asked by a reader how to convince their partner to seek a diagnosis for their child . . .

Chapter 5

Say the Word:
On the Importance of "Labels"

Somewhere out there right now is a parent who just heard something they didn't like. Someone who loves or works with her child suggested her precious, perfect baby may have a form of autism spectrum disorder.

There are signs. Their child is most likely developmentally delayed in significant ways. He may have walked late, often skipping crawling altogether. He may lack the fine motor skills other same-age peers have already mastered. Physically, he may lack the strength, balance, and coordination to do the typical things young children do, such as ride a tricycle, jump, run, or hold on tight when taken for a ride on Daddy's back. Perhaps most significant is a speech delay. He may have developed a few words and lost them, or he may have never made any kind of vocalizations. In addition to not speaking, he may not understand the speech of others. And, if his name is called, he may not consistently respond—if he responds at all.

In addition to developmental delays, he probably has exhibited some seemingly odd behaviors. For example, he may not play with toys appropriately, preferring spinning, lining up items, or flicking strings or non-toy objects. He might not be able to tolerate certain textures, sounds, or lighting. He may throw sudden "tantrums" that go far beyond any prior conceptions of the word. He may appear to be present physically—but live in a world of his own. It's also possible he may not have any physical developmental delays. But he's unable to authentically connect to others, read social situations, or tolerate transitions from one activity to the next.

And though his mother probably already noticed these delays and odd behaviors, she is angered when the subject of autism inevitably comes up. She thinks she has good reason.

She remembers a time in which "the short bus kids" were never seen in school. A time in which children with disabilities were not invited to access the world of their same-age peers. When "special needs" was a stigma—and autism a kind of death sentence in the minds of those who didn't understand it. She's afraid. She doesn't want this kind of label for her child, doesn't want the world to discount him before he learns, grows, and reaches his potential.

So, she refuses to say the word "autism"—and refuses to allow anyone else to say it or dare suggest her child needs therapeutic services or counseling.

Her fears are understandable. But she's wrong. The worst thing that could happen to a typically developing but slightly delayed child is not an incorrect autism diagnosis. For if that diagnosis is wrong, it'll eventually be evident. And they'll be undiagnosed.

No, the worst thing is for an autistic child to not be identified.

That's because we know so much more about autism today than we did before. We know, for example, that the younger a child receives intervention services, the better the outcome over his life span. The earlier an autistic child learns to adapt to the demands of his world, the greater the possibility of future independent living. The ability to communicate their needs, fears, wants, and pain *matters*. The ability to access and nurture their interests and passions. The possibility of a career, relationships, and a family of their own. The statistics on autistic children who do not receive early intervention services are dismal indeed. The capacity for children to learn to compensate for the more disabling aspects of autism—while still utilizing some of its strengths—is heightened at this tender age. To throw away these vital years over fears of him "being labeled" is a mistake—a mistake that will likely haunt both the child and his family. Neither labels nor autism itself is the enemy; *time is*.

For labels serve more than one purpose. In education and medicine, labels equal *services*. Labels are the keys to the locked doors of help and hope for a brighter future. Yes, they can be harmful when used to exclude or when used as weapons. Yes, they can be misleading to those who don't understand them. But without them, there will be no access to therapeutic services for anyone but the independently wealthy.

Labels also serve an equally important purpose: for the child to learn who they are, why they think and experience the world the way they do, and how to find others like them. Meeting others who understand them and learning how to navigate a world of those who don't. To value their own unique minds and perspectives. And to recognize those who haven't yet met their own tribe and reel them into the fold. Every soul needs to find their tribe in life. We all deserve to know who we are. Everyone. For autism is not an add-on. It is woven into the fabric that makes the individual. So it's wrong to deny a child that self-awareness, no matter how good the intentions.

If you are sitting on that fence, parents, jump off on the side of awareness, intervention, support, and hope. Read and learn about the many autistic individuals out there who live rich and rewarding lives—lives that have joy and value and contribute to our communities and our world.

Go on. Stop hiding and procrastinating. A diagnosis won't bite but regret just may.

Autism. Say the word.

Chapter 6

Snake Oil:
On the Money to Be Made Off False Hope

Feeling lost, crazy, and desperate belongs to a good life
as much as optimism, certainty, and reason.
—Alain de Botton

You know the story. The one of the mother who lifts a car off her child with nothing but love and a surge of adrenalin. Maybe you've seen the movie *Lorenzo's Oil*. The true story about parents with no medical background who tirelessly learned, researched, and fought to create an actual treatment to benefit their dying child. For most parents, there is little they're unwilling to do or try to save a beloved child.

As Callum began therapies, I started "researching." I put that in quotation marks in the ironic sense. Because despite being reasonably well-educated, I didn't yet have any training in evaluating research studies. I went to Google and read everything I could find on autism and autism treatments and used every search term combination I could think of. Without understanding the research process, I didn't know how to evaluate my scientific sources.

But I was determined to "cure" my son if a cure existed. And it didn't take long to come across the Defeat Autism Now! (DAN!) movement.

Now, I'm a naturally skeptical person. I don't read my horoscope. I'm suspicious of most social media "news" shares. And I don't believe most people with strong opinions on subjects they haven't formally studied know what they're talking about.

But love feeds desperation, and I kept telling family and friends:

> *"I'm not saying I believe this, but it won't hurt to look into it."*
> *"It sounds plausible."*
> *"I don't want to look back and say I didn't try everything. I want no regrets."*

So, off I went in search of a DAN! practitioner. The website I searched listed eleven of them in Florida. To my then delight, I discovered that one of the most famous in the world had an office not two hours from me. I called and scheduled an appointment several months ahead with Jeff Bradstreet, MD, in Melbourne, Florida. And in February 2011, Sean, Callum, my dad, and I made hotel reservations and headed toward our first appointment.

DR. Bradstreet's office was in a strip mall in a busy stretch of Melbourne, next to an excellent sandwich shop. My first impression walking in was how bare it was. A train set up in the center for the kids made sense (autism). But other than that, it was devoid of brochures, health posters, etc. It did have pictures on the wall of cute, smiling young patients with parent testimonials below thanking Dr. Bradstreet for "recovering" their children. And there were strict notices about refills on supplements and vitamins.

We were ushered back into Dr. Bradstreet's office. On his walls were pictures of his own autistic son, grown and never looking into the camera. (I knew about his son from my reading.) And there were a lot of Christian plaques, paintings, and knick-knacks along with degrees and framed articles about him. But it was mostly his son, family, and images of Jesus. Scattered everywhere were books, papers, and conference materials on autism and alternative therapies.

He asked us a lot of questions about Callum (not yet formally diagnosed). First, we discussed our family history of autism, vaccinations (I hadn't given him the MMR yet), ear infections, and therapies. Then he told us how excited he was to treat Callum and that Callum was the youngest patient he'd ever had in his DAN! practice.

He said, "Most people don't bring them to me until it's too late to do much. With this little guy, we can do a lot." We grabbed for hope like a drowning person does a lifeline.

For the next forty-five minutes or so, we heard a lot of impressive-sounding "science." We listened to a lot about yeast, parasites, fecal fat, bacterial sensitivity, immunoglobulins, and more. When asked about vaccines, he dismissed that as "no longer his primary focus" and stated he no longer believed them to be the leading cause of autism. Then, according to Dr. Bradstreet, we needed to order up a bunch of tests. One series of tests would go through Quest Diagnostics, which our whole family (and probably most of America) had used at some point. The others needed to go through specialized labs. Dr. Bradstreet explained that most labs didn't "do the kind of testing needed" to analyze Callum's gut, allergens, and other things I've now forgotten. One was Genova Diagnostics in North Carolina. And the other could be done only via the Laboratoire Philippe Auguste in France.

Dr. Bradstreet wanted us to try the gluten-free/casein-free (GFCF) diet while waiting on our test results. Unfortunately, the tests would take weeks due to their complexity. He then prescribed a cocktail of vitamins and supplements, including Cal-Mag/Chela-Max, Arctic Cod Liver Oil (in peach), Zinc Mini-Minerals liquid, Selenium Mini-Minerals, Ther-Biotic Complete Powder, Vitamin D3 Liquid, and Nutrivene Longvida Curcumin. He also prescribed IVs of glutathione. His official diagnoses? "OTH Symbolic Dysfunction," "Colitis, Enteritis & Gastro Infect," and "OTH Select Immunoglobulin Deficient."

By now, alarms should have been ringing in my head. Ashamed as I am to admit it, they *did*. But I'd checked his medical license. He was mentioned in many, many books on autism and even wrote a foreword or two for others. I found him on YouTube speaking at conferences around the world. But, as has been proven time and again, *wanting* to believe is the strongest placebo of all. So I ignored my gut in deference to love—and hope. Which was exactly what he sold us that day for a low, low price starting at around $2,000—which, of course, insurance didn't pay.

Following a trip an hour out of town to Whole Foods, we started the GFCF diet the next day. We began with a toddler who was still eating most things for us. We tried so hard. I made muffins and pancakes with gluten-free flour. Every GFCF frozen product available, we tried. We pushed fruits. But ultimately, the only thing Callum would eat was French fries. He went from not being overly selective to being suspicious of every texture we introduced in mere days.

Months later, his test results came back. Callum was negative for every possible allergy-induced "cause" of autism. Dr. Bradstreet informed us we could stop the diet as it didn't apply to *Callum's* autism. Instead, we needed to focus on ridding him of "oxidative stress" from the environment because autistic kids were just more sensitive to it. This would be done in the form of chelation IVs and hyperbaric chamber therapy (in a few months when he was older). Sean and I kept looking at each other. We decided those procedures needed further research on the ride home, but figured there wasn't any harm in nutritional supplements. We scheduled one such treatment, a glutathione IV.

My friend Sandy accompanied me for that visit, and we had to hold him down for the nurse to insert the IV. My mind was screaming at me the entire time, but I tried to reason it was the same as when he had blood drawn for ear surgery. It was for his own good, right?

But he cried the whole time. He wasn't the only one. Sandy begged me to never have to help hold him down again. And I began to feel what I expect all mamas in the wild feel—a *knowing* that something wasn't right.

Before paying and starting the drive home, I asked to use the restroom. I knew it was located through the hyperbaric chamber room, but I hadn't been in it before. As I walked through, I was struck by how surreal it all was. How the tanks looked like futuristic stasis pods. How expensive the "supplements." How suspicious the need for medical testing that couldn't be performed in the United States.

What medical testing couldn't be performed in the United States?

Something was very wrong, and I had been ignoring my gut. With a sense of disgust and shame, I knew we'd never be back. There wasn't going to be any chelation. We weren't going to purchase any more supplements. At that moment, reason overtook desperation, and I gathered my child and left—never to return.

It shouldn't have taken me even that long, and I have to live with that.

IT wasn't long before my Internet searches began to find the pseudoscience behind the snake oil. I took a deep dive into searching the terms, test names, and "diagnoses" Dr. Bradstreet spoke of so authoritatively. Instead, I found medical terminology and conditions that didn't exist in legitimate medical resources. "Researchers" with no background in science. "Doctors" . . . of nutrition. And I found a mess of conspiracy theorists convinced all of the non-DAN! scientists and physicians in the world were part of a vast plot to hide the truth and pad the bank accounts of pharmaceutical companies.

I thought about doctors like my friend Beverly, who incurred $200K in student loan debt to research cancer and heal others, only to see "holistic healers" talk her patients out of lifesaving chemotherapy. And I learned about Dr. Andrew Wakefield, who—now stripped of his medical license—is responsible for thousands of preventable deaths after his fraudulent study and "findings" about the dangers of vaccines. The very same doctor mentioned in the indexes of almost all anti-vax books on the market. If he's not, go one step deeper, and check the sources of *their* sources. It will *always* tie back to that man.

I learned how easily desperation can make fools of us.

Dr. Bradstreet seemed kind to me. His love for his adult autistic son shone through in conversation and in the photographs adorning his walls. I know his medicine now to be without merit. But I learned something from him that is even more disturbing.

Despite obvious profiting from the sale of dubious treatments, he was a true believer.

And as with religion, politics, and even science, the most dangerous among us aren't liars and snake oil salesmen. The most dangerous are always the true believers. Because they have the power to spread their beliefs. And almost always, people suffer.

IN June 2015, the Buford, Georgia, office of Dr. Jeff Bradstreet was raided by the FBI due to an investigation into his GcMAF (controversial chemotherapy) treatments for autism. His Melbourne office had already been shut down.

Later in the same month, Dr. Bradstreet was found dead in a river in North Carolina from what was determined to be a self-inflicted gunshot wound to the chest. His death aroused suspicions in the anti-vax community, who believed Dr. Bradstreet to have been murdered due to his criticism of vaccines. In 2017, the TV show *Scene of the Crime* with Tony Harris explored his death and the various theories behind it.

I have no idea what happened to Dr. Bradstreet. I'll concede what authorities allege he did—extraordinary pain followed by drowning—would be a peculiar way for a *physician* to kill himself. But I'm fairly positive he wasn't murdered by the government. As the majority of true crime docs reveal, the truth is usually more personal.

AUTISM is *not* a disease. You can't catch it, and it definitely isn't the result of a lack of essential oils. It's a neurodevelopmental disorder. No supplement, oxygen therapy, music, bleach enema, diet, or exorcism will regrow a brain. No matter what your mom, neighbor, pastor, friend, or boss says, *you cannot cure autism.* Like Down syndrome, it just is. Putting someone autistic on the prayer list in the hope they'll learn to communicate is a lovely gesture. But putting someone on the prayer list to be cured of autism is ridiculous. You don't pray an extra chromosome away in Down syndrome. You don't pray a severed leg will regrow from an accident. People and their conditions often just happen. Autism happens. Yes, it changes some things. Now, move forward.

And avoid all snake oil along the way.

Chapter 7

Getting Stuck:
On Moving *Forward*

'm an only child, a teacher, and a former school librarian. So, as you might imagine, I sometimes struggle with correction. Oh, I'm nice about it. But once I've researched an issue and formed an opinion, I'm a smidge confident of it. I'm unlikely to be swayed until *proven* wrong.

To make matters worse, I was raised by a lawyer and an English teacher—so I handle myself reasonably well in a debate. By now, you're probably feeling sorry for my husband, and rightly so. It can be wearing to live with someone fact-checking multiple times a day. But, in my defense, I can't help it. It's a compulsion. I even watch TV with a laptop, looking up related topics while watching.

During the diagnosis and early therapies period of Callum's life, I immersed myself in what I do best—hours upon hours of research. I didn't think I was in denial. Instead, I *thought* I'd accepted the situation and was leaving no stone unturned in learning everything I could to help my son.

So, I stayed up late at night trying every Boolean search string I could think of.

Even though I had dismissed DAN! treatment as an option, I was still mesmerized by stories about globally delayed autistic children who learned to speak and went to college. In particular, I kept trying to find studies of indicators of future speech and "functioning." For example,

I researched whether eye contact was predictive of a more favorable out-come of autism severity. (Because Callum had always made a lot of eye contact.) I studied whether frequent displays of affection and sociability were a sign he would one day talk. (Because Callum had always loved being around people and was physically affectionate.) And I kept search-ing for an autism-version timeline for communication and when we would know. I read books, highlighted studies, and watched videos in my effort to be the Energizer Bunny of Never-Giving-Up-on-My-Child.

I wanted assurance he would ultimately be okay. I wanted to hear he could communicate his needs, form meaningful relationships, and have a career and a 401(k). To me, that was the definition of okay. And the part of his diagnosis I found the most troubling was the uncertainty. I was raised by a mother who believed, when encountering resistance, to push harder. But there is no way to try harder to know the future. I wanted to *know*. Right then. And I didn't yet realize my tireless research was my own attempt to gain power over what I couldn't control.

Each week, I took him to therapy with Megan, a passionate and ener-getic speech-language pathologist (SLP). She focused on teaching func-tional communication to Callum. She often welcomed me into the therapy room to watch and learn while making suggestions for what to work on. At every visit, I told her what I was reading. What study I'd found that sup-posedly suggested he would be verbal and what did she think. We were many months into this new life, and I was still deep in research mode. In the meantime, Megan was attempting to introduce Callum to picture ex-change. I thought that was really nice and all, but I was holding out hope for spoken speech and figured all these efforts were in aid of that surely inevitable outcome. That was the goal, right?

Each week, Megan would suggest practicing more of this and trying more of that. She'd ask if we made lists of Callum's favorites and family, etc. Had we done the thing she had advised? Because he wasn't showing much progress. And, in his frustration with communicating, he was be-coming more challenging to work with.

I listened and took notes. We tried the things she suggested. But I had my eyes fixed on spoken communication, and that was pretty much all I wanted to talk about, think about, and read about.

Late one afternoon, Callum was the last appointment of the day. She worked with him some one-on-one and then invited me to the back. After which, I told her all about the latest thing I'd read.

That's when Megan directed Callum to something that would hold his attention and turned to me. She took a deep breath and adopted that expression teachers in parent conferences do when they have to be careful in what they say. I knew that look. I'd performed that look.

She began by telling me she didn't know what it felt like to be in my shoes. She didn't have a child with a disability, and she would not pretend to know what that was like. She told me I was clearly a devoted mother and how glad she was that Callum was in a loving family. I sensed the "but" coming.

"You have done so much. You got your son diagnosed early. And put him in therapy early. You learn everything you can. And you're a wonderful mother. But I think in focusing on all this research, you've gotten . . . stuck."

Stuck?

Megan then pointed out that while I was busy focusing on a possible future, we were losing valuable time in the present. Because while she hoped Callum would one day talk, *he might not.* And if we spent all our time researching, waiting, and hoping rather than teaching him an accessible form of communication, we would be doing him a disservice. Worrying about the future wasn't productive. Giving him a means by which to express himself *now* was.

She talked about the (research-based!) fact that alternative and augmentative communication facilitates later speech. Since Callum wasn't functionally communicating, the increasingly frustrated behaviors he was showing in therapy weren't a surprise. Callum clearly wanted and needed to communicate. But right then, his brain wasn't yet wired to do so verbally. Because of that, he was a little boy locked inside himself—without a way to express his needs.

"I'm not trying to criticize you. But what Callum needs is less research . . . and more *action*. What I'm trying to say is I think you've gotten stuck spinning your wheels on the future—out of love for him—when we need to focus on the little boy he is *today*."

Well, I didn't like this conversation *one bit*. I *had* been trying. I'd been fighting so hard to ward off a future I didn't want for Callum. My eyes began to water, and I could hear my voice shaking with effort to remain steady as I mumbled in shock and attempted to defend myself from what *felt* like an attack.

But it wasn't an attack. Megan was right. I can't say I left there with perfect clarity. Deeply shaken, I found it easier to be annoyed and hurt than to be honest with myself. But her words followed me. And slowly, I began to spend less time searching for nonexistent predictors and more time on research-based methods for improving functional communication. I'll always be grateful for that difficult conversation.

It was a mindset shift I didn't fully understand the importance of at the time. But looking back, I know that was the day I stopped mourning a child who'd never existed and began to focus on the one who did.

THE subject of grief in a parent of an autistic child is a touchy one. Autistic advocates understandably do not like the implication that their existence is something to be lamented. After all, they aren't dead; they have a disability. And they will tell you that to mourn a living person with a disability is to devalue their existence. From that perspective, it's hard to deny their argument.

But that's a realization it can take time to reach. I know it was for me. Yet, I hear some suggest this is a manifestation of hatred for the disabled.

Cruelty exists, I know. Unfortunately, one has only to follow the news to hear horrific stories of abuse perpetrated on the disabled—some by their own families. By supported living facilities. By schools.

However, what the parent of a child with autism *should* feel when first faced with a diagnosis has little to do with how fear for one's child can override reason. And that fear is primal. We don't want our young to be vulnerable to predators. When we discover they are, it can induce panic. That panic might manifest as denial, anger, or too much googling. But it's real, *and it stems from love.*

But you can get stuck in it. And if you do, then you're depriving your child of being loved as they are. You're also depriving yourself of the joy of fully loving the child you have. So it's lose-lose all around.

If you need to grieve—and you might—go ahead and do so. *Privately.* And then dry your eyes, wash your face, and move on to *action.* Every parent who has ever loved a child has known from go they'd walk through fire for them. Well, statistically speaking, some of us will get the three a.m. wake-up call of a fire. We can freeze where we're standing, or we can suit up and carry our children through it. I know my preference.

What's sometimes hard for parents to process is that *the fire isn't autism.* The fire is a combination of a lack of services, family support, adequate education, and long-term planning. The fire is a society that does not go far enough to protect the most vulnerable among us. The fire is indifference, intolerance, and a lack of awareness and acceptance.

The fire is not your child.

But the fire surrounds your child. And fully loving them means snapping out of denial and grief and leading them to safety and the best life they're individually wired to live. It's really that simple. Now, suit up.

Chapter 8

Growing Calluses:
On Gaining Resilience

've observed that a person's best qualities are almost always their worst. They're just flip sides of the same coin that make a person who they are. By nature, I'm a people-pleaser. I don't like seeing others feel awkward or be embarrassed or inconvenienced. Confrontation raises my blood pressure, and I feel compelled to smooth over conflict. That's not to say I can't get riled, but it takes quite a bit to incite my fury. Usually, I'm the person who tells the cashier in the drive-thru how pretty her eyes are. I'll trip all over myself to make the newbie on her first day feel welcome. Saying no isn't easy for me. I give too much thought to what others think. Unfortunately, the flip side of that coin above is not conducive to raising a significantly developmentally delayed child.

When I first began to suspect Callum was autistic, I spent a lot of time talking it over with my sister-in-law Julie. She was then a school-based occupational therapist. I fretted and obsessed and obsessed and fretted. I lamented how loud he screamed in the restaurant. I worried what fellow parents in the therapy waiting room thought when he melted down on the floor. I cringed, relating how he pulled down the backdrop to the church's Christmas children's play. But she knew me well, and a decade of working with developmentally delayed children and their families gave her insight into our future. And she realized some of the realities of this journey were going to be particularly hard for a people-pleasing softie like me. Julie and

I have always joked that I say what she *should* have said, and she says what I *wish* I would've said.

But one night, she bluntly and prophetically told me what I needed to hear.

"Girl, you're going to have to grow thicker skin. Because people suck. And if you don't, things are coming that are going to tear you apart. So start growing that skin now. You're going to need it."

I didn't know what she meant—not really. But I do now.

WHEN Callum was almost three and Bronwyn four, we took them on our first road trip to visit family in North Georgia. It was an eight-hour car ride, and things had been going quite well. Callum had always enjoyed riding on the open road and was so easygoing, happy to look out the window, stim, babble, and giggle. Bronwyn christened us into traveling parenthood with endless bouts of "Are we there yet?"—which, at four, was not unexpected. Although my preferred stations are the seventies and classic rock, there's something about a car trip that begs for classic country. I found a fantastic old country station on the radio. I got my Southern belle on belting out heartfelt power ballads with George Jones, Patsy Cline, and Conway Twitty. I felt normal. Positive. High-spirited even.

Just a couple of hours away from our destination, Sean and I decided to break for lunch. We chose a McDonald's with a play area—determined to allow the kids some time to run their little legs off a bit. And it was a really nice play area—sectioned off, indoors, safe, complete with tables and even a toddler zone. The parents were all lovely—smiling at others and encouraging their children to be careful with the little ones. It should have been ideal.

But soon, Callum began attempting to climb up the main slide from the bottom. He didn't understand he needed to go up into the maze and slide down. Developmentally, Callum wasn't able to do that anyway. He climbed up a bit—and just sat in the middle of the "hamster tube," partially blocking the children anxious to get around him. A line of impatient children was forming. Sean and I were both too big to crawl up to get him out, so we had to verbally coax him to come down, which seemed to take forever. Finally, we directed him to the toddler zone, where his differences became apparent to the other children who stopped and watched.

A couple of sweet kids came up and attempted to engage with him. He smiled in their general direction and backed into a corner, flapping away and making odd vocalizations and facial expressions. And I saw for the very first time the strange expressions on the faces of those children—who were realizing there was something different about him. They didn't even back away. Bless their little hearts, they again attempted to engage him before walking away confused and looking back curiously. There was no malice, just curiosity and an awareness of his . . . otherness.

And then Callum took an interest in all of the tables nearby. He started walking up to them, reaching for their food and drinks. Every parent waved away my apologies and smiled at Callum, happily flapping away. Not one single soul rudely stared or showed any kind of disapproval.

But I noticed. Oh, how I noticed. I saw the future—Callum, so happy to be in the middle of such fun, yet not knowing how to join in. I saw these children, a bit older and less tolerant of Callum's differences. The now-smiling parents—no longer able to dismiss his odd behaviors. People visibly relieved they aren't in our shoes. I saw the future in the past I had already (due to family and professional experience) seen before. And it hurt. Another layer of understanding was revealed. And the realization that there was so much more underneath, also waiting to be discovered.

All the while, my daughter was pressing her little face against the "hamster tube" sides, calling out, "Mama, look at me!" Over and over—"Look at me!" Finally, in my concern to get Callum out of the maze, I lost sight of her and panicked, only to find her in a tube, making silly faces to get my attention. A moment frozen in time—and yet another layer of understanding revealed.

I couldn't calm down. Couldn't reason. The air was too thick to breathe. I had to get out of there. But, in my urgency, I didn't do such a great job of warning my daughter of our impending departure. It was sudden, and she was having fun. So she threw the mother of all tantrums. And in her howls of protest, I heard all of the future wrongs that would be perpetrated upon

There are better photos of us, but this one is hilarious to me, because it was still early and we didn't *really* know. But in hindsight, it was all captured in this one moment—with neither one of them looking at the camera.

her. When she'd want our attention, but it must—by some necessity—be directed to her brother. When she'd want for all the world to have a special moment—only to have it distracted by her brother's immediate needs. When she'd realize her brother wasn't *really* a baby and worried what her friends would think. I knew she'd survive it and be a kinder person for it. But she, too, had challenging times and lessons ahead.

Something in me broke amidst the chaos of that play area and my daughter's screaming. And in my own panic, I committed an injustice upon her. In the middle of trying to drag her out of there, I thought she had picked up another child's toy and demanded she leave it behind. Not realizing or listening to her crying that it really was hers, a toy from her Happy Meal. I made her abandon her My Little Pony on the table, desperately trying to escape that room. I won't be getting Mother of the Year for *that*. If it hadn't been for my husband realizing I was unhinged, suggesting I go to the car, and sorting it all out, her toy would have been left behind forever, creating a memory I'd rather she not have.

In the car, I attempted to recapture the mood. But I could no longer find that station on the radio. Instead, I heard echoes of the last song playing when we stopped, in Conway Twitty's ragged baritone: "It's the soul afraid of dying that never learns to live."

========================

I didn't grow up in the church, which was rare for a child raised in the Bible Belt. However, because I was born after September 1, my parents sent me to a private Baptist church school to avoid being held back for a year. So, despite being christened Episcopalian and briefly attending a Methodist church during one of my mercurial mother's momentary whims, my religious instruction was Baptist. That's not a good fit for me theologically. I pondered everything from Judaism to atheism before finally landing on sticking to my Episcopal roots. Both Sean and I wanted that for our family—a sense of tradition and community—so we set about getting confirmed and getting church-based marital counseling before we wed. Following Bronwyn's birth and even briefly after Callum's, we still managed to attend quite regularly.

But as Callum's autistic traits became more noticeable—and loud—attending church was a bit rare for us. I hadn't grown that thicker skin yet, and every vocal stim reverberating throughout the sanctuary set me on edge. In addition, our church has an older population, and Episcopalians are somewhat of a tame bunch as it is. Flapping, spinning, shrieking little boys tend to stand out. And in my way of handling most public family outings at the time, I wanted out.

At some point, I commented on a church member's Facebook post to the effect of it being difficult to take him to church—not wanting to disrupt the service. And that's when several members of the church took notice and reached out to me.

> *"Oh, honey, please bring him! We don't care about that."*
> *"A church without noisy children is a church that's dying. Please come!"*
> *"We know he's autistic. We love him. We don't care about any of that."*

All of that felt welcoming, and I knew they meant it. So, one Sunday, we dressed for church, prepped the diaper bag, brought the stimmy toys, put on brave faces, instantly stopped the bickering typical of two frustrated parents trying to get little ones ready, opened our car doors, and showed up. Those kind souls who had reached out to me smiled their welcomes and hugged us. The service began.

And so did Callum. He stimmed and squealed and whined over things he wanted. But it really wasn't too bad, considering it was a new experience for him. I kept looking behind me, worrying his outbursts would hinder others from their worship. I got a few curious looks but mostly smiles. Sean, better at riding it out, still had to stop me from scooping Callum up and whisking him out the door a couple of times in my paranoia and a misplaced sense of propriety.

Following the service, we walked over to the parish hall for a luncheon for the visiting bishop. It was there we paid for our lack of planning. For when a bishop visits, the church goes all out with a banquet. But Callum, being food-aversive, wasn't interested in any of the hot lunch offerings where foods touched, and ingredients were mixed. However, he was *very* interested in the dessert buffet—most unfortunately located directly in front of our table. Back then, I hadn't yet learned to roll with the punches. I hadn't yet figured out that the simplest solution was simply to survive the immediate crisis and go get the child a cookie right then for the sake of everyone's sanity. But I didn't do that. No one else's child was beginning with dessert, and mine wasn't either. I didn't want to be judged.

That's when the real meltdowns began. And Callum wasn't the only one. As Callum fell apart on the outside and Sean unsuccessfully attempted to distract him by carrying him kicking and screaming to the playground, I melted down on the inside: panicking, hearing every comment real and imagined, and worrying what all those experienced mothers were thinking about us now.

It was at that precise moment of paralysis—staring through a stained-glass window and wondering what I should do next—that someone approached me.

"So, has the doctor told you when he's going to stop making all that racket?"

I can tell you all the things I fantasized about saying. But I can't remember my actual ineffective and non-kickass response. Because I didn't have one. I stared and froze and mumbled something, but I don't know what. Soon, one of the kind ladies who had reached out to me on Facebook walked up and saw the look of shock on my face. I told her what had been said as I scrambled to gather our belongings and our four-year-old and find my husband and son and leave. She begged me to stay and tried to assure me no one else felt that way. But due to just one comment, I convinced myself my child wasn't welcome by some and that the welcomes would continue to dwindle as he grew older. I left, and it was years before we returned. Was that person solely responsible for our lack of attendance? Of course not. But people don't realize how hard it is for families like ours to get out the door somewhere together.

So, churchgoers, if you're trying to increase church participation, be really sure what message you want visitors and members to walk away with.

I wish I could say there was a single transformative experience when I tossed aside my misplaced self-consciousness and overdeveloped people-pleasing tendencies. But there wasn't one. There were no epiphanies.

However, skin is a clever organ. It gets abraded, burned, and cut, but it regenerates. And if it's repeatedly exposed to friction, it gets tougher or grows calluses. We don't tend to think they're beautiful. But when it comes to weathering some of the tough stuff, they're helpful and protect the soft skin underneath.

The only way to grow that thicker skin is by repeated exposure and time. If you're new to high-needs autism, you might still be in a place where you don't want to leave the house. That's understandable. I've been there. But it's self-defeating, and it doesn't help the child. If we don't wish our children to live in prisons of our own design, we must teach them how to get about in the world. And just as watching a YouTube video is unlikely to successfully teach a person how to ride a bicycle, we cannot hope to teach our autistic children about the world if we don't actually take them out into it. Which means we must go with them. We have to shake off our fears of others' perceptions, the what-ifs, fears for the future, and *try*.

By "try," I don't mean jumping into the spring all at once. Here in North Florida, we have lots of lovely freshwater springs. Conventional wisdom—because they're freezing at first—is to "just jump in and get it over with." As I write this, I'm forty-seven years old and still refuse to do that. No, I'm an enter-one-inch-at-a-time spring swimmer, and I find introducing Callum to new experiences to be best achieved in the same way. If we're visiting a new doctor, I drive to the parking lot of that office one day. Another day, I might take him inside and let him see the lobby, say hello to the receptionist, and give him a little treat before leaving. It desensitizes his anxiety for the actual appointment and usually works out well for all. There are lots of ways to do this for many situations, and it's a worthwhile investment. Over time, your child's ability to acclimate to new experiences will improve. There's no rule you have to stay but a few minutes. And once a new experience is repeated, it becomes a familiar experience. Then you think of another new one, and your worlds will expand. Promise.

In the meantime, you will acclimate, too. You'll learn how to proudly stare right back until people look away. You might even manage to come up with a good zinger or two to put rude people in their place. Of course, it doesn't say much for my spiritual growth to admit that can be fun. (But it can be *super* satisfying.)

You'll grow that thicker skin. And in doing so, you'll be sending your child an important message—that they belong in their world, too. They have just as much right to experience, learn from it, and enjoy it as everyone else. That's important, and your willingness to defend that right for them is your job. Because playgrounds are meant for all children. Movies on the big screen with popcorn and candy should be accessible for everyone. And if you believe in God, then you must believe He wants your child in His presence, too.

So, take a deep breath, mamas and daddies. Shake it off, and introduce your children to their world and their world to your children. They'll both be better for it.

Chapter 9

The Island of Mispurchased Toys: On Acknowledging Pain

Why must the corners we turn be so sharp?
Why must I keep all these things in my heart?
Why must I silently give in to time?
Forfeit a childhood to boxes and twine.
—Ann-Jo Hale

Many years ago, my mother wrote a song about the day she packed up my Barbies and toys to redecorate my bedroom for my thirteenth birthday. There's one stanza I've always remembered for some reason. Perhaps because I remember her sitting on the floor next to my bed, carefully packing items she thought to save in under-bed storage boxes.

One afternoon, my good friend Sandy came over to help me whittle down the kids' toys in preparation for a room reorganization and makeover.

I expected to feel sad and a little reluctant (thus the need for Sandy to keep me in line). I knew it would be hard to part with toys I associated with my little ones' baby and toddlerhoods. I didn't want to give away my daughter's first baby doll, the first blocks she stacked, or her favorite chunky books.

But what took me by surprise was the sheer number of toys of which the only memories I have are *buying* them—for Callum. Buying them in the hope that one would be just the right toy to trigger Callum's interest. Then, unwrapping them and setting them out for him, only to find them ignored when he returned to banging his pink plastic baby hanger.

I know all the correct answers when people ask why he is playing with some non-toy household item. I have read how to engage him with the things he is interested in. And I know how to find companies specializing in high-interest toys for autistic children.

I don't know how to explain how it feels to acknowledge that your little boy *doesn't know how to play*. I don't know how to convey that sadness in a parent's heart. And I don't know how to avoid those moments of unbearable clarity watching him throw a toy truck down repeatedly—while the other children push their trucks down imaginary roads. Moments when the walls close in, my mind tunes out the chatter and background noise, and all I can see is that truck landing over and over again.

It has been nearly fifty years since King Moonracer and A Dolly for Sue tugged at the hearts of movie watchers who empathized with those unloved toys from the Island of Misfit Toys. Everyone watching *Rudolph the Red-Nosed Reindeer* wanted those toys to be played with and loved. We humans attach meaning to things. It's not because we believe objects feel; it's because we yearn for those carefree moments of childhood when building blocks become castles and empty boxes rocket ships hurtling toward Mars. These are the moments when I confess to hurting.

Yes, the autism spectrum has bestowed many gifts to the world among the fascinating autistic people who have lived and live. Great advances. Breathtaking works of art. Visionary minds.

But for some, it *has* been a thief. It has so overtaken their ability to access the world—independence, work, romance, parenthood, career—that they indeed are profoundly disabled. Their lives, of course, are of just as much value as any. But they cost a whole lot more to keep happy and safe. And there is an alarming number of long-term supported living establishments that don't begin to achieve that. Thus for some, autism combined with intellectual disability has stolen a rich and full life.

Stealing the play of childhood hurts. Because play is how our young learn—from toddler humans to lion cubs. And it is part of the joy of loving a child.

Autism can steal that—leaving behind memories of unfulfilled play—dump trucks, puzzles, and stuffed animals doomed to exile on the Island of Mispurchased Toys. Toys that dredge up only memories of dashed hopes for birthday parties and Christmas mornings.

And it leaves behind mothers and fathers, putting those toys away in boxes to give to somebody else's children—children who *will* play with them and will love them as we hoped our own would have. We want to give to our children. We want to delight them. So we buy, thinking this will be just the thing. Only it isn't.

Leaving castles to be built in someone else's home. Missions to Mars not bravely accomplished. Sounds of "Vroom, vroom!" that will never be uttered. And evildoers not vanquished.

This is just one truth of many in the story of parenting an autistic child: that silence can be overwhelmingly loud.

Chapter 10

Savoring the Now: On Living *Anyway*

Shortly after Callum was diagnosed, I called my aunt, who raised two autistic children herself, by then mostly grown. I was still in my "research" obsession phase, and I rattled on at length about all the therapies and interventions I was exploring. She shared their family's experiences with all of those, what helped, and what didn't. (And to her credit, she warned me about all that snake oil!) I continued talking about every book I'd read so far and what I planned to do next.

And that's when she shared some wisdom that remains a guiding principle in raising my son.

She explained that once her children were diagnosed, she, too, had scrambled to do all the therapies and implement all the interventions, and research everything she could in hopes of helping her children. But one day, she looked up and realized that while she was so busy organizing and worrying and researching, her children had grown into young men. They were still significantly autistic—still unquestionably disabled—and their childhoods had flown by.

She said, "There are a lot of things that can help an autistic child develop and communicate. But there aren't any miracles. In the end, I learned that they will ultimately grow up to be who they are. And I realized that I had spent the years they were little too busy to simply savor that time as I should've. You have them little for only so long. And you can worry yourself out of the joy of being a mom. If there's any advice I can pass down to you, it's not to do that. Enjoy him and all the little moments now. Don't regret not doing that."

He was not yet three years old, but I saw myself in her words. For once in a lifetime spent rarely taking other people's word for it (and needing to experience every mistake on my own), I chose to listen. It's a rare day when I forget her advice. I've remembered it more than any other.

At the time of this writing, Callum is twelve years old. Developmentally, various experts have placed his age somewhere around two. As his mother, that feels mostly correct to me. In addition to autism, he has a profound intellectual disability that I sometimes believe impacts him more than autism. He does things that two-year-olds do. He experiences separation anxiety like a young child. He wakes in the night and seeks the comfort of our bed in the same way as well. He's snuggly and loving and still wants to crawl into our laps. He still gleefully insists on being tickled. Still wants to play toe and finger games. Still carries a bright orange lovey/stim ball everywhere. He pretty much just wants Mama and Daddy.

And we just let him be him, mindful of pushing when we think a new skill will be beneficial for him. We enjoy him as and who he is. One day, for his sake, we will have to seek a supported-living home for him in adulthood. That's not because we don't want him at home. But one day, we will die, and we don't want everything in his world taken from him at once. We want him to have his own life, own home, own friends, routines, and interests. Because there will come a day when we aren't around to pick him up for outings or visit home. We don't want that to devastate him. We don't want him waiting at the window for hours with his shoes on.

So, we push all the love we can at him now. We take pictures and videos of all his cute and sweet moments  we *actively* cherish. Because she was right. The time is flying by just as it does raising any child. And I refuse to miss the sweeter moments of it worrying, obsessing, and seeking. I don't need to seek. He's right here. Right now. And I'm going to be present as well.

Chapter 11

A Funny Thing Happened:
On the Kinship of Community

When my friend Jenni was diagnosed with breast cancer, she turned to another breast cancer survivor. She needed to talk about treatments, what-ifs, decisions to be made, and how to cope. Later, when one of my family members was diagnosed with the same cancer, Jenni called and offered her the same.

When my friend Vernieca lost her child in an accident, she believed she was losing her mind. Unable to sleep or function, she drove herself to the emergency room. The staff tried to offer her a sedative to go home, but she refused to leave and pleaded for them to find her a doctor somewhere who had lost a child themselves. She wanted that doctor to tell her she wasn't crazy and how to move forward.

Amazingly, one was on hand that night. He came and sat with her, held her hand, listened, talked about his own story, and told her that she was definitely not losing her mind.

We human beings do this. We seek those with shared experiences when overwhelmed by the sudden and the unknown. Friends who can't relate may be wonderfully supportive. But it isn't until you talk to someone who truly gets it that you can finally speak what feels unspeakable. When you can remove the mask and just be.

A few months after we got everyone on board with a likely autism diagnosis, I got the utterly unoriginal idea to start a blog. (According to Google, there are over five hundred million blogs on the Internet.) I wasn't seeking to become the next Dooce. But I thought maybe I might get a following of thirty or forty to share with and get advice. I spent a few days thinking up a name that didn't include "puzzle" or "warrior." Somehow, I heard somebody say, "Happiness is a plate of warm cookies" right about when I looked over at my toddler flapping happily. Eureka! "Flappiness Is." As in, it just *is*. It doesn't need to be changed. Merely accepted. The name felt right. So, I ran to WordPress, bought my domain name, followed the advice to secure the same name on Twitter, Facebook, Pinterest, and Instagram, and launched my first "Here I am, World!" post. Quite naturally, nobody saw it. And it wasn't terrific anyway.

But within a few days, I knew something I needed to write. Something long overdue to people I'd never be able to track down. People who had been haunting my thoughts.

By 2011, I had been teaching for thirteen years. During that time, I taught many students with disabilities, 504 plans, and IEPs (individualized education plans). I sat across from their parents at teacher conferences and IEP meetings and listened to their concerns and suggestions. I read their IEPs. And I *thought* I understood. After all, we had autism in our family, and I'd even read Temple Grandin. So I made sure to put them toward the front of the class and allowed them to turn in assignments late.

Wasn't I doing my job?

But life is funny, and it has this way of running up and knocking you over on the playground. Your glasses get broken, and you find you need a new pair. Only you've needed them for quite some time, and suddenly you find yourself looking through new lenses and seeing more clearly what is in front of you, including what was always there but you couldn't see before. So, I wrote a post titled "Apology from Your Child's Former Teacher"— addressed to parents of children with disabilities from the perspective of a teacher who had just become one of those parents herself. It just *flowed*, and I think it took no more than twenty minutes to write. I posted it to my brand-new Twitter account, where I had followed and been followed back by some autism bloggers and authors. And I forgot about it.

But one of those authors, Bobbi Sheahan (*What I Wish I'd Known about Raising a Child with Autism: A Mom and a Psychologist Offer Heartfelt*

Guidance for the First Five Years), noticed it and retweeted it. It then got shared on Facebook. Suddenly, my phone was blowing up with notifications. First a hundred, then a thousand, then over twenty thousand in a day. And it kept going and was even shared by some significant disability-related groups. Every day for a few weeks, I kept getting notifications, shares, emails, and new followers. Three weeks later, another post was "Freshly Pressed" on WordPress (an editors' feature that picked around ten blog posts each day out of approximately nine hundred thousand new posts). I went from complete obscurity to having a nice little niche following and getting interview requests in less than a month. The Internet is funny that way. You just never know what's going to happen. I won't lie. The best part was how proud my dad was, bragging to others and keeping up with my stats. I'd always wanted to write. A blog about raising a child with autism wasn't what I envisioned. But it's where I found my voice, and it was a lucky distraction for someone who badly needed to talk.

I didn't get any money from it as my blog wasn't and still isn't monetized at the time of this writing. So I wasn't interested in that. But what I did get in return was something priceless. Thousands of people reached out with comments and emails. Some said, "Thank you for the apology I never thought I'd get. I forgive you. You can't know until you do." Others said, "Honey, take it from an experienced mom. It's going to be okay." And a few chose to blast me, saying I should have known and done better. This is an understandable criticism, so I won't complain.

Suddenly, I had readers from all over the world. Europe, Africa, the Middle East, and Australia. I "met" people from different cultures, religions, and backgrounds. The only thing we shared in common was loving someone on the autism spectrum. In some cases, these parents were autistic themselves. That was new. Because until then, higher-needs autism was all I knew. I had not yet interacted with autistic adults who were entirely verbal, living independently, and with careers and raising children of their own. (Or at least I thought I hadn't. My "autdar" has gotten pretty good since then.)

I learned about how autistic children are educated in South Africa, Saudi Arabia, Ireland, and Greenland. Readers shared stories about seeking diagnoses and therapies from all over. I learned about disability stigmas in some countries and cool initiatives in others. Indeed, it's luckier to be autistic in some places than in others.

But it was interactions with autistic people themselves (#actuallyautistic) that truly altered my perspective. They generously shared ideas about my son's behaviors and related their own experiences. And sometimes, they checked my somewhat able-bodied misconceptions. Some of them have become dear friends over the past decade. I've even been able to meet some of them in person. Not only are they friends, but they are also invaluable resources and wise advisers.

My point here is not to convince you to start a blog. There are umpteen thousands of them, usually adorned with puzzle pieces and a whole lot of complaining. Some are very good and helpful. But many are harmful and achingly exploitative. Worse yet are the ones who compromise their children's dignity with videos of head-banging and pictures of teens wearing diapers. It's best to stay away from that sort of stuff. Because if you don't, the negativity can seep into your pores. Kind of like the employee lounge. It's generally best to keep away lest you catch what they've got—which is usually a seriously sour attitude. And sometimes, though it's hard to contemplate, you have to wonder just who it is they're speaking for. Those inclined to attention-seeking can get an awfully big reward from oversharing.

The point of sharing this story is to stress the importance of finding your tribe—made up of understanding people seeking to connect and share resources and, more important, to seek out spaces online or in real life where you will interact with those most knowledgeable about autism—autists themselves. Isolation is common in our families. Don't give in to it. Seek out doers, thought leaders, and different perspectives. Attend conventions and learn more about your child and how to help them navigate adolescence and adulthood.

There's a community out there. But like all communities, there are places it's best not to hang and people you ought to avoid. So I'm including in the Places to Go and Things to See section a list of pages and personalities you might want to follow if you're just delving in. But do delve in. It's life-changing and affirming in ways you won't understand until you do. And on the most challenging days, those folks can cushion your fall.

Chapter 12

Apology from Your Child's Former Teacher: On What I Wish I Knew Then Based On What I Know Now

Dear Parents of Special-Needs Children I've Taught in the Past,

I need to make a big apology. You see, I've been teaching now for fourteen years, but I have only just recently joined your ranks.

I didn't know. *Not even a clue. I thought, mistakenly, that having two special-needs children in my family made me more sensitive to your needs as a parent. It didn't. And I'm so sorry for operating under the assumption that it did. I'm not attempting verbal self-flagellation here. I meant well. I knew a lot about autism and some about other special-needs conditions. I did care about your child. And I did want to do right by them. But, like a lot of teachers who Just Don't Get It, I thought doing right by them meant giving them extra time on assignments and not allowing them to fail my class. I thought being extra nice and seating them at the front of the room was what you needed from me.*

But you needed more, and I didn't understand that. You needed communication. A lot of it. You needed me to understand the depth of your fears. You needed me to realize that if you've met one special-needs child, you've met one special-needs child. *You needed me to understand that I was teaching your child, not an IEP. You needed to know, not assume, that I would go out on a limb to ensure your child's needs were met all over the school and not just in my classroom. You needed to not worry that, when your back was turned, I was still doing everything that I promised as well as thinking of better ways to meet your child's needs. You needed to talk about your child in meetings and not worry about the clock.*

I know better now. In just a few months, I will be placing my special little boy into the hands of the public school system. Because he is non-verbal, I will have no way of literally knowing how his day went, if he is being treated well, and if the people and agencies to whom I am en-trusting his care actually care about him. That kind of fear is paralyz-ing. And more so because I know just how little training (read: almost none) that most of the staff in a public school have in dealing with chil-dren like my son. They, too, will mean well. But they won't know. I now understand why you carry what I call The Binder of Epic Proportions to every meeting. Mine is getting bigger by the day.

I look back now at all of your children and wish that I had picked up the phone more, written quick notes home more often, challenged your child more often rather than less, and made you feel confident that someone else loved your baby in your absence. For that, I'm sorry. I promise to do better for those kids in the future. I promise to not as-sume anything about your children's unique situation and needs. And instead of merely reacting to any bullying of your children, I will ac-tively be on the lookout for it. I will remember your children and their possible confusion on activity bell schedule days. I will take more time each day to get to know them. I promise to do my best to push, per-suade, inform, and even take to task my colleagues who don't get it in the years to come. I pray that teacher training will improve in the fu-ture and that my son will reap the rewards of that. And I hope that I am just as patient, kind, and understanding with his teachers and schools as most of you were with us.

And those of you who weren't? I get you, too.

Sincerely,
Your Child's Former Teacher

Breakdowns, Closed Shoulders, and Lost Signals

I think nighttime is dark so you can imagine your fears with less distraction.

—Calvin, on why we're scared of the dark
Calvin and Hobbes, by Bill Watterson

Chapter 13

The World Doesn't Stop:
On Compounded Grief

When I was a tiny girl, maybe four, I remember my dad pointing up to the clouds.

"Did you know that those clouds are made out of water?" he asked.

"They're not water!" I insisted. "They're made out of cotton balls."

"No. They look like cotton. But do you remember when we were up in the clouds in the mountains this summer? Do you remember how the air felt so cool? That was the water in the clouds," he explained.

"No. I saw it on the news, Daddy. Scientists flew a plane up to the clouds, got out, walked around and looked at them, and they were made of cotton!" I fibbed.

I have lines of lawyers from both sides of my family, so it could be argued the instinct for debate runs in my blood. Fortunately, an appreciation for facts and scientific evidence later took hold. But my dad, gentle and attentive to young children, must have been amused by my creativity. And then he laid a response back on me that made even a young little me take pause.

"*Oh.* I see. Well, I hadn't heard that. I must have missed that on the news," Daddy replied. And then wisely and craftily he looked me in the eye and said, "But if *you* say you saw it, then I have to believe *you*. So it *must* be true that clouds are made of cotton." And then he changed the subject.

His testament of trust in me, combined with the knowledge that I'd feel my lie, was brilliant. I've never forgotten it.

That was my father. Wise, loyal, funny, playful, and described by many as the person they came running to when they were in trouble and didn't know what to do. Daddy always knew what to do. And I've never felt safer with any human being in my life.

A few years ago, my daughter came across an old postcard in storage. It was a 1976 image of the Bay Area Rapid Transit, sent to my father by a high school friend, Tommy. His friend entered the military during Vietnam. Unfortunately, his friend began to mentally unravel during boot camp, was arrested for assaulting a superior, was thrown in the brig, and was later determined to be suffering from paranoid schizophrenia. This condition often doesn't present itself until early adulthood. It attacked his mind as it does with so many. It followed a typical childhood and interrupted what should have been a bright future.

His mental illness was severe and completely disabling. As he spiraled into delusions, conspiracy theories, and bizarre middle-of-the-night phone calls, his social circle disappeared, leaving him to the family unable to help protect him from himself. As is typical, no one could keep him on medication for long.

But he had one true friend. My father. Daddy didn't brag about his kindness toward his friend. He never made jokes or tried to duck out of his calls or spontaneous visits. All he ever said was that the disorder was random, that it could have been any of us, and that he thought his friend would have remained loyal to him under the same circumstances. Tommy often called the house, launching into stories of government agents watching him from the trees, the city water supply being tainted with mind-altering drugs, etc. Sometimes, I answered the phone, and he shared his delusions of a Vietnamese daughter with me (he never made it out of boot camp) before asking to speak to my dad, who listened for as long as Tommy wanted to talk.

He often showed up unannounced at Daddy's law office. Everyone knew that if Daddy was free, his friend was to be welcomed inside. Daddy would listen to him ramble and offer him a sympathetic ear and general inquiries about his well-being. An hour of an attorney's time is expensive, but Daddy always welcomed him back freely with a respectful handshake and a warm hello.

I didn't understand then that my father's patience and kindness were unusual. But I now realize I learned much from his example.

I learned that differences in the mind are no more shameful than differences in the pancreas. I learned that everyone deserves friendship, understanding, and compassion. I learned about the randomness and privilege of good health. But, most important, I learned that you're not supposed to pat yourself on the back for being a friend to someone.

I'm not sure he realized that he taught these things by example. But of all the things I lament, it's that my children didn't have him around long enough to learn from him as well. Bronwyn was five and Callum was three when he died. Bronwyn's memories are limited to sitting on his lap and playing with the blue fine-point Pilot pens he preferred and always carried in his front shirt pocket. I know she loved him because even though five-year-olds aren't supposed to understand the finality of death, at his wake I found her standing alone in front of a table, looking at his picture, with a single tear running down her cheek. Of course, Callum didn't understand. But he lost a good buddy in my daddy, who always seemed to know how to just *be*, how to accept and enjoy the autistic children in our family. He would have loved taking Callum fishing on the beach and wouldn't have minded the lack of conversation. Heck, he'd have *preferred* it. I've often smiled, thinking how well their relationship would have worked out. Daddy would be able to share his passionate and *unabridged* tales of Allied naval war victories. And Callum wouldn't have known what he was talking about but would have loved the time together. It would have been a beautiful bond. They should have had that. They should have had him.

So, in the rambling words of an unmedicated paranoid schizophrenic's postcard, I told my daughter about her grandpa and the kind of man he was and the principles he lived. I hope I conveyed it well.

THREE weeks after Callum's official autism diagnosis, I was at school and gathering materials to administer makeups of the state FCAT (Florida Comprehensive Assessment Test) exam in the library. My cell phone rang, and I saw the caller was Vicki, my dad's longtime legal secretary. It sent a chill through my spine. Vicki had only ever called me once before at work—sixteen years earlier when my grandmother had a massive, fatal heart attack. She was flustered and not sure what was going on but told me that a man named Derry had run five blocks in the Florida heat to alert her that he'd seen my dad being loaded on a stretcher by an ambulance and saw blood on his head. (Derry was a young boy whose mother my father had helped, pro bono, to get him back from Puerto Rico when he was taken by his noncustodial father. Derry was troubled and suffered from alcoholism issues that kept him without employment or transportation and still living with his mother. But my dad would hire him for lawn care, odd jobs, etc., and sit and regale him, too, with stories of Allied naval war victories. Derry was fiercely loyal to him, which is why he ran five blocks in the Florida heat.)

After leaving school in a hurry and racing to the hospital, I sat for a long time in the lobby before they would let me back to see him in the ER. It hadn't been like that ten years earlier when he'd had a Wallenberg syndrome stroke of the brain stem. (He recovered almost entirely, with a few "glitches," and returned to work, fishing, and his longtime lady love, my "stepmother," Sheila.) During the last stroke, Sheila and I were allowed back quickly. But I was in the lobby a long time alone on this one. And, sadly, Sheila had died six years earlier from pancreatic cancer. I remember the parent of a former student recognizing me and striking up a surreal conversation about what her child was doing following high school. I remember the style of the chairs in the lobby, the frustration of having to continually walk outside to get a cell phone signal, and being afraid I'd miss them calling my name. I remember Jerry Springer on the hospital TV.

It's funny the details that forever impress in our darkest moments.

They finally let me back. Daddy was conscious, speaking, and continually pulling on the sheet to cover his chest. Always a modest person, I'd never once seen him without a shirt.

His previous stroke had been a blockage. They didn't diagnose his TIAs (transient ischemic strokes or "mini-strokes") the day before and had withheld invaluable clot-busting medicine for nearly ten hours on the day of that stroke. So, understandably, in his mind, nobody was listening when he repeatedly requested "the clot busters." He kept asking for Dr. Anderson, his doctor, whom he trusted. (Our whole family had switched to Dr. Anderson following the death of Sheila due to his gentle and kind bedside manner in her last days.)

Knowing Dr. Anderson was just across the street, I ran outside to get a signal and frantically called his office. Within minutes, he arrived, let my dad know he was there, and went off to look at his scans and find out what was going on. Soon, he came back with a neutral but kindly expression, put his hand on his shoulder, and explained that this was a different kind of stroke. It was hemorrhagic, and clot busters for this stroke would thin his blood—a bad thing when your brain is bleeding. Daddy was comforted that the right things were being done and rested a bit better. I remember Dr. Anderson looking down at his closed eyes, telling him he'd check back soon, and smiling. *But I knew that smile*, and my stomach cramped. Six years earlier, when he informed Sheila the chemo had caused total kidney failure and dialysis was not an option, she had cried, thinking she'd had more time and understanding the immediate significance. And then she asked if she could still have Popsicles. He'd smiled the same gentle smile then and told her she could have anything she wanted.

Dr. Anderson gestured to me to come out into the nurses' station area, where he showed me the CT scan. An English education major, even I knew that much of a brain shouldn't be so dark. Dr. Anderson told me he was amazed my dad was still conscious and talking, but that swelling would likely be coming and that they were getting ready to life-flight Daddy to Shands Hospital in Gainesville. He told me, in his gentle way, to make all the calls.

I called my husband, Daddy's brother, my stepbrother Tyler, and my stepsister Trisha. I arranged childcare, rang some more people, and waited. During that wait, we made small talk and jokes. But his head hurt badly. Trisha arrived. We took turns rubbing his temples to relieve the pain. It was the only thing that seemed to help.

And then life-flight was there. Even in a daze, I noted the quiet and the careful kindness of the medical flight crew. I remember the arms of the nurse as she hugged me tightly. I remember thinking how unbelievably gentle and compassionate they were with us. Though most ER nurses have been kind in my life, I don't usually get hugs from them. I didn't yet realize why.

ON the hour-long drive to Shands Hospital, my mother unexpectedly called from Georgia to tell me they were doing some tests and were suspicious she had cancer. Mentally, I set that aside, prioritizing crises, and made more calls. (Days later, it was decided she didn't have cancer.)

And every year since, Facebook has helpfully reminded me of that long hour to Gainesville by sharing the memory of my desperate pleas to friends for prayer.

DADDY was immediately transferred to the Neuro Intensive Care Unit (confusingly called NICU). I notified the NICU of my presence, sat, and waited. In that room, I remember the corkboard on the wall, a tear-off sheet for somebody seeking a roommate, and an informational poster about symptoms of a stroke. I recall the color of the chairs in that small lobby, and I can still feel the weight in my hand of the coiled red phone outside the NICU doors families had to use to call the nurses' station. I'd be using it a lot over the next twelve days.

The neurologists and neurosurgeons were also amazed at how alert he was—sitting up, talking, and still complaining about those pesky Democrats in office. I remember him wishing he had his trusty sound effects machine he kept in his office drawer. It had sounds of bombs, explosions, and gunfire. He liked to use it to call friends, declaring, "Help! The Demo-crats are coming! We're under siege!" And he'd laugh and laugh. He thought that would be funny to share with the nurses.

Somebody came in to ask all the questions about insurance, living wills, and his religious affiliation. Still himself, he gave his favorite answer: "Druid." Technically, he was Episcopalian. But he'd always thought it would be hilarious if, on his deathbed, the hospital had to scramble and round up a Druid priest somewhere. But, of course, you see lots of unusual stuff in a university town because she didn't blink and dutifully wrote it down.

He wasn't *supposed* to be conscious. Not with that much blood on his brain. But he was. The neurologist explained that swelling might become an issue and that they'd need to use a shunt if he were to start showing symptoms of cranial pressure. But he was wide awake and talking for three days before he suddenly believed it was 1973, the year I was born. I was quickly ushered out of the room so they could insert an emergency shunt to relieve the pressure. It worked—mostly—and he was back to being lucid. That was wonderful, but I still remember staring a long time at the tufts of his beautiful silver white hair on the floor from when they'd had to shave part of his head in a hurry. As the days passed, he began to simultaneously live in two worlds. Imagining that the hospital staffs were sailors or ne'er-do-wells and ordering his ship to be ready for battle. Yet he still knew we were there and was laughing with us at the amusing orders he declared and inviting us into the adventure. Despite that man's love of war history, he didn't have a mean bone in him, so it was just part of his playful nature.

I didn't realize his occupancy of two worlds was a sign he was leaving us. But *he* knew. One afternoon, the respiratory therapist came in to work with him. Uncharacteristically grumpy, he declared he wouldn't partici-pate until somebody moved his bed closer to the window (not an option in intensive care). The therapist left with a threat to return later. Since he was beginning to develop fluid in his lungs, I was worried. And after days of living in the hospital from seven a.m. to eight p.m. daily (Trisha and her love Brent took the night shifts while I crashed at a nearby hotel), I was frustrated by this lack of cooperation.

I remember turning to him in exasperation, saying, "Don't you know how lucky you are? Nobody even thought you'd be conscious! You have zero damage to speech, swallowing, writing, walking. When the swelling goes down, if your lungs are clear, you're going to get to go to rehab here in Gainesville. They're already discussing it. If you would just cooperate, you could go back to lawyering, fishing, and your life! Don't you realize that?"

But Daddy turned piercing brown eyes at me and dropped the expression from his face. He held my eyes as I stood there, and with a grave expression, Daddy slowly, ever so slightly, shook his head. I still had hope, so I didn't see that for what it was—Daddy trying to prepare me for what even he, in his sometimes-confused mind, already knew. Looking back, I know what he was trying to say: "No, Punkin. Not this time."

FROM there, he began to decline. He was on oxygen and had a feeding tube. They tried to keep him comfortable from his headache, but it still plagued him. The only thing that seemed to make it better was rubbing his forehead and temples. If you did, he'd go back to sleep. Trisha and Brent came over every night, sleeping in chairs. They hadn't been together long enough for me to know Brent well yet. But I learned all I needed to know during those awful days and nights. Because Brent, kindhearted person that he is, sat up all night watching for any look of discomfort on Daddy's face before tirelessly rubbing Daddy's brows and temples to alleviate it. He did that for a man he barely knew, simply because Trisha loved my daddy so. As long as I live, I will never forget his kindness to my father in his last days.

On the eleventh night, after two weeks of Sean having to bring Callum and Bronwyn to me at the hotel to see me, I went home for the night, intending to return in the morning. We left Trisha with Daddy and drove the hour home. I crashed immediately. About an hour later, close to midnight, my phone rang. Trisha told me she didn't know what was happening but that I needed to come back right then. She had dozed off for a bit and had been awakened suddenly by a flurry of medical staff. When she looked at the shunt, the bag was full of blood. They raced him into emergency exploratory neurosurgery in the middle of the night. Sean stayed with the kids while a dear friend arrived to drive me to Gainesville.

Around three a.m., the neurosurgeon came in and said they'd looked for an active bleed but couldn't find one. So they really didn't know what happened. But it wasn't good. That they knew. It wasn't good. Soon, they began to wheel Daddy back into the NICU. When I walked over, his eyes were open. But when I looked into them, I knew he wasn't behind his eyes anymore.

That's when I lost it. When I *knew*. When Trisha and I fell into chairs, wrapped our arms around each other, and sobbed. Just as we had done six years earlier as her beautiful, loving mother Sheila (and my daddy's heart) slipped out of this world.

The rest of the day was tests, more tests, and tests to confirm. By then, everyone had arrived. We talked with one of the doctors, who was a bit too gentle in discussing the prognosis. Briefly, some in the room interpreted what he said to be hopeful. But it's what he wasn't saying that I noticed. And I knew my father's greatest fear was to become vegetative. He'd even set up his own living will to ensure that in such an event, we'd turn off life support. So, interrupting the others, I looked the doctor in the eye and asked point-blank what percentage chance he had of communicating consciously. I remember him seeming surprised by my directness. But all I could think of was Daddy's eyes as he shook his head at my question days earlier. He'd been trying to tell me something. I understood now. His life was over. And a sense of desperation to relieve any possible suffering of his being trapped inside himself took over. To love him, I had to let him go.

We had to wait for another few hours for that process and a third doctor to confirm the prognosis before we could turn off the machines. I've said before I'm not a crier. But I had been sobbing since three a.m. and not leaving his side. Finally, my uncle, his brother, arrived. After hearing it would be about three hours, he looked over at me and suggested I leave for a bit and take a break. Overcome with grief, I refused and laid my head on Daddy's chest. At which point, he declared there was no way his brother would be happy with him if he allowed me to remain like that. That I needed food and fresh air. And speaking authoritatively, he looked at Sean and told him to take me to get something to eat before returning to the hospital. Daddy had that same way about him—he just knew what to do and declared it. So we went to a nearby Olive Garden. I must have looked as I felt because the whole restaurant stared at my swollen face. We ate.

And then we drove back to the hospital to sit with my father as he died.

It wasn't like those scenes in movies where they flip the switch and they instantly flatline. Instead, it took about forty-five minutes. I held Daddy's hand, stretched my arms around him just like I did as a little girl, whispered into his ear that Granny and Sheila were waiting on him, and laid my head on his chest until he took his last breaths.

And then my rock was gone. When we left the hospital, the sky opened and began to pour.

IN just a month, my child had been diagnosed with severe autism and my father died. In my head, it certainly seemed like the universe was picking on me something awful. You'd think that you'd get some time to process one life-transforming event before another comes along. But life doesn't work that way. The world doesn't simply stop because you're overwhelmed. It keeps spinning all the same, and the operator will not let you off the ride just because it's making you sick. Your employer still wants you at work. The electric company still wants to be paid. And you have no other choice but to keep getting up, going through the motions of living, and learning to live with your new normal.

It continues to spin. But having lived through those weeks of heart-ache, I gained some perspective. I now know what constitutes an emergency—*and, more important, what doesn't.* I know what to let bounce off of me and what I must prioritize. Autism is not an emergency. It just *is*. Losing a child is an emergency. I've mourned the loss of my friends' children too many times. That's a whole different kind of loss. And I haven't lost mine. He's here. Happy, healthy, and delightfully mischievous. Do we have hard times? Yes. But we get through them. Do we have joyful times? You betcha.

And I promise—*so will you.*

Chapter 14

Triage:
On Shortcomings, Siblings, and Attention Equity

When it comes to loving, nurturing, and meeting the needs of our children, the term "triage" doesn't usually come to mind. No mother holds a sleeping baby in the wee hours of the night and ever imagines a reality in which that child's needs rank below another's. I certainly didn't.

I know differently now.

On the battlefield, triage is a necessity. It's a cruel necessity, but triage saves more lives. When there aren't enough resources, you must choose who gets attention first. Unfortunately, like all the hard decisions in life, triage sometimes fails. You thought the gentleman walking and talking would be okay while you were treating a possible head trauma victim for what later turned out to be a minor scalp laceration. But the gentleman died of a heart attack while waiting in the lobby.

When you have children with widely varying needs, triage becomes your new reality—not in the lifesaving sense, but in every other way that matters. If the choice is gymnastics lessons for one and speech therapy for the other, you pick speech therapy. And, if one child is having problems organizing her room, that problem gets trumped by the other's penchant for throwing household objects. No, it isn't fair. It just *is*.

In the ER, the limited resources are beds, imaging, and experts. In families, they are Mom, Dad, time, money, and energy. As a parent, you'd like to think you're limitless. But, unfortunately, it's a lie we tell ourselves. Because the only thing a parent has without limitation is love.

And children need more than love.

Bronwyn was twenty months old the day Callum was born. She doesn't remember a time when she was the sole focus of our world. Of course, that's not so different than other kids, and parents do their best to love them equally.

But it wasn't long before Callum's needs began to take a lot more than 50 percent of our parental attention. While we were running around getting evaluations, doing therapies, talking to insurance companies, and so on, she was often without an attentive audience. Instead of being a kid, she was sitting in a therapy lobby waiting on her brother or hanging out with Grandma while we took Callum to a specialist. And of course, she was always present for the early behavioral problems—probably frightening to a little girl—accompanying his frustration in not being able to communicate.

It never let up after that.

All those years with Callum up all night and waking everyone. The times we had to leave the party or the restaurant early. The places we couldn't take them both, so we didn't go or couldn't go as a family. The years of encopresis (you'll want to look that up) misery. The times we had to jump to react to whatever her brother was doing—interrupting the performance she was putting on for us.

Bronwyn's never had 50 percent of us from the time she was too young to remember. Yet, she's never complained. But, of course, she doesn't know different.

She doesn't know about the doll dresses I wanted to sew for her. The antique shops I wanted to explore with her. The plays and musicals I would've bought tickets for. The Girl Scout badges I once dreamed I'd sew on her uniform. And how badly I wanted to create the home where all the neighborhood kids wanted to hang out. She doesn't know the interests and skills I wanted to pass along to her—calligraphy, jewelry making, and poetry. There wasn't the time or opportunity for any of that.

And I fear she'll remember too well that day, following too many Callum-related days off work, I wasn't there when she won the Principal's Award. It was the only awards day I ever missed. But she got to shine, and I wasn't there to witness it.

You might expect her to resent him. Yet she's kind, helps him find his favorite videos, laughs at his antics, and sometimes graces him by letting him sit in her saucer chair in her room. There's no sibling rivalry. She learned early that sometimes life isn't equitable and accepted it.

But I haven't. I know the mother-daughter moments I'd envisioned but wasn't able to have. The stories there hasn't been enough time to share. I see how few years I have left with Bronwyn, and I want all of what I missed back.

I adore Callum. I regret nothing about him. Of course, we don't resent him. Ever.

Still, if only she knew how much I've wished I could make time freeze and just be with her. How much I worry I didn't give her the emotional foundation and attention she needed. How I hope she knows how much she's loved and how badly she was wanted. Mostly, I hope.

Bronwyn doesn't remember all those sweet middle-of-the-nights with just the two of us. Her soft head tucked under my chin, her little fist clutching my nightgown. Singing to her and rocking, holding her and thanking a God I wasn't even sure about for her warm little body and sweet, milky breath against my neck. How I'd stay just

This picture of my girl and her perennially untied shoes captures her spirit.

like that, long after she'd fallen asleep and could have returned to bed. Life being fragile and random, I wanted my love to seep into her pores.

But a few years later, she asked me how much I loved her. Before I got to the part about "all the way to the moon and back," she said, "I know you love me a lot. But you love Callum just a little bit more, don't you? Because he's special, right?" A little part of me died inside. I quickly corrected her. Tried to find the right words. Prayed she'd never forget them. It was a great many more words I can't and would not quote verbatim. But their essence was, "Before you were born, I dreamed of you. *Just* you."

I hope she believed me. I hope that one day she knows I did the best I could. I hope she'll forget all the ways I could have done it better and will remember all the ways I loved her instead.

And I hope she knows that while triage is a necessity in this world, it has never been recognized in the heart of a mother.

========

There's nothing quite like parenting to make us confront our short-comings.

We were first told Bronwyn would be a boy. I had desperately wanted a daughter. I spent an entire week apologizing to my belly and assuring him I loved him. A week later, a nervous ultrasound technician carefully asked, "You said the other ultrasound showed a boy?" When she had to tell us otherwise, I whooped and cackled with glee. (Later, I read Hope Edelman's books and realized that's a common thing for women lacking a relationship with their mothers. They seem to overwhelmingly want daughters the first time around to try to get a mother-daughter relationship right by other means. It was true enough of me.)

I called *everyone I knew*, bought all the dresses, and dreamed of reading beloved books together. She would inherit my grandmother's jewelry and my china. With dreams of slumber parties, pedicures, and shopping, I cherished my baby girl. And I wanted to give her a mother she'd grow up to always want and need in her life.

Sean and Bronwyn are so alike. They both have been diagnosed with ADHD—the kind that puts the H in ADHD. But they have the other delightful traits that those with ADHD often have—the creativity, quick thinking, and passion that those of us who love them adore.

But because they are so very alike in temperament, interests, sense of humor, and ADHD, they are close. They get a kick out of each other. Bronwyn often prefers him to me, me being a little too low-key. They're kindred souls, my baby girl and her daddy. Sometimes, I'm envious of her relationship with him, although I do understand it. If ever a woman were a daddy's girl, it was me.

I still remember running to him every evening and screaming, "Daddy!" before jumping into his arms, confident I'd be caught and hoisted into the air. I have memories of being curled up on his lap watching *The Rockford Files*, *All in the Family*, and *Sanford and Son*. My oldest friends will often laugh at the way I say something and declare, "Oh my God, you just channeled your father!" My dad and I were kindred souls as well, so I love her having that with her daddy.

But I'd dreamed my entire life of having a daughter I was close to. For reasons it would take a separate book to explain, I'm not close to my own mother. We're not estranged exactly. Sean and I help when we're needed, and we do holidays. It's complicated, but that mother-daughter bond I've envied in others isn't possible for us. I was close to my grandmother and my stepmother, but both are long gone.

BRONWYN has always been a delight to me. Still, in the way of children and their oft-perplexed parents, we're pretty different personalities. She's more courageous than I am, willing to put herself out there. I love how she dismisses popular opinion in favor of truth. It took me longer to sort that out, but she's had it from the get-go. It has never occurred to her to wish anyone harm, even if they harmed her. And her loud, snorting laughter isn't the least bit reserved.

Sean is on the road often, and that's always been hard. Bronwyn has always taken it hardest. One morning a few years ago, she woke early and came in to snuggle with me. She talked about how much she missed her dad and said, "The truth is, Mom, Daddy's just more FUN than you."

Ouch.

Once again, I wished the homebody, introvert, and lover of air-conditioning in me were all less so. I acknowledged the difficulty she was having. I told her I was sorry I'm not as much of her kind of fun (theme parks, producing videos, games) as her daddy and wished I were better at those sorts of things.

Then I felt her little arms wrap around me before she clarified, "Mom, Daddy is more fun than you. But you're more loving. I go to Daddy for fun and you for love. That's what I love about you best."

Well, hell. That's for sure a conversation I've replayed in my head obsessively as I continue raising these two. But the combination of those big beautiful blue eyes—my grandmother's—and those words? Deep breaths kind of love right there. Words that feel a little like absolution just when I'm sure I'm failing.

SHE *comes to me for love*—for the stuff that's hard to talk about. And sometimes, if I'm lucky, she shares her secrets with me.

I may be doing lots of things wrong. But I hope that statement counts. I have to be doing something right, right?

Chapter 15

Losing My Convictions:
On How We're All Changed *Somehow*

N ot so very long ago, I knew what I thought about things. I could
debate them point by point with relative ease and felt comfortable
with the conclusions I reached. Or rather, conclusions reached for
me by articulate and plausible political philosophies ingrained in me in
an echo chamber of D'Souza, Buckley, Sowell, and conservative radio. I
identified myself as a libertarian-leaning Republican—conservative both
fiscally and in terms of defense, but socially liberal. Central to my thinking was the sincere belief that most of what the government takes on turns
out to be disastrous. I'm still naturally suspicious of decisions made by
committees and generally believe the fewer cooks in the kitchen, the better. And raised by a lawyer, I'm equally skeptical about proposed new laws
and constitutional amendments, suspecting them to be the result of emotional reactions and political machinations rather than well-considered
policy or a workable plan for funding them.

But convictions are a funny thing. Sometimes all it takes to shake up
your belief system is a personal experience with what you didn't know
before.

From the fundamentalist Christian mother who finds herself loving a
gay child to the pro-life couple whose amniocentesis shows a baby whose
genetics are incompatible with life. The anti-cannabis-legalization police
officer who is racked with pain from bone cancer and nausea from chemo,

and the fiscally liberal woman who finds taxes and regulations strangling her small business.

Life is like that sometimes, and irony mocks us.

Fourteen years ago, I had many convictions. One of them was a sincere belief that the Department of Education was the worst thing to ever happen to US public education. My opinion wasn't based merely on my party's official stance. Unlike most politicians, I graduated from the University of North Florida with bachelor's and master's degrees. I have been trained in the latest fad learning theories, participated in wastes of expenditure, and seen firsthand the effects of an educational culture that values test scores over knowledge. From twenty-three years of experience, I know a typical US public school education is insufficient for too many of our children. I know we can do better.

Only we don't vote to have enough living, breathing people to do it properly.

With the diagnosis of Callum came the absolute certainty of my own hypocrisy. When Callum was born, I was a College of Education graduate with a degree in secondary education—English ed. I had once attended an all-day Saturday seminar in educational law. I knew that IDEA stood for the Individuals with Disabilities Education Act. I knew that an IEP (individualized education plan) is a legally binding document. I had a quick, factual recall of features of specific disabilities and knew that visual aids were necessary.

That's it. That's all I knew. I didn't know that:

- Prior to 1975, schools weren't required to educate children like Callum in any way.

- The reauthorization of the Americans with Disabilities Act (ADA), the IDEA, wasn't just a reauthorization. It included potentially life-changing rights for special-education students: FAPE (free and *appropriate* education) and LRE (least restrictive environment), which together mean that a child has a need and right to learn in the least restrictive environment possible, and reasonable efforts and evidence-based practices and resources must be used to ensure success. Gone were the days of putting a bright child with language but no speech in a room full of nonverbal classmates—simply because the adults weren't trained how to use AAC (assistive and augmentative communication) methods or equipment.

- The only thing stopping states from returning to life before 1975— without compulsory, free, and appropriate education the law of the land—was the Department of Education.

- IDEA has never been fully funded. Congress promised 40 percent of the funding for its mandate, with the states to pick up the remaining 60 percent. Its current funding rate is somewhere around 14 percent.

- ADA/IDEA are the only assurances disabled children in all fifty states have.

I suddenly realized I was a hypocrite because I now depended upon the Department of Education and federal law to protect my child from a substandard education. If it were not for the ADA and IDEA, my son would not have any of what he has now. If it were not for federal oversight, school districts would not provide for his needs. So, IDEA safeguards became the only big sticks available for me to carry as I began to walk softly through the Land of IEPs. Now I knew myself to be dependent upon the same agency I generally abhorred. So, I was a walking, talking hypocrite.

And that had a lot of implications.

What else do I hold to be true—until I have walked in the shoes of one directly affected by it? What other political philosophies are incompatible with the needs of human beings I love? How can I now gratefully accept that which I have decried and voted against? Because of *taxation*?

Only now, I had at my keyboard and fingertips people in the autism community *from other countries*—those same countries I had read about and heard about on conservative radio that were so miserable, what with their universal health care and high taxation.

And I found them looking at Americans with pity. Which was a strange thing to a curious person.

So, I decided the only way to be confident in my convictions was to systematically educate myself—from scratch—issue by issue, assuming I'd confirm my bias.

Only I *didn't*. Thinking like the school librarian I was, I went to primary and the most politically neutral sources to learn, avoiding commentary. I read both sides of most of the issues dividing our country—and followed all the links on their sites to ensure I'd considered everything. *Then* I listened to the commentary. With some degree of shock and horror, I realized I'd made a gradual, years-long transformation. I was not a fiscal conservative anymore. I wasn't even a libertarian. To this day, I don't know who is more shocked, my lifelong liberal friends or me.

Becoming the mother of a high-needs autistic child didn't just shake up my world; it shook up my *mind*. I became more aware of the things I don't know the slightest thing about, and I want to know—but from unbiased sources. I'm suspicious of every viewpoint I hear. And for a straightforward reason—people don't always know of what they speak. Not really know. They've heard about it. They've read about it on Facebook. They don't always care if it's true or bother to fact-check. They imagine how they would feel if it were them. They listen to their favorite talking heads shape their opinions (that they now consider facts). They compare it to something they know that isn't entirely (or at all) related. They espouse—and vote—from the comfort of their unaffected lives. Not because they're evil. They just don't know otherwise. And they won't until someone they love becomes someone they once professed to disapprove of.

That realization has left me without the foundation that built me, out of sync with a community that no longer understands my way of thinking—even if they still love me. And meeting new friends whose views align more than my previous party but who aren't necessarily looking at the world from behind the eyes of somebody who spent most of her life as *one of them*. We have many of the same goals but not always the same ideas of how to change them. I haven't found my place yet.

In the meantime, I'm reading social media commentary from friends and family who don't yet realize the ease of becoming a hypocrite as well—when life might run up and knock *them* over on the playground, breaking the lenses by which they currently view the world. People who haven't yet had to fight for the well-being of someone they love. Who haven't been desperate, mentally ill, shunned, violated, sick, disabled, disenfranchised, broke, addicted, or any of the various occurrences that can shake up one's world. Instead, they're just loud people who are clueless about what they would really think if it happened to them.

No, I didn't convert to someone who hates conservatives. It wouldn't be fair, honest, or even possible. I live in the red county I was born and raised in. I still love everyone I've ever loved. Still know their hearts. Still remember their arms wrapped around me in my darkest moments and losses.

But these new lenses showed me other things more clearly as well, people I hadn't noticed as much before Callum. I can no longer reconcile my previous beliefs with my current ones. For a born people-pleaser surrounded these days by more people she disagrees with than agrees, it's all a bit of a soul-searcher. I ask myself if it's worth trying to change some perceptions. And then I remember I once couldn't be convinced, either. People learn. They grow. The things that make them the wonderful people the younger me remembers are still there. And since I do love them, I'm just going to keep relentlessly reminding them. They'll continue sending me shares, arguing on Facebook, and praying for me. And somewhere along the way, I hope good conversations happen. Good conversations are the only things that have ever opened hearts and minds.

That's the most profound thing the experience of being his mother changed in *me*. I'm not saying it will do the same for *you*. It might not change your politics, values, or religion at all. But I've not known any parent who has ever loved a permanently vulnerable child who remains the same person they were before. In some way, you are forever different.

I still have imaginary chats sitting in Daddy's car, with the cold air blowing while we hash out our thoughts on matters. What I loved most about him was his calm in all situations. These days, we'd disagree about a lot of things. But he never disrespected those who disagreed with him. A lawyer, he didn't resort to logical fallacies, and he wasn't a bully. When I think about how being Callum's mother changed much of what I believed in, he remains the sole person I ache to talk it all over with. The person I most want to tell what I learned. How I've changed—what I've lost and what I've gained.

I see very little of the world in black and white these days like I used to. It's all shades of gray now. Which makes it hard to wholly embrace any one viewpoint. Instead, my mind immediately goes to "What if it was Bronwyn? What if it was Callum?" And then I have my answer. When you've loved someone disenfranchised by their very existence, you better empathize with all those who are disenfranchised.

Meeting the needs of the developmentally disabled across their life span is not a priority in this country. Thousands of pro-life activists march demanding every child be born, but they aren't willing to contribute tax dollars for education and lifetime care if they are disabled. (If protestors only knew what many states consider ethical and legal lifetime "care," perhaps they'd march more for those already born.)

Until then, we're not justified in letting up on night watch. Some would deny my child a happy and fulfilling life when I'm gone. They vote for it. And friends, family, and genuinely liked acquaintances vote for it, too. Even those who love us or claim to. I have few remaining illusions that most people will do the right thing unless the opportunity is standing before them and impossible to ignore or deny.

Of the things I've lost, the only one I miss is my faith in the inherent goodness of the collective—not as individuals, but within the anonymity of community. But, unfortunately, that naïveté is a luxury my son could end up having to pay for.

Therefore, it will always be too expensive an indulgence. I must represent my son's interests to the best of my ability and in conjunction with like-minded others.

Because the world will not.

Chapter 16

The Bears in the Park:
On the Effects of Hypervigilance

n folklore, the witching hour is that time of night in which demons and their supernatural companions are most likely to appear and bedevil a soul. Not being the superstitious sort, I've never feared ghosts and goblins. No, my fears have always been more practical and less fanciful. At the three a.m. "witching hour" of sleep loss, I worry about things that can actually happen—cancer, crashes, predators, and the certainty of one day not being here to protect my son. But despite not believing it, the witching hour has haunted me for years.

Because in the busyness of daytime life—the laundry, haggling with insurance reps, and ferrying children to various therapies—the demons assigned to parents of high-needs autistic children make themselves scarce in daylight. However, they know to lie in wait and return when it's quiet, and no one is around to distract us from our fears.

IN October 2013, a New York mother's worst nightmare came true. She received a phone call that her fourteen-year-old autistic son Avonte had eloped from his school. Worse yet, it took many minutes for school officials to realize he was missing and more than an hour for law enforcement to be called. Avonte's image was plastered everywhere. Those of us in the autism community shared, hoped, and prayed this one would come home.

Because so many *don't*. We held our collective breaths. But the days turned into weeks and then months. Finally, three months following his disappearance, Avonte's remains were located on the Queens side of the East River. Unfortunately, the condition of them were such that a cause of death was never determined. As a result, his family will never know if he was simply drawn to the river like so many or if his life ended at someone else's hands.

SIX months following the recovery of Avonte Oquendo, Callum eloped for the first time. He was five years old, and it was the Fourth of July. He'd shown a tendency to elope (bolt from safety), which approximately half of autistic children will do. ("Elopement" is the preferred term over "wandering.") We knew that danger, and we thought we took suitable precautions when we arrived at Sean's brother's home for the cookout and festivities. Everyone, including the children, gathered in the kitchen for a quick reminder of the importance of keeping all the exterior doors locked (as Callum didn't yet have the dexterity to operate locks). And we reminded everyone of how autistic children tend to be drawn to water. We discussed the mantra whenever a child on the spectrum disappears—"Search water *first*." Everyone agreed. Sean and I took turns being on Callum-watch, following him everywhere, and switching off to give the other a chance to visit with family.

But no situation is 100 percent safe, and human beings aren't perfect. So, while Bronwyn and her cousins were busy chasing one another about the house and family arrived carrying in platters of potluck, Sean was watching Callum. And two things happened simultaneously.

The timer went off, and Sean turned his back briefly to check the contents of the oven. And somebody—we never discovered who, nor did it matter—left the front door unlocked.

In the thirty or so seconds it took Sean to peek in the oven and turn back around, Callum left the room. First, I heard Sean calling Callum's name, followed by the alarmed calls of his grandparents, before I took off running toward the front door, pulling my phone out of my pocket to call 9-1-1.

We were lucky. I didn't have to call. As everyone searched and shouted Callum's name, Sean heard a faint giggle and yelled for everyone to be quiet. He took off running across the street to where our sister-in-law's parents lived, a place Callum visited often *and knew to have a swimming pool*. That's where his daddy found him. Standing outside their locked gate to the pool area, splashing delightedly in the puddles from recent rain. The entire ordeal took less than two minutes.

But I remembered Avonte and all the other autistic children over the past decade who didn't come home again.

And no matter how long I live, I'll never forget looking out from their front porch, shaking with terror, and the surreal observation of how the St. Johns River glints silver as it flows north.

THE second significant time Callum eloped was from the playground at school when he was nine years old. Ask anyone who has witnessed the devotion of Callum's 1:1 aide, Ms. Dawn, and they'll all sing her praises. But as we've learned personally, sometimes perfect storms arise, and people are imperfect. The video later showed the split second Ms. Dawn turned her head to answer another student's question coinciding with Callum bolting around the side of the building. In the video, Ms. Dawn immediately turned her head back to the playground, didn't see him, and walked out to look in the hamster tubes he is fond of crawling through. The tape shows her instant panic, shouts to the teacher, and Ms. Dawn taking off at a run for the front office and screaming for them to activate all the cameras. They did, and the principal and resource officer took off out the side doors to search. There was no delay.

As they scanned the video monitors while others searched in person, a phone call came in. A sobbing parent leaving the campus after dropping off her children late that day had spotted him. He'd made it past the parking lot and out the main gate of the school, crossed a busy, rural road, and was standing inches from the road—excitedly flapping his arms and squealing as pickup trucks drove around him. Two school employees (one my stepsister Trisha) heard the shout from whoever picked up the phone and raced to bring him back to safety. (The sobbing parent didn't exit her car to shield him. She instead filmed herself going off on a rant about it for Facebook as my son stood in harm's way.)

As quickly as it all went down, I was unaware until I got a near-hysterical call from Ms. Dawn, sobbing and begging my forgiveness for letting us down. I have never blamed her. I know all too well how quick and cunning my playful and curious boy can be when finding trouble. I know her love for him and how fiercely she protects him. These sorts of incidents are simply the reality of having a profoundly intellectually disabled and sensory-seeking child who has no understanding of danger.

And it's why the Pied Piper of Hamelin comes to mind every time an autistic child elopes, never to go home again.

———————

I read with interest one day a post by psychiatrist Dr. Gail Saltz, "This Is You on Stress." Being stressed all the time, I'm well aware of its effects. Dr. Saltz says stress is an evolutionary thing, a fight-or-flight response triggered by perceived danger. In dangerous situations—such as the possibility of encountering bears in a park—it keeps us aware and can save our lives. The problem, she says, is when you are removed from the danger, but the fight-or-flight instinct is still going. That kind of anxiety is harmful. She suggests some strategies for breaking the cycle of unhelpful stress when danger isn't actually nearby. I thought about that and how to use those strategies to stop the witching-hour anxiety attacks and how to calm down. I thought about those bears in the park.

And that's when I realized. It's no wonder parents of severely autistic children are increasingly getting diagnosed with anxiety disorders, PTSD, and depression.

It's not because of their children. No, our children give us just as much joy as any others. It's because there is rarely a time when you aren't in the park looking around for all those bears.

And the bears are many: elopement, bullying, failure of school districts to provide an appropriate IEP, medical and dental appointments, unfamiliar situations, loud noises, lack of autism awareness, lack of autism acceptance, loved ones who don't get it, judgmental stares and comments from strangers, accessibility, respite care, insurance battles, lack of appropriate housing for autistic adults—and on and on.

So, we *never* leave the park. And we stand, perpetually in a state of "fight or flight," clutching the hands of our children and scanning for trouble—while trying to live our lives in all the necessary ways. Meeting the needs of other children. Nurturing our marriages. Paying bills. Working. Caring for older family members. Then taking care of ourselves—which, on that list, always comes last.

But we do all these things simultaneously while anxiously looking around, listening, and facing those bears when we encounter them. The hypervigilance required to keep them safe can be exhausting in body, mind, and spirit.

I'd like to follow Dr. Saltz's suggestions. I'd like to try meditation, breathing myself calm, and reminding myself that I'm out of the situation. Except I'm not out of it, and I already know we'll never leave. Not alive anyway.

I don't have the luxury of letting down my guard. Because if I do, the bears are still there. My child might not receive an appropriate education. He may be traumatized by people not trained to work with autistic children. Someone might forget to latch a door—a door within minutes of busy intersections and bodies of water. He might be targeted by those who would do harm to the defenseless.

No, the only time I can relax is when he is safely in bed and the house alarm is engaged. But, even then, fears of my own mortality (who will take care of him?), his education, his health (feeding issues), and his future wake and haunt me in those middle-of-the-night hours of worry.

The problem is that these fears aren't unjustified. My anxiety isn't occurring in the absence of danger. It's not a simple matter of my brain being chemically imbalanced. These dangers are *real*, not catastrophized, because this world is not yet ready to welcome my son. A son who will one day outlive me. A son whom I fear will not be cared for by those with good hearts and a desire to allow him as much independence as he is able to handle.

A child whom—in the wee hours of the night—I lie awake envisioning as an old man. An old man—with no family of his own—lying in a bed and taking his last breaths with no one to hold his hand.

That's the demon who haunts my personal witching hour. That one right there. Yes, those bears are all around me.

I don't want anxiety to win, but it's ever-present. It steals from me sleep, laughter, and peace. Joy? It's fleeting. Found in bits and snatches—and always bestowed on me by my children. Yes, it's there. But it's often stolen by the thieves of anxiety and fear.

And in my darkest moments, I fear that lack of joy is turning *me* into a bear. Someone who sometimes fails to appreciate the little things. Someone who will fail to pass on joy to my children, who deserve that in their mother.

So, I do what I can to repel the bears. I involve myself heavily in autism-related causes. I see an excellent therapist who helps me to sort out all the feelings. I take antianxiety meds so that I can sleep—hopefully right through the night, but not always. I try to keep my eyes on the horizon and live in the moment. I inhale his little boy scent when he creeps in early to snuggle. I sing our songs together in quiet moments before dawn. And I record all the little moments, laughter, and successes as they come—so that anxiety doesn't do me in by stealing any more joy than it already does.

And in the meantime, I remain perpetually on watch for bears.

Including the one who lives permanently in me.

Chapter 17

Picking a Lane: On Controversy and ABA (Applied Behavior Analysis)

I n the autism community, the subject of applied behavior analysis (ABA) is, to put it mildly, controversial. Everyone who knows anything about it has an opinion they'll be sure to tell you about. A person new to the subject and googling will find descriptions that range from "form of torture" to "dog training for people" to "changed our lives for the better." So if you are a parent making decisions for an autistic child or a teacher weighing using recommended ABA techniques, how do you know what to do?

As I've said before, I view these things through three lenses—teacher, parent, and autism specialist. But I didn't begin with all three of those titles. I was a teacher who became a parent who returned to school and became an autism specialist. My perspective evolved along with me.

ABA is considered by most professionals who work with autistic children to be the gold standard of therapeutic approaches to learning. It has lots of research-based studies over fifty years that support its use. It and its verbal behavior approach to functional communication teaching is responsible for thousands of children learning to communicate in whatever manner best suits them. Picture exchange—the gold standard of teaching communication to nonverbal children—also benefits from behavior analysis. Which leads to AAC (assistive and augmentative communication) methods and devices, which we're all in support of.

We know behavior analysis and associated derived interventions work because they work on everyone who's conscious. It's not an autism science. It's behavioral science. It works on rats, pigs, dogs, children, adults, and members of Congress. We know that mammals will behave in specific ways based on changing factors.

But professionals and parents aren't the only stakeholders on the subject. And there's a large number of autistic adults who tell horror stories of their experiences as children.

Why the vast difference in perspectives? Well, as with many things, the truth lies somewhere in the middle. And a person's view of ABA may be significantly influenced *by the era in which they were ABA patients.*

A simple definition of ABA is using knowledge of human behavior to shape future behavior. ABA itself doesn't adopt any position on what behaviors should occur. It merely acknowledges that intelligent creatures can usually be counted upon to react in certain ways based upon rewards and deterrents. Which is something we already knew.

My employer wants me to work. Every two weeks, they pay me to continue doing so. The desired behavior is me working. The reward is the pay. The pay shapes my behavior when I wake up and want to go back to bed. Now, if I commit an offense, such as posting something inconsistent with the company's values on social media, I might get suspended without pay for a couple of weeks. The desired behavior is me not doing that again. The deterrent is not getting paid. So, there's a very good chance I would choose not to post something like that again.

In a nutshell, that's ABA. Some of it is obvious and doesn't require formal behavior analyst terminology to understand. Some of it is subtle, and you wouldn't notice without a practiced eye and the religious use of data.

Prisons use Board Certified Behavior Analysts (BCBAs) to shape prison practices. Corporations use behavior analysis when trying to effect a change in workplace culture. Animal trainers use ABA for service dogs. Law enforcement uses it in investigations and interrogations. Grandma uses it when she gives out cash to grandkids for good grades. And evildoers in the movies use it to train their microchipped super soldiers. We all use behavior analysis, rewards, and deterrents in some way—from leadership to parenting to personal relationships. Behaving, analyzing behavior, and shaping behavior are what we do *naturally*. And then, helpfully, some people made a study of it.

It isn't behavior analysis itself that's bad or good. It's what behaviors you concern yourself with and how you're going about doing that that's right or problematic. In the early days of ABA used with the autistic, the "applied" part for many therapists was misguided at best and abusive by some.

And that's because of the behavioral goals they valued. The idea was to relieve the child of all autistic traits—flapping, eye contact avoidance, repetitive behaviors, etc. Worse yet, it was in an era in which corporal punishment with almost all children was favored over positive reinforcement. Like everything else, I'm sure that varied with the therapist. But there are stories of trauma out there. Even in cases where therapists weren't abusive, one intervention, discrete trial teaching (DTT), was sometimes applied to autistic children without spoken speech *but who had perfectly normal intelligence and capacity for nonspoken language*. Thus, some kids who didn't need it and understood just fine suffered hundreds of hours of repetition. That certainly does sound like a pretty miserable education. All they needed was an alternative means of communication and an intuitive teacher to show them how to use it. Only they didn't get it, which led to frustration and more "behaviors" and more punishment. That many adult autists abhor the term "ABA" is unsurprising.

And they weren't lying. If you do a search online, you can find old therapy training videos that illustrate their objections. I remember one black-and-white clip when everything seemed nurturing and positive—until the autistic child made a mistake and got slapped for it.

ABA and associated teaching methods for autistic children have changed dramatically over time. So have all teaching methods and attitudes toward healthy development for children in general, I might add. We no longer stand students in front of the room to be punished with a ruler, right? I haven't met any behavior therapists who recommend spanking. And judging from the way Callum runs to them affectionately, I know his aren't practicing punishment. Times do change. So has ABA. I hope those who practiced it abusively are no longer in business. I know from my own behavior analysis training what's taught now. And the subject of punishment never once came up as a solution. It was mentioned only briefly as a past practice.

Before behavior analysis even begins, first, you need to know if there is a behavior that legitimately needs changing. For autistic people, repetitive behaviors and lack of eye contact are a sort of defense against an overwhelming world. Sometimes, depending on the person, they can remain present if one form of sensory input is turned off (eye contact) and focus is placed instead on listening. Repetitive behaviors can be soothing in a seemingly chaotic world. The "behaviors" most associate with autism are simply how their brains are wired. To force them to fight their instincts all day long doesn't benefit *them*. Instead, it benefits the person they're talking to by lessening that person's discomfort with atypical neurology.

What do I care if my son flaps his hands when excited? It's how he expresses himself (not having the ability to exclaim, "I'm so excited!"). And knowing that eye contact issues aren't about stubbornness but about actual physical discomfort for autists, why would I set a goal of teaching anyone to tolerate extreme discomfort *for my sake*?

Again, it's not the teaching or unteaching of behaviors that are necessarily good or bad. It's *what* you're teaching that makes behavior therapy excellent or purposeless. And teaching autistic children to stop using self-soothing behaviors in an overwhelming world isn't best practice.

If an autist later in life wants to increase her own tolerance of eye contact for job-related purposes, that's up to her. But it isn't reasonable of me to demand she look me in the eye if I know it makes her uncomfortable. So, I can simply learn to expect that and adjust. That would make eye contact not a problem, not painful, and we could just stop worrying about it and move on to something that matters.

Another complaint about ABA is that it's overly repetitious and humiliating. Had I not had experience as a parent and watched discrete trials in ABA therapy, I might feel the same. It can appear rapid-fire, mand after mand.

But discrete trials weren't intended for use with every autistic person. That's because every person doesn't have the same needs. My son isn't autistic only. He's also profoundly intellectually disabled and has apraxia of speech. Though not currently popular in regular education, drilling is still begrudgingly acknowledged to aid in basic fact retention. (Spelling and multiplication tables come to mind.)

When teaching those with intellectual disabilities, increased repetition and opportunities for practice are essential. For Callum, he might have to have twenty to one hundred experiences with a concept in order to catch on, while his sister might with two or three or even just a verbal explanation. So, for Callum, discrete trials aren't a mindless repetition of what he already knows. He *does* have to think and work. He *learns*.

They're just practice—occasionally interrupted by a favorite snack or stimmy toy—laughing and giggling with somebody he absolutely adores. Ms. Dawn gives him choices and tunes in to his moods. If he needs to go for a walk, they go for a walk. Sessions are done a few times a day in a side room to work on his communication and social skills, but most of his day is spent with his class. When he masters those concepts, new ones are introduced, with the old ones coming back only every now and then so as not to forget (no different than I did with eighth-grade language arts students).

So, no, I don't hate discrete trials. That said, I wouldn't recommend them for any child who would learn better differently. It wouldn't make sense. I don't disapprove of ABA. I do disapprove the intent of some ABA goals—like attempting to make an autistic child not autistic. (You can't.)

ABA in the hands of an intuitive and kind practitioner *should make life better*. BCBAs are excellent at figuring out what seems to be the actual trigger for a classroom or home problem rather than the one assumed and ineffectively addressed. They're good at breaking down new learning into digestible chunks that make sense both conceptually and developmentally. They can see the dynamics of a situation and help propose solutions that work for everyone. ABA and the BCBAs who practice it with autistic children are not evil. They aim to teach significantly disabled children the value of communication to achieve their wants and increase independence in daily living. School-based BCBAs analyze a classroom setup for what isn't working and help the teacher make it work. The best of them teach parents how to teach their nonverbal children, understand the root causes of problematic behaviors, and teach new behaviors to replace them.

What would I say from the perspectives of a parent, a teacher, and an autism specialist to a parent considering ABA therapy?

1. Interview them first. Ask a lot of questions. Be concerned if they don't ask *you* a lot of questions.

2. Focus on communication goals. Behaviors we view as negative are generally the result of frustration over not being able to communicate effectively.

3. Make clear they won't be trying to exorcise the autism out of your child. That is not a goal. Decide what the actual goals are. For example, hand-flapping is not a problem. Stripping naked in public *is*.

4. Ask for opportunities to observe and learn. If they say you can never attend a session, turn around and leave. Many ABA centers have waivers other families can sign for just this purpose. How are parents supposed to support and emulate therapy if they never see it?

5. At the same time, it isn't necessary to be underfoot with a therapist you trust. All children behave differently around their parents, and they might get more from your child if you aren't *always* there. That said, your child's reaction to the therapist should be telling, and you should be listening and watching for it.

6. Follow the plan without fail. I know you don't want to get up from the couch every ten minutes to check if all clothes are still on and give a reward. But it works. It's a few days of doing that, increasing the time intervals, and reducing the frequency of rewards until it

just becomes a new habit. The investment pays off. No tears. No humiliation. No denying your child the right to be themselves. Just, you know, *pants stay on*.

In the profoundly intellectually disabled and language disabled, those little achievements add up. They make life easier. They make the world more accessible for your child. Which makes life better for *everyone*.

Applied behavior analysis and associated teaching methods for autistic children have significantly changed over time. The best behavior analysts respectfully approach the child's challenges and preferences and consider what will make the child and family happier and more functional. They seek to help children navigate and access their worlds. They don't belittle or shame. They don't use punitive or abusive measures. And they understand that for their most severely disabled patients, what they teach will ultimately determine how many choices those patients get in life—and how to advocate for themselves to the extent they are able.

That's everything. That will let you sleep easier.

So, yes. If you have an autistic child who is melting down left and right and everyone is miserable, definitely go find yourself a good BCBA. For a "functionally nonverbal" child to show a spark of understanding that things have names and you can ask for them is a beautiful, pivotal thing. It's the start of autonomy in a world that's been making all the decisions for you.

Give your child the power and dignity of functional communication as soon as you can in the manner in which they best learn—whether that's speech therapy, functional communication training, or ABA. Everything else will follow. For a child who cannot speak or control their impulses, the quality of their tomorrows may ride on it.

Chapter 18

Somebody's Knockin':
On Depression and Anxiety

Depression and anxiety are like an old lover, the lover you successfully managed to get away from to begin a new life. A life where laundry gets done, friends get visited, lists get checked, balanced meals get cooked, and the things you usually enjoy get enjoyed. But something or a lot of things happen. Usually in succession and often involving sleep loss, grief, financial or marital stress, among others—and, under the weight of exhaustion, your resolve weakens, and that's when he comes looking for you. Whispering in your ear. Telling you your efforts are futile. Crooning the familiar songs he sang to you before. Knock, knock, knocking at your door.

Until you give in, open the door, and invite him inside—where not long after, his seduction is complete. And the following day and every morning you wake up beside him, you know you knew better. But now his clothes are in the closet. His toothbrush is beside yours, and he is ingrained in your life once more.

I haven't been writing much lately. Some people have noticed. I've noticed, too. I've noticed lots of things. When I do, I race off to create a post, give it a title, and even jot down some of the words that are clamoring to be released. But it isn't long before he begins whispering to me.

This post will take a lot of time. Of course, if I write it, I'll likely infuriate someone and I'll feel the need to respond. Which will just upset me more than I already am. I'm tired. Tomorrow—I'll write it tomorrow.

But, of course, it doesn't get written, the meeting doesn't get scheduled, and the insurance company doesn't get called. Thoughts and emotions keep coming, and my startle reflex becomes more pronounced, from the dishes being unloaded to the dogs' incessant barking to Callum's persistent vocal stimming.

It's all so very *loud*. And all I want is to sit on a porch overlooking the mountains on a cool early morning and hear . . . nothing. Nothing but the wind blowing and perhaps a little rain or moving water. No voices. No screaming. No phone ringing. No cacophony of everything undone. To sleep. To read. To write. To recharge. Because I am depleted. I attempt to get my head together and manage to accomplish a thing or two. But my constant companion draws me back into myself. His incessant whispering for me to lighten my load and sit down for a spell. To put it off for another day. To pull the covers over my head and attempt to hold the world back. Yes, he knows how to talk to me.

My heart aches, and my fears bully me. Even my bones feel tired.

I'm starting to see the things I feared and knew were coming. I see my sweet boy, excited by the mere presence of other kids his age—but oblivious to their activities and most of the conversation. He jumps, laughs, and flaps away—and has no understanding that he isn't a part of it all. Part of me is grateful he doesn't understand, while the other part is terrified because he doesn't.

Everywhere we go, we take two cars. There are few new things we can confidently plan as a family. It's too crowded, too bright, too large, too hot, too long. Too everything. People not seeing the delightful boy he really is hurts. His sister having an uneven share of our time and attention hurts. The annoyed looks we get hurt. But his discomfort hurts the most.

Sometimes the view from this ride is beautiful. Sometimes it's fun. But today, it's making me sick. And I want badly to be let off. I want the support of my father, my stepmother, and my grandmother. I want them to tell me it will be okay. But they're all gone now. And every time I get on the highway or have a strange pain, I fear dying myself. Not for me, but because who will take care of him? Who will fight for him? And how do I ensure that his sweet sister will understand that I love her equally though I cannot give of myself to her equally? Some days, some weeks, it's too much.

And I begin to suspect that *I'm* not enough. That I'm doing this all wrong. Making the wrong decisions—not doing enough of one thing and doing too much of the other.

Yes, I have been to see my doctor. I have taken my antidepressants. They help some. The doctor and I are trying again with another antidepressant, but she and I both know there's no pill for *too much*. But we'll continue to fight it because there is no other choice.

Because the alternatives to managing it are unacceptable. My children need all of me; therefore, Depression can't have me. There simply isn't enough room for him in my house. I've told him he must leave. To pack his stuff and get out. Good riddance and all that. So far, he hasn't budged and has turned into a squatter instead.

But I know something he doesn't. I know the unconditional love and trust of two children who depend on me. I know the maternal bliss of snuggling against their sleeping forms in the wee hours of the night. And I know, in this battle between him and me, who I'm really fighting for.

In nature, whoever gets between a mother and her young is always at a disadvantage. He'd do well to remember that.

Chapter 19

You're Not Doomed:
On Autism Parenting and Marriage

t's bad enough parents new to a diagnosis are inundated with advice on how to cure it, beseeched to not "give up hope" that their child will turn out normal, and are terrified how the world will treat that child. And then, sooner or later, somebody comes along helpfully informing them that parenting a child with autism significantly increases a couple's likelihood of divorce. So, it's hardly a surprise they find themselves clutching each other, convinced their family's future is doomed.

I was told the same thing and even repeated it in well-intentioned advice to make sure couples remember each other. It's good advice, but it's good advice for all couples—children or no.

It's a little like the oft-repeated guideline to drink eight glasses of water a day. Everyone from nurses to your grandma insists you should. But no one can trace that advice to any scientific study. Instead, the advice appears to originate from a 1945 guide from the Food and Nutrition Board of the National Research Council—*which also stated most needed water is contained in food*. Somehow the advice spread worldwide and became one of those myths most people assume to be fact.

Parents of autistic children do *not* have staggeringly high divorce rates. At least not in comparison to the divorce rate among all couples. No, marriage isn't easy. But we can all stop blaming our autistic children now. Circumstances—financial hardship, conflicting work schedules, political differences, infidelity, and more lead to divorce—not autism. A lot of couples face the same challenges and weather them.

By communicating effectively, squeezing in together time as a priority, and seeking marital counseling if needed, your marriage can be as strong as anyone else's. I know *a lot* of still-married couples raising autistic children.

That's not me denying that some aspects of raising autistic children can strain a relationship. They can and do.

Almost every parent of an autistic child could speak at length with zero preparation on the subject of sleep loss. And it's not like the sleep loss you experience with a newborn. Eventually babies will sleep through the night, and their grateful parents look less frazzled walking into work each morning.

But autistic babies? Callum was waking approximately every two hours *for the first seven years of his life.* You better believe that was stressful.

The human body isn't meant to do that. It can handle it a few weeks or months. Several years or a couple of decades of it is an entirely different thing. Sleep loss heightens emotions. It can be easy to resent the partner who gets more sleep, and unless you acknowledge that and try to work out solutions benefitting you both (and your child!), that particular stressor can literally be a killer. And let's not forget that sleep loss contributes to challenging behaviors in your child as well. Addressing that issue with a specialist will help *everyone* in the family.

How parents react to meltdowns is another issue. It's essential that *both* partners learn about autism, sensory processing disorder, and all the factors contributing to meltdowns. If one partner does and the other doesn't, the one who does may find themselves having to defend their child's behavior against the irritation and possible mishandling of it by the partner who doesn't. Meltdowns and temper tantrums are two different things. But if you don't know the difference, you might lack compassion for the one and treat it like the other. Not understanding the neurology and behavior of an autistic child can put partners in adversarial roles. This is why it's essential to locate nearby services offering parent trainings, grandparent trainings, sibling workshops, and other supports (see "Places to Go and Things to See"). Having an expert explain sensory integration, meltdowns, and effective strategies for preventing and/or mitigating them can take the pressure off the parent who "gets" it—so that the whole family "gets" it. Their merely accepting the diagnosis isn't enough. They need to *understand* it.

And then there are the little things that can wear on a parent. Verbal stimming can be quite loud, and it can go on for *hours*. For years. It fulfills a need your child has, but it would be a lie to deny that the volume or pitch can't dance on your last nerve. It's certainly not your child's fault.

But your all-too-human response isn't your fault, either. Let me repeat that. Finding yourself irritated and exhausted after hours of screeching isn't a failure of your humanity. It's a known feature of it. Otherwise, annoying and loud music wouldn't be blasted 24/7 during standoffs. In some situations, it can be used as torture. The problem is in remembering that torture isn't your child's intent while cutting yourself some slack for feeling it.

How you choose to cope *is on you*, however. And how you choose to support one another is *everything*. Redirecting your child to another activity, going outside (where it doesn't reverberate quite so much), having a friend or family member come over to let you get out of the house for a couple of hours, or buying a set of noise-canceling headphones are good ways of coping. Screaming, drinking at noon, yelling at the partner who wasn't home for it, or posting about how much you hate autism are not.

Some autistic children and adults do not master toileting or they master it years after their classmates. Many struggle with encopresis (holding back bowel movements), which can cause diarrhea and other miseries. For some parents, this will mean they'll be handling personal hygiene for their children long past the toddler years. And in perhaps what might seem to be the most horrific sentence in this book, *toileting issues can merge with sensory-seeking ones.* This can result in unspeakable messes and wall art using an unpleasant . . . medium. Feeling a smidge sorry for yourself on your knees with a bucket of bleach is understandable. Jumping on Facebook to tell the world how bad you have it because your child painted the walls with poop isn't. Would you have wanted your parent to share that on the Internet?

It doesn't matter if your child is intellectually disabled and unaware of that post. It matters that you've compromised their dignity—when they can't safeguard it themselves. It's a betrayal, even if the betrayed is blissfully unaware. Worse yet, it promotes the autism-as-tragedy perception, which serves no useful purpose whatsoever.

Sensory-seeking behaviors are completely natural for some autistic children and adults. But depending upon their developmental age, some of those behaviors can create spectacular messes. I couldn't begin to count the disasters I've cleaned. The times he got into the butter and rubbed it all over his body. The Nutella incident. Cold cream. His fascination with my scented wax warmers. A green facial mask from head to toe. Red nail polish all over the furniture and heirloom quilt. Those sorts of messes can be frequent. Again, how you feel about it on the inside can be different than how you *choose* to handle it. We all have unpleasant thoughts and emotional reactions. We all hear negative voices in our heads. You aren't a bad parent for feeling or thinking them. But like all negative thinking, what we must do is pause, take the thought or emotion out into the light of day, and look at it. Then acknowledge it for a moment, decide how we'd rather view it, and go with that decision instead.

Sean and Callum.

I choose a moment of silence to process it and take a few deep breaths. And then I go with laughter at the absurdity of what I now must clean up (as well as instruct my son how to help as best as he's able). Often this involves a shower for him.

But I'm telling you learning to laugh is the way to go. I have any number of cute pictures of Callum immersed in some sensory delight/disaster over the years. I'll share them with friends and call them "sensory extravaganzas." Have I ever, exhausted from already being up all night, wanted to cry? Sure. I'm human. And so is he.

But instead of crying, scaring him, and giving myself a headache, I laugh. My Millennial Therapist Extraordinaire Justin has confirmed this to be a healthy coping mechanism. (I encourage everyone to find a millennial therapist. That generation invented the "Every body is a beach body" concept, and they have a great generational perspective on self-acceptance.)

Laughter is also a healthy marriage saver. When we're run-down and frustrated, it's human nature to seek to blame. Unfortunately, the closest target can be our partners. The thing you must keep reminding yourself is there's no blame in these situations. That's because there hasn't been any wrongdoing. It just . . . *is*. Like the common cold and taxes.

Do I know divorced parents of autistic children? Sure. The causes of those divorces involved infidelity, alcoholism, and marrying too young. But I know a lot of intact families as well. There is no human being in this world who loves my son as much as Sean. Nobody else who has traveled this path of diagnosis, challenges, acceptance, and joy in loving this child as my husband. Callum can do some little thing, and Sean and I will meet eyes and smile. No words are needed. It's a bond I can't imagine forever broken. Learning to accept people as they are is a skill we're acquiring from raising this little soul. And I think that can make you both better people and partners.

But a memoir is no place for hypocrisy. If you don't already have some healthy coping mechanisms in place, extra stressors can overwhelm. If you're already struggling with mental health, trauma, or substance abuse, any major change to your life can make you not right in your perceptions and reactions. It can make you assign motives not there, cast blame, lash out, get inebriated, or become clinically depressed.

Here in Florida, we talk a lot about hurricane preparedness. There's a whole agreed-upon list of things we should have and do. Of course, many don't—and end up either riding it out the hard way or getting rescued. I believe raising children with significant disabilities ought to have such a list. I'd go so far as to say that any couple whose child has a diagnosis ought to go to a few counseling sessions with an aim toward assessing your storm readiness as a couple, or as an individual.

I'm not sure this is related to the well-established tendency for native Floridians to ignore storm warnings, but Sean and I sure did. We both brought individual issues we probably needed to have dealt with previously into this marriage. And they didn't magically go away. They manifested in the evolved roles we now had. We went from Sean and Leigh to Sean, Leigh, Bronwyn, Callum, Autism, and Advocacy pretty quickly. (I don't like using the term "caregiver," because it isn't quite an accurate description for loving and caring for your own child. But I will say there are stressful aspects to it that echo such a role.)

And, as we are wont to do, we coped in the ineffective ways we'd always coped.

For me, I dealt with fear for the future by obsessively researching, procrastinating, being anxious, being depressed, escaping into books, isolating myself, etc. My desk is always scattered. I have piles of folded, clean laundry not put away. I go on subject binges late into the night and sometimes overspend on whatever new thing I'm fascinated by. And I keep the world at a distance while I'm—ironically—writing *to* it.

For Sean, a textbook case of ADHD, he deals with it in ways perhaps known to those of you with knowledge of it. Tending to see the trees before the forest, he often doesn't know where to focus. His overcharged self gets distracted by things that don't matter. He forgets little details, and we end up arguing over what the expert said. He's impulsive. He wants to handle a parenting situation but forgets what we agreed on and goes with his first reaction. This all leads to meltdowns or disagreements. And adults with

ADHD who feel overwhelmed and frustrated tend to lean toward substance abuse. He's been there. Done that. Still fights it.

As we've faced challenges related to services, behaviors related to communication, a change in lifestyle, and the ever-present hypervigilance every parent in our son's situation experiences, we've handled things the wrong way sometimes. We've not asked for help when we needed it—not gone and found it when it wasn't readily available. We've had to learn new ways together.

But we play to our strengths.

Sean is the fun parent, the one who enjoys going, going, going. Since Callum likes to go, go, go, too, they have fun together. It's because of Sean's tenacity in pushing him to have new experiences (versus my being afraid of the results) that has led to some of our happiest memories. He has that wisdom that dads often have by nature of being men. It's a completely different kind of wisdom from moms. We tend to play defense, while they tend to play offense. Of course, winning football teams must have both. He's a get-down-on-the-floor roughhousing kind of dad, and that's a beautiful thing to be. Our children laugh a lot with their daddy, and they do more things than they would with their homebody mama.

I'm the rock. I keep us grounded. I remember the details, read the things, write the letters, and kiss the boo-boos. Like I said, we play to our strengths. We give each other me-time. We often fail at managing *we*-time. We laugh a lot. If we get in a rough patch, we seek out a weekend away or therapy. Mainly, we try to extend the same sort of grace to each other. We're not always successful.

Raising a child with a profound disability just makes things . . . *more*. It takes more time to get places. Activities require more planning. You need more hands on deck. There are more messes, and you'll need more patience. If you work together to recharge your batteries, you can absolutely be a team. If you let each other get too depleted, then one or both of you needs to step up.

But raising a child with a profound disability makes things more in other ways, too. Witnessing the patience and gentleness of your spouse toward your child or catching them snuggled together in a nap is more beautiful. The first time your child uses a fork or communicates or tries something new, that's more meaningful. Bigger smiles. More pride. When it comes to raising an autistic child, life can also be *more* in a way only we know.

No, your marriage isn't doomed because of autism. Just take care of each other.

Chapter 20

What I'll Never Know: On Inexplicable Tears and Autism

Sometimes, with no warning, Callum suddenly bursts into tears. We all run around like the Marx Brothers trying to figure out what's wrong. Because it's not whining. It's real tears and a quivering lower lip. It's not when we're out and about or in new situations or noisy environments—where you might expect his senses to get overloaded and him to get emotional. It's home, during quiet moments. Where he's relaxed and comfortable. It's after joyful bursts of hopping around, doing ball tricks, and playing endless repetitions of tickle-me. When he's just been laughing and loving on us. When you'd never expect it. And nothing I can do that he usually loves as comfort will soothe him. No back rubs or snuggles dry his tears. He cries for a long time. He usually doesn't want us there when he does and may gesture for us to leave the room. Only rarely do we get to stay. And then all we're allowed to do is sit there and be quiet.

Then, just as inexplicably, he stops and returns to his usual happy mood and playful self. I've often tried to figure out what's happening, what's wrong, what he's thinking. But I can't seem to do it. Nothing I offer he wants; nothing he loves will distract him. He cries it out until he's done. And then he goes on his way.

Right now, I'm watching him looking out the front window after just such a crying spell. And reflecting on it not being my job to get to the bottom of his every emotion. He gets to have them, too—no justification or explanation required. Perhaps he expresses them differently. Maybe he saves them up—stored until he's in a safe place to process them all at once. The tears being the frustration of the words he doesn't have and can't express—but like every other human on the planet, still needs to. Maybe he remembered something that made him sad. Or had a frightening thought. He could have a headache. The guessing annoys him, but the mother in me can't help but try to make it all better. I must remember that's *my* need, not his. His need right then is to cry and to be given the space to do it. I need to remind myself often that even if he were neurotypical, he'd have emotions I couldn't "solve."

In those rare moments he invites me to share space while he cries, I know I've been honored.

So, I think—other than quickly ascertaining if he's in pain or wanting something I can provide—I'm just going to do better at not trying to solve him like a puzzle and instead let him cry it out. To sit with him quietly and stop peppering him with questions about the cause. To let him be himself, to feel, without me implying something is wrong in how he does it. Besides, he might just be more efficient at it than the rest of us—getting it all out at once as he does.

We're not given instruction manuals for any child, but with children like Callum, you can't help but feel the lack of one even more. I hope he senses I'm doing the best I can. I hope he knows how absolutely he is loved.

Driver's Ed

Autists are the ultimate square pegs, and the problem with pounding a square peg into a round hole is not that the hammering is hard work. It's that you're destroying the peg.

−Paul Collins

Due Process and That Year I Haven't Talked About: On What I Learned and You Must, Too

didn't want to write this. I didn't want to write it because I'm not sure there's a way to write it that's fair to all involved. When Callum was in preschool seven years ago, I filed a due process complaint with the Florida Department of Education (FDOE) against his school district. Only with one minor complication—I was employed by the same school district in a small city—with an elected superintendent. Some of my family goes back six generations in this town. So, this was no small thing.

Outside of my father's death, our due process case was the most stressful time in my life. While it would have made a tremendous continuing drama for blog traffic, I kept it quiet publicly. I personally knew many of the people involved (or their mutual friends and loved ones), and I didn't want to hurt anyone.

Most of what happened with our case was due to a lack of understanding of autism, a lack of funding, and fear for one's livelihood. It wasn't because evil people got together and decided to target one little boy. That never happened.

Knowing that didn't change the roles we were all assigned.

Because my four-year-old wasn't talking, wasn't learning, and was hurting himself in his frustration at being unable to communicate. A developmental pediatrician two years earlier had matter-of-factly told us, "Bring him back when he's five, and we'll be able to make some predictions." As his fifth birthday grew closer, I knew what kind of predictions they might be. Time flew, but Callum's struggles got worse, not better. And in my desperation, I began asking the questions I should have known to ask before but didn't.

I'M sure it's true in many lines of work; there are perks to being an insider. I'm sure doctors afford courtesies to other doctors. And if you know the manager of McDonald's, it's a little easier to get a donation of Happy Meal toys for a good cause. Who you know shouldn't give you an edge, but we all know it can make a difference.

By the time Callum was born, I had been working for the school district for thirteen years. I was first in multiple schools as a substitute teacher while attending college and the remainder during my professional public school career as a middle school teacher and library media specialist. In a small town with only one high school, I knew *many* of the people later involved in his education. Our superintendent had been my own third-grade teacher, *and* she had been a high school student of my mother's. I grew up and attended school with many of my colleagues. I'd laughed and cut up with them, mourned with them, knew their mamas, and taught their children. And some of them had done me great kindnesses over the years.

So, when I began having him evaluated for prekindergarten ESE at not quite three years old, I felt good about how it would go. After all, I was among my people. I trusted them to know their stuff, and I thought (because I'd attended a mandatory one-day educational law seminar in college) that I knew, too. I felt confident my colleagues would make decisions for my child in the same way I would. I never thought their information might be out of date, their pockets would be empty, or their hands would be tied behind their back. That some might know less about autism than I. And I didn't realize that standard practice was to inform parents of their rights—but not necessarily to tell them about services and placements that might actually be better for their child. That's frowned upon by those with the impossible task of stretching too few dollars among too many students. It can get you reassigned somewhere you'd rather not be.

I confused their being friendly with being entirely forthcoming. Little did I know—in that early, unsure, vulnerable stage of transitioning Callum to school—how wrong I was.

ON Callum's first day of school in early 2012, just before he turned three, Sean and I drove him to school together. Parents everywhere worry on the first day of school. It's certainly not unique to parents of developmentally delayed children.

But placing your nonverbal child into the care of a stranger unlocks an achievement level of anxiety you can't know until you've lived it. I couldn't ask him about his day. He couldn't say, "Someone hurt me." He never had (and still doesn't have) the language to tell me his worries or understand comforting words.

So there I was, standing in a busy cafeteria, giving the class paraprofessional Mrs. Brenda information sheets on him and handing over supplies. I must have looked as terrified as I was trying to not let on. Because she took my hands in her own, looked deep into my eyes, and said, "He's gonna be fine. I'm gonna take care of your baby, Mama. It's gonna be okay. You'll see." And then she wrapped both arms around me for the tight hug I didn't know I needed. That hug allowed me to steer myself out of that cafeteria and go about my day.

Both she and his teacher were lovely people, and Callum loved them. His therapists were kind and dedicated. The guidance counselor was a sweetheart. The school psychologist was extraordinarily gentle in providing his test results, doing her best to keep me from crying, and admitting there's much we don't know about his mind. His staffing specialist made a point of saying she'd never fault a parent for advocating for their child and was always helpful and courteous. They were all kind to us.

Which is what made the drama two years later even more stressful and painful.

CALLUM had been in school for nearly two years, but we weren't seeing any evidence of learning. He refused to sit for longer than thirty seconds for group time, didn't participate on his turn, shut out everyone to stim nonstop, and was prone to frequent meltdowns that had him banging his head on the floor. Mrs. Brenda was functioning practically as a 1:1 para-professional for him because of his high needs. She was even having to feed him if it involved holding a spoon. Of course, this meant his teacher didn't have the intended benefit of her paraprofessional and had to manage the rest of the class by herself.

My sister-in-law Julie had been a pediatric occupational therapist for the district previously, so I talked to her. She recommended that I get in touch with the OT at his school. When I asked his teacher and para how I might get in touch with the OT, they told me she'd left the district six months earlier and that they'd been told the district was still looking to hire a replacement. I immediately wondered why I hadn't been informed by the district, went back to Julie to update her, and she reacted with surprise. I thought I knew all about special education laws and individualized education plans (IEPs). But I was a "regular ed" teacher, and I really didn't have a clue.

As it turns out, if a service is listed on a student's IEP and a district doesn't have someone to provide it, they must subcontract that service temporarily or provide transportation to an outside service. But that didn't happen. No mention was made. Worse yet, through the ever-present grapevine, I learned a local pediatric therapy practice had become concerned about a lack of school-based services for some of the patients they shared with the district and had reached out to offer subcontracting services while they sought a replacement. But, unfortunately, the therapy practice wasn't taken up on their offer. I don't know why. I don't know who their offer reached. I don't know if there were funds available to the decision makers. I know only that six months later, students at affected schools still weren't receiving services, and the district didn't inform the parents.

That was the moment I realized the system didn't really have my back or my child's. They had their own back. Yes, they informed me, sometimes twice, of his legal rights. Then, dutifully, as required by law, they mailed and handed out the same little yellow brochures explaining.

But they didn't notify me when needed services were stopped entirely.

Let's be for real. That's not because the district had spare armies of qualified occupational therapists sitting around bored. It's a poor county. Schools are partially funded by property taxes. And politics in this town is about how to shift the ever-dwindling money. Being one of them didn't afford me any extra notification. I had naively assumed efforts would be made to inform me of issues, and I didn't dig deeper. That assumption had left my son without the free and appropriate education he's legally entitled to. My own lack of knowledge failed him.

That very day, I jumped online to find some training in special education law. The book that kept coming up in searches was *Wrightslaw: From Emotions to Advocacy* by Pam Wright and Pete Wright, written for families and professionals needing to understand the law, IEPs, and disputes between families and schools. I spent two weeks with highlighters and page flags, reading and working through a section at a time. In the meantime, I casually placed a formal request for a copy of his entire cumulative file. During this time, I talked nightly with a dear friend, Jackie, who is a retired self-contained ESE teacher.

When the file arrived, and I'd finished the book, Jackie invited me over for chicken and dumplings. Then we sat down with a cumulative file two inches thick and began reading, periodically stopping to exclaim "oh my God" and marking pages. We quickly realized we would have to go about documenting the IDEA violations in a more organized fashion. After getting the file copied to not ruin the original, we spread it all out. We sat down for most of the weekend to assemble our case for IEP noncompliance and failure to provide "free and appropriate education" (FAPE).

Having been raised by a lawyer, I grew up with an appreciation for direct and decisive action in matters of conflict. My problem was that I'm not a naturally confrontational or litigious person. But I'd learned from my dad that you must get their attention quickly and be willing to follow through to prevail.

We sat at Jackie's kitchen table for hours, talking about my next move. Should I just call the ESE office? Talk to the principal? Write a letter? Or hire a professional parent advocate or lawyer? Jackie, herself a veteran of the district and a beloved, maternal busybody, knew everyone involved, their extended families, *and* associated scandals. She was uniquely suited to understand the ramifications of a potential fight with a school district that also happened to be my employer. Moreover, Jackie knew almost all of the district's ESE secrets—which families had sued and what arrangements had been made for some students but kept quiet to not tip off parents who might want the same services for their own children. While she wasn't worried the superintendent in office would come after me, we didn't know who might take office after *her* or who might be promoted after other administrators moved on.

It was clear I had to advocate for Callum. But I also had to clothe and feed him. I needed my job. We debated the pros and cons until after midnight.

Ultimately, I heard my dad's lawyerly wisdom playing in my head, telling me that I didn't want to give the other side too much time as an advantage and reminding me that you teach people how to treat you by what you're willing to tolerate. Had he been debating at the table with us that night, he would have told me it was time to declare myself—as a mother who wasn't going to tolerate anything less than an appropriate education for my child. A mother willing and fortunate enough to hire professional representation and who had a small platform. The list of IDEA violations and failure to provide FAPE was long. I knew revealing it wasn't going to bring about change for those students whose parents are gaslighted by educational jargon. I knew the district had ready access to legal representation. I knew they would argue the reason Callum wasn't learning was because of his "behaviors." And I knew they'd assemble a response to intervention team (RTI) to look at it (which takes months). But he was four years old, and he couldn't communicate in any form but whining, tantrums, and severe meltdowns. He didn't have months.

Callum is considered Level 3 Autistic Disorder or "high-needs." And among those with high needs, he'd be ranked even higher due to a comorbid diagnosis of "profound" intellectual disability. Yes, we can have a chicken-and-egg argument about language disability and intellectual disability. They are not necessarily related, and there are nonspeaking autists with perfectly normal intelligence. But intellectual disabilities *can and do* coexist in others. And they do for Callum.

As of this writing, he is twelve years of age. His developmental age is somewhere around two. And this was confirmed by an outstanding pediatric psychologist, Dr. Mary Alston Kerllenevich, who, from the very start, admitted that it's just one number and that a test result doesn't mean he doesn't have moments in which he demonstrates higher-age proficiency. But it does mean that on a day-to-day basis, his understanding of danger— other people, poisons, traffic—is *nonexistent*. He cannot defend himself or communicate in nuanced ways. He cannot identify his parents or address. He doesn't know what a phone number even is, much less how to use a phone. He cannot even pronounce his name clearly enough for anyone else to understand.

It's why we're afraid to die, to leave him at the mercy of others.

He doesn't have enough language conceptually to convey anything but the simplest of requests. He can't describe pain or emotion. So he is *completely* vulnerable to harm. Which disability applies to him more is somewhat irrelevant to us. We love him. Almost everyone who meets him loves him. And I've done my best to put the world on notice that my child is accompanied by terrible consequences if he is harmed in any way.

As I read night after night, looking for studies, following top minds with an interest or stake in policy affecting the disabled, I realized research-based methods for teaching students with nonverbal autism weren't being utilized in our school district. They'd existed once a decade earlier in a successful verbal behavior program that had been terminated due to the teacher leaving. Unfortunately, they didn't have someone local to teach it, so it was disbanded.

I realized with lightning clarity just how many IDEA violations I personally knew of as an educator. I looked at older, nonverbal autistic students and knew they'd never been taught to communicate. The realization stunned me. And it provided a glimpse into Callum's educational future. Looking over the list of violations with accompanying documentation, I surmised we'd prevail. I also guessed they'd be worried I'd want an expensive, private autism school out of town, requiring tens of thousands of dollars in tuition plus hiring a 1:1 para to accompany him—*along with a driver and their insurance and pension benefits.* I worried the rumor mill would paint me as greedy for settlement dollars. And I knew the probability of eventually being supervised by someone who wouldn't appreciate what I'd done.

I was damned if I did. But Callum was damned if I didn't.

I'm going to now say something perhaps unpopular to my colleagues in education. But there is a psychological state of numbness you can reach in the caring professions. Loving and interacting with society's most vulnerable—and seeing the system fail them repeatedly—can sicken your soul over time. It happens to child protective investigators, emergency workers, therapists—anyone who must process the suffering of others daily.

Future teachers declare their majors confident they'll stand up for their students and not be complicit in a subpar education. Few teachers enter the field without stars in their eyes and dreams of making a difference in the world. But nobody tells them about the shocking systemic failures of the American educational system. Students not identified for needed services. Or food. Or a winter coat.

You dutifully report the horrors they confide but are told that nothing can be done. And their revelation to an authority figure makes their circumstances even worse when they return home later that day after the investigator knocked on the door. The times you couldn't get anyone to listen, and yet another kid fell through the cracks *hurts.* Looking away rather than screaming out alone that the emperor is naked gets easier over time. And if you remain in education long enough, you see many once-sweet young faces, now hardened habitual offenders in the jail log. It compromises hope, and people without hope tend to give up. They stop advocating for students and count the years till retirement.

Being a Floridian who has experienced hurricanes and their aftermath a few times in my forty-seven years, I've learned that people weather storms differently from one another. That's a truth applicable to every situation on the stress event scale. Some of us are just tougher than others.

And some of us are ill-equipped to process the more traumatic aspects of what we see, hear, or sense and are afraid to think about it too much. Because it might create a moral quandary and a call to action. That doesn't make us evil. But it makes us complicit in not stepping in to help a student *we all knew needed it*. But we had our own to feed.

Teachers who've sat in emotionally fraught meetings know not to mention expensive interventions and services to desperate parents, lest they have to answer to being the one to suggest what a school district can't afford (or didn't allocate funding for). Overworked staffing specialists and their assistants know to schedule IEPs in quick succession. In regular ed, administrators rarely attend. It's not uncommon to list an elective teacher or the school librarian as the "Regular Education Teacher" whose presence is required—for students they might never have met. They breathe a sigh of relief at four p.m. that a parent is a no-show, sign the IEP (perfectly legal when a parent doesn't "show"), quickly check off the required boxes, and get out the door as soon as possible.

Apathy takes years to develop. But it originates from love, big dreams, helplessness, and all the ways the world disappoints.

We're in a state that allows elected rather than appointed school superintendents. No matter one's opinion of such, small-town politics and history are assuredly always in play. Hiring representation might be viewed as an aggressive move, but I didn't want to fight for months and years. I didn't want to slowly move up the chain. I didn't want meeting after meeting while my child's ability to communicate with the world was threatened. And I needed to settle the question of whether or not I was serious once and for all. If I was going to do this, I didn't want to have to do it again.

Because educators do discuss that among themselves, which parents are likely to know the law and which ones aren't. Therapists privately lament to each other that a beloved student's parents sadly don't know their rights. Staffing specialists who *ought* to know better wait for a parent's reaction to "We don't have that here"—and cross their fingers that parent can't recite the legal definition of FAPE (free and appropriate education), thus shooting the ball back over to the district's court. And forcing the staffing specialist to meet with administrators who aren't going to like what's proposed because it will cost money they don't have. IEP battles are much like games of chicken. The side that swerves first loses.

Districts know a certain amount of grease must be set aside for the squeakiest wheels. As a result, children of squeaky wheels get the interventions and services they need. And other children don't—simply because no one at their home knows how to demand them.

Essentially, my task was to get myself identified as a wheel it's easier for all to just go ahead and grease. And to somehow figure out how to do that respectfully so that one day, when some of those people might become my coworker, principal, or superintendent, I could weather their possible dislike for me and not wind up transferred to the boonies to teach underwater basket weaving in a portable.

And all while managing to make perfectly clear I wasn't objecting to a single person who had ever worked with him. I was objecting to services he *didn't* receive and training his team *had never been provided*. The last thing I wanted was to cause those people problems.

Yes, my first obligation was to my child. But my dreams were grander. I hoped this process would open the eyes of the district to the unmet needs of language-delayed and autistic students. I hoped it would inspire serious discussion. I dreamed of creating something that would make other school districts visit and want to emulate what we came up with. I wanted an advisory panel to the district made up of parents, therapists, disabled students, and community members. I dreamed of one day creating a public school for autistic students that would be modeled after the Florida School for the Deaf and the Blind, a fantastic campus nearby I'd been able to visit. I wanted to put it in our city, central to nearby cities I knew didn't have such schools, either. It could be significant for our city in terms of employment and new residents. I knew families outside our county would certainly move here for that (more property tax revenue!), and nearby school districts would bus their students over. They were big dreams, I knew. But somebody has to dream.

I *never* wanted litigation. I just wanted my son to learn to the best of his ability. And I needed that sickening feeling in my chest every time I worked with an autistic student whose educational needs weren't being met to *end*. Because in public education, it's often. Because by not reaching out to the evening news, I was essentially complicit, too. I didn't want to punish anyone. I just wanted us to start doing right by these students. And I figured the best way to achieve that was to first get their attention.

THERE were nineteen issues (later twenty) we documented by their own paperwork. They included: violations to the family transition plan, multiple violations of his IEP, failure to identify his needs and provide needed services, a behavioral assessment required by Florida law to be performed by a behavior analyst or school psychologist that was carried out in fifteen minutes by a paraprofessional, an unmet need for assistive and augmentative communication (AAC), speech and behavior services, and more.

After assembling them into one document, Jackie and I sat looking at it with grave expressions on our faces. More so than others, she knew the significance this battle with the district could have for me personally and professionally. She also understood the ramifications of his being four and a half years old and not being able to communicate. Valuable time had been lost we'd never get back. Time Callum would never get back. We knew there was no decision to be made. No phone calls. No letters. The system was dysfunctional. It needed to be addressed. And Callum was still waiting for what he needed.

But looking into those knowing eyes of hers, I knew she was worried about how easily careers and reputations are destroyed. And we knew that people I genuinely liked were going to be sitting on the other side of the table from me. They would put on their best smiles. But it was going to be awkward, and people would talk. No question, this was going to suck a lot.

However, it had to be done. And unlike some families in our desperately poor county, I had the resources from which to fight should that become necessary. I wanted big things. Not just for Callum but for other kids like him. I wanted training, programs and services, and a county-wide team approach. I wanted *change*.

But I was terrified. I knew I needed someone speaking for me to balance out the unfamiliar awkwardness of intensely polite district responses of people I'd been raised with, graduated with, taught by, hugged by, and eaten lunch with. I could go with a lawyer who specialized in educational law or an experienced parent advocate. Parent advocates in Florida are a little like paralegals given authority to represent in IEP cases. It's about half the cost, and I already knew that many are hired by disability rights attorneys to assist them (and probably advise them on details of workable IEP solutions). Hiring a lawyer right off would be an open declaration of war. Not wishing to do that, I went with the advocate I assumed would be a kinder, gentler version. (Um, he was not.)

I remember standing in a Chuck E. Cheese parking lot while answering a phone consultation with the parent advocate and reading out my credit card numbers for the retainer. Jamison Jessup would now be representing me. He was delighted to take my case. For one, it was his first visit to the district. Two, he was impressed by the level of work Jackie and I had done already with the documentation. And three, he was confident we would win. Those nineteen violations were flagrant. He didn't think they'd attempt to fight it, and he was sure we'd prevail in arbitration and never need a day in court. Since then, I've obtained a state teaching endorsement in autism spectrum disorders, become ESE certified, earned a master's in autism spectrum disorders, and become an IBCCES Advanced Certified Autism Specialist. From that perspective, I now smile, imagining just how delighted he was to take this case because it really was going to be that easy. But I didn't know all that then. You'd think I would have.

But I didn't. I didn't know. And that's coming from a fairly privileged background—having never known poverty, low wages, lack of education, racism, ableism, and all the other -isms. These were my colleagues. Their suit jackets didn't intimidate me. I had one of my own. I knew the teacher jargon, jokes, and small talk. But even with those advantages, when I walked into my own child's IEP for the first time and saw the long table, the well-oiled machine that is a traveling IEP setup, and the professional countenances of those assembled, it *was* intimidating. That, combined with my lack of background in ESE, and I trustingly signed what *sounded* good. Most parents do.

Is it any wonder then that a tired, just-got-off-from-a-double-shift parent with an incomplete education and no resources shows up and defers to what the experts are saying (who are all smiling and being so lovely)? Assumes this is the best their child can get and heads home quickly before going to their other job? And when their autistic child is "bad," they dutifully show up at school and thank them for their patience—not knowing that those problem behaviors are usually *a direct result of our collective failure to teach the child to communicate.*

Jamison found the violations so egregious in duration, involving much documentation, and having so many people involved that we were well within our rights to just file due process. Callum was so obviously struggling, it was hard to believe he didn't have more intensive services. Jamison declared the district had had all the time in the world and that it would be in our best interest—both for Callum and for me professionally— to just get it over quickly. He said they'd learn within days after we filed and that he would make it clear that they needed to go through him rather than call me in to discuss it. That was the part I liked best.

ELECTED superintendents—no matter how nice—turn the politics involved in teaching in a small community into a sort of chess game. Do you dare come out in support of Bob? Or stay silent because you were best friends with Sue's sister? Your principal is possibly related to high-level district officials. Nepotism abounds. Employees who've angered higher-ups have been known to be relocated thirty miles out of town to teach unfamiliar subjects. Leadership staff is frequently relocated or fired for their misplaced loyalties with the ushering in of a new administration.

Jamison understood the potential fallout involved and offered to find me help in the event of future retaliation. In my mind, using a parent advocate as a buffer made an emotionally fraught situation more tolerable for me. I had hoped they'd note the lack of an attorney from an attorney's child (who tends to believe in lawyers) and interpret that as less aggressive. Before our scheduled meeting with ESE district officials, however, I heard through an administrator friend that word was I'd "struck a low blow out of nowhere." I heard that coworkers and friends had been warned not to speak to me. District friends confided in me that my money-grubbing due-process case was the topic of lunch that day.

So, I knew even before the first meeting that this would echo for a long time.

WE met Jamison face-to-face for the first time at our initial hearing at the district office. On an uncharacteristically windy and cold day for North Florida, we huddled in a hallway to confer. The superintendent made her office available, and soon we were ushered into a room with district leadership. That's when we were informed the meeting would be slightly delayed *due to their attorney needing to take a phone call, but he'd be here soon to start the discussion.* I remember glancing at Jamison, who merely smiled and politely nodded before I glanced at one of the officials. She was nothing but cordial, but I saw her eyes go straight to Jamison as if to gauge his reaction. I knew she knew and was wondering if he did, too.

Within a few minutes, the school district's attorney bustled in, with a file folder, some hearty handshakes with the men, and an address to me, asking if I was Lew Merryday's daughter. Upon confirmation, he proceeded to tell me that he knew my daddy "very, very well" and "had worked with him many, many times." He made reference to a relative of mine who holds an important position, and I responded politely.

He then took a seat at the end of that long table. Noted.

He opened his folder and proceeded to announce that we were there to discuss the due process complaint. He had a meeting agenda available and was prepared to lead it.

If ever I thought my daddy was shining down on me, it was right then. Because that's when Jamison politely informed him that his presence was a violation of IDEA procedural safeguards. I waited—fascinated—for his reaction. For a lawyer, this was lose-lose. A reaction of surprise would indicate he didn't know the law. No attorney wants that. But agreement would suggest he was well aware of the violation and made it anyway. So it was awkward, all right. Jamison merely smiled and waited.

The attorney blinked a few times, made sustained eye contact with the district officials, stammered a few times, yet soon realized he had little recourse but to leave.

He stood up, took his folder, patted at his pockets, and announced he'd just go somewhere nearby and to call if we needed him. The look on the faces of the officials remaining and the unspoken tension in the air was a little awkward, but they rallied. I caught the slightest hint of an "I told you so" smile from the one who'd watched Jamison earlier. I don't know that for sure. But she was said to know more about IDEA and Florida ESE law than anyone else. I realized she'd probably warned the attorney that that wasn't allowed, and it had been assumed we wouldn't know. So her turning out right became item number twenty on our list.

The rest of the meeting was a blur. I remember the director choosing her words politely and carefully as if someone had slowed down our track just a smidge. They were suddenly having to take over a meeting the lawyer was supposed to be running. Of course, they understood the issues (certainly better than he did) and remained professional, but it rattled them. The whole thing seemed surreal. We broke with an agreement to seek out various evaluations—including private—and to schedule a time for the big IEP. I remember walking out in my new cream-colored coat and heels that day, hearing Katy Perry's "Roar" in my head, and feeling like I could take on the world for my son. It would be over soon. Maybe it wouldn't be such a big deal.

I didn't understand then that taking on the world might be good for some things, but it has repercussions.

WHEN I was a school media specialist, I often had to host big meetings. Everything from district training to manifestation meetings. I remember one such meeting after school. Person after person filed in: district security administration, a school psychologist, teachers, guidance counselors, police. I remember turning to the visiting IT tech and commenting under my breath, "Army, Navy, National Guard . . ."

And I recall the almost blank expression of the student, his jaw tight—but still young enough to not know how to control his telltale big eyes. He was at the mercy of these people, and he knew his fate had already been decided.

But as a librarian, what I had previously noticed about that young man was that *he couldn't read*. And he was embarrassed by it. So, he defended himself against those feelings of stupidity. When he realized I liked him irrespective of his reading ability, didn't think he was dumb, and would keep him emotionally "safe" by never revealing what we both knew, he took a liking to me. I never pointed him in the direction of books on his reading level. I pointed him to ones with sports on the cover. And then I would slip a slim Reading Counts book in with it. That's how he got his points and preserved his dignity. I had no problems with him. But a lot of other people did. I wasn't there for those moments. Nor was I invited to this. This time, he'd somehow taken it too far. His mother didn't know how to advocate for him, despite his ESE status, and the school was "sad"—but they needed others to learn and felt they'd done all they could (we hadn't). He had to go, so of course, no one explained to his mother what a "manifestation of disability" is. She didn't know to ask. But I knew of his disability. And I knew the behaviors they were discussing were absolute manifestations of it.

So this kid, with his educational needs unmet, was sent off to an alternative school. I'm sure he learned many things there, but probably not what his mother was hoping for.

That student didn't even cost them a lot of money. Mine almost certainly would. So, for our meeting, they pulled out *all* the big guns: director, compliance person, guidance counselor, speech teacher, district speech-language pathologist (SLP), district "behavior specialist," district occupational therapist (OT), district physical therapist (PT), ESE secretary, staffing specialist, principal, assistant principal, teacher, and school psychologist. In addition, our team added a private OT and director of a large pediatric therapy facility, a private SLP, a private PT, a Board Certified Behavior Analyst (BCBA), a Board Certified Assistant Behavior Analyst, a parent advocate, his assistant, and us. I think I counted twenty-seven chairs in that little conference room. The only people who seemed to be missing were the Army, Navy, and National Guard.

We came prepared. Armed with best practices, research studies, and a professor of autism education on standby, we were ready to refute any arguments they might make.

Only we didn't need to refute anything. The meeting opened with the district pushing the proverbial silver platter in our direction. We didn't even discuss his need for a 1:1. It was simply announced he'd be getting one along with a contracted *authentic* BCBA who would train his 1:1 paraprofessional as a Registered Behavior Technician (RBT). He would receive compensatory OT services for six months and 1:1 functional communication training services all summer. His speech therapy time was doubled. Rather than a speech teacher (who was a lovely, dedicated SLP student), a certified SLP was assigned. He would be receiving AAC technology as well. And there would be a separate space made available for his 1:1 functional communication training.

That was it. We didn't even have to argue. Jackie had told me she knew the director to be a good person who wanted the best for students but wasn't given the financial resources to do what was needed. I believe that to be true.

Because in an offer of extraordinary kindness, she walked up to me and asked if I had anyone in mind for a 1:1 who would fit the bill. I knew she was asking both as a parent and as a professional. She didn't have to, but she did. As it turns out, I had the perfect person in mind. And although she probably doesn't know it, her generous olive branch changed the trajectory of Callum's life.

ENTER Ms. Dawn.

I'd known Dawn for a few years as our school's favorite volunteer mom and soccer coach. She was the parent who stayed all night for library lock-ins—rare birds indeed. I'd known she'd recently applied for a 1:1 position for another autistic boy but hadn't yet taken the paraprofessional exam. She had been the principal's first choice if she had. When I mentioned that to the director, she said it wasn't a problem because she would be paid out of temporary service employee funds until the position received a new allocation the following year. Temps didn't need paraprofessional exams. There was time, and Dawn already had some college. She could pass it.

I got Dawn's number from the school secretary, called her, and invited her to spend a day with him. The first thing she said at the end of the day was, "Where do I sign up? I just love him." What I loved about Dawn was the open-mindedness she'd taken when learning about autism and behavioral modification with the therapists. Dawn became somewhat of a lay expert. Even the district's contracted BCBA pleaded with her to return to college and become one herself. She just got it, and she got him. Dawn has this magical blend of powerful observation skills combined with the tenacity of mamas who've raised three boys. Loving, gentle, patient, and unflappable determination was precisely what we needed.

Dawn was by the book. She wore clickers to keep track of data demonstrating the need to change something. She understood he wasn't whining because he wanted to annoy others. He was attempting to communicate something, and our job was to figure out what and teach him more effective ways to express it. That's what we focused on from the start and continue to this day. We don't care about eye contact or flapping. That's just him. What we care about are choices. And you get more options in life only by cooperating, communicating, and using good manners. Like Helen Keller in *The Miracle Worker*, he didn't yet know that communication served a purpose. He didn't know there was a picture for "cracker" and that by pointing to it, he could have one. That was her job. The BCBA, Ms. Dawn, and I all had the same vision. It was beautiful.

AND then things started to go south. While Callum was making gains in attention time, requesting items, following simple procedures, etc., Ms.

Dawn was getting the runaround from others. If Callum was late from a doctor's appointment, she was told to go home (unpaid) rather than being used to help other students.

The therapy room promised in the IEP was still just old book storage at the end of a hallway—with electrical wiring coming out of the wall. When she asked if she could have the junk hauled off and the room cleaned, repainted, and repaired, she was told they'd do that later—*on days Callum was going to ABA out of town.* When she replied that Callum wasn't doing that anymore because *she* was providing those services along with the BCBA, she was looked at with suspicion. It became clear that despite everything we'd just been through, some folks *hadn't read the IEP.*

And then I saw the photos.

That therapy room wasn't merely dusty and full of books. It was filthy. As in years of dirt in every corner combined with old gum wrappers and even dead spiders. Because of the years of accumulated storage, they had only a tiny space in which to work. So Ms. Dawn was having to haul things back and forth daily rather than have the dedicated space promised. She also had to keep her back to the wall of electrical wires. Because they were directly at Callum's eye level.

I was told that the PT took one look at that room and flat-out refused to be in it. So she took Callum elsewhere, but she made clear to others it was unsuitable. And bless her heart, she documented it. A lot.

But the photos. Lord have mercy those photos. My sweet, smiley little boy being assigned to a filthy closet—all while Ms. Dawn was reporting unfriendly behavior from others. Some were kind, but others didn't understand why she was there or what she was doing—only that it had something to do with a demanding mom and a lawsuit.

However, in just a few weeks we had a calmer child who was learning routines, who loved all his people and went to school happily. Our lives had changed for the better.

But that room was disgusting. It was unhealthy and an insult. So, hearing my father's voice tell me it was now time to swing the proverbial stick, I located a disability rights and education attorney, retained her, and informed the district. I wasn't there, but I'm told they were not happy with this turn of events. Because according to witnesses, a district official showed up and pitched a very loud fit, informing them Callum's IEP would be followed *to the letter.*

I then sadly had to inform an understanding Jamison that although I had no doubt of his abilities, my daddy would have never forgiven me for possibly going to court without a lawyer. He was great about it, provided records, and has remained friendly. I still recommend him to some families and believe in the value of what he provides. He got my son "the prettiest IEP in the State of Florida," and I'm forever appreciative.

Our new lawyer, Nancy, was a completely different personality. Her philosophy was to get what the child needed while doing the least amount of harm to the parent-school relationship. So when she quoted Sun Tzu's advice to "build a bridge by which your enemy may retreat," I got it. And she pointed out that allowing district employees to "save face" and "look like they came up with the idea" was a tool I needed to learn.

Because one day, this would be over. And real people with really cool ideas might be scared off by a history of litigation on my part. She asked me if I wanted his IEP team afraid of me.

I knew she was right. I never wanted that, and that I had to figure out a way to make this better. To prove good things could happen if we dreamed big enough.

Nancy met with the superintendent, who asked her point-blank, "What is Leigh wanting?" Considering that a fair enough question, Nancy informed her I just wanted what we'd agreed upon in the IEP. I wanted Ms. Dawn to have what she needed. I wanted everyone on the team to be treated well. And Dawn was on that team. All of that sounded reasonable to the superintendent (who hadn't ordered anything to the contrary anyway). So a final meeting with all the parties was scheduled. This time, since we had a lawyer, the district lawyer joined us. He didn't speak as glowingly of my dad this time. Issues were sorted out. The room got cleaned. I thought it was over.

Wrong.

All during that summer, while working with him, Ms. Dawn watched for the job posting for Callum's 1:1 to come up. She'd see one on the Human

Resources site, but when she asked, she kept being told, "No. It's not that one. Probably the next one. We'll let you know."

And then one day, I walked into Ms. Dawn's temporary summer therapy office to find her in tears and being consoled by the speechless school psychologist who'd been sharing a space with them and who'd witnessed Callum's gains firsthand.

Unfortunately, Ms. Dawn had just been informed they'd "made a mistake." Oops! The most recent job posting she'd asked about really *had* been the job for Callum, and sadly, she'd missed the application deadline. What a shame. But the good news, someone informed her, was that there were plenty of other positions she could apply for in the district.

I knew what this was. *Everyone* knew what this was. Ms. Dawn was the whistleblower who'd brought a lot of aggravation to others by sending me those photos of that room. Somebody wanted someone new—who wouldn't be texting with me.

I had spent the last few weeks addressing the needs of my elderly mother, who'd fallen and broken both her tibia and her fibula. That morning, after running some errands for her, I had started repainting Bronwyn's room. Covered in that paint and still wearing my paint clothes, I left Ms. Dawn in the care of the sweet school psychologist, who was equally incredulous at this turn of events. And I drove to the district school board office unannounced.

A new director had just taken over following the previous one's retirement. This one I happened to know reasonably well, having taught with her years earlier. This was to be my last-ditch effort before I commenced raising hell.

I walked into her new office, looking a sight, I'm sure, and by then a little beside myself. In my hand, I held a letter I'd written just the night before announcing I would not be seeking the recovery of attorney's fees or any other financial compensation. I wanted them all to know I'd eaten $15,000 in expenses because what I really wanted was change. I wanted the district to *learn* from what we were providing Callum. I wanted other children to have it, too. They owed me that money, but I'd decided not to ask for it. Instead, I felt there was a sincere effort to explore an improvement in services. And when it was all said and done, I didn't want anyone believing I'd sued the district for profit. I wanted everyone who I heard made snarky or suspicious comments to be proven wrong. I was in the right. I cared. And so could they.

She dropped everything she was doing and listened to my whole story from beginning to end. Suddenly, I got a "Wait a minute. They got rid of the only employee in the district with the training we agreed to in legal arbitration? I'm calling right now." I don't know what was said by the recipient of that call, but the part I heard on the director's end gave me hope. Now, of course, the problem was that some innocent, perfectly nice person just got the happy news they'd been hired. That didn't seem fair. I mentioned I'd lost trust with the school (not the teachers, therapists, or aides, mind you) and felt like maybe I ought to call my friend, principal of another nearby elementary school. The new director had her on the phone in seconds and sent me for a visit—telling me the principal said to "bring that IEP and that baby to her." Callum would be welcome there. I was told the director needed to get in touch with HR first about the other hire and allocations, and she'd be in touch with me ASAP.

Within an hour or two, the HR and ESE directors worked magic and ended up getting approval for the new principal to take both the new hire *and* Ms. Dawn from the other school. And Callum was officially transferred.

The principal took his IEP home to read that weekend and scheduled a new IEP team meeting *before* the new school year would start. Ms. Dawn moved in that very afternoon. And with that, I turned in my letter to the superintendent.

Since this was a new school, there was a new team. A couple of them were common to both schools, but most didn't know our story. At least our side of the story. One employee walking down the hallway with Ms. Dawn commented, "I hear this mother is difficult and will sue. That's okay. I've got experience handling difficult parents." Ms. Dawn tried to explain I wasn't difficult at all and that the only difficulty had been with the district—not the teachers, aides, and therapists who worked with him. But the employee had been warned I needed to be handled and was on her guard.

We also had the new ESE director present, and the principal had been sure to include anyone she could think of who would contribute to his learning. I walked in and saw a lot of friendly, curious, wide-eyed expressions. Oh, yes. Callum's case never made it to the school board's ears, but all present were ESE department insiders whose work friends had been involved in some way. I don't blame them for their ready expressions. In their shoes, I would have had the same one. It was bound to be an interesting meeting.

I remembered what Nancy had advised us. It wasn't a win if the IEP team hated one another or me. Nothing good or extraordinary has ever come from that.

I realized this was a rare opportunity for me to correct some rumors. So, I somewhat impulsively decided to set the record straight.

"I'm going to go ahead and address the elephant in this room. You can try to tell me you didn't hear all this through the district rumor pipeline. But I've been one of you for longer than I've been one of me, so, I know better. Right now, I'm not an employee. I'm the parent. So, I'm free to say whatever I want. And, I'm sure as district employees, you can appreciate the beauty of this moment."

A few of them laughed. Some began to look around ever so slightly to catch one another's eyes. Some maintained an impenetrable professional countenance. I continued.

"I've heard a lot of rumors recently. Some made me mad; some made me laugh. Some worried me. Some hurt. It boils down to a lot of district employees hearing that I'm a litigious parent out to get people. That I'm after every little mistake and am at war with the district. And that you'd better watch your back around Callum. I've even been told some have expressed genuine fear of working with my child because of me.

"Normally, I'm not one to air my dirty laundry, but if this team functions as a team, you can't be afraid of me. Fear and collaboration don't mix well. So, I want you to know you have nothing to fear. The district and I indeed had some issues regarding his needs as pertains to services. We resolved

that. But I want you to know not one teacher, aide, or therapist has ever upset us. It was a lack of services we had a problem with, not the services he was provided. We've loved the staff who've worked with him so far and have never done anything but sing their praises.

"What I'm trying to say is, if you have one of those days and remember at ten p.m. you were supposed to call me? Just call the next day. I'm a teacher. I know why you're busy, and I know why you're tired. And let's not forget I also live with the student in question. I'm not coming after your teaching certificate for a slip of memory. If Callum trips, and skins his knee bloody, you don't need to send a contingent of district officials and the school board attorney over to my school to inform me in person. Little boys trip and fall and get skinned knees. You're human, and he's a child. Things happen. Don't be afraid of me, and please don't be afraid of Callum."

That's when a couple of them who'd worked with me in the past began smiling and nodded. And I felt the slightest release of tension in the air. I ended my spiel with a thank-you and a smile, and everyone adjourned. I wasn't sure if my impulsiveness in speaking was good or not. But just following, a team member I knew caught up with me to whisper, "I'm glad you spoke up. They needed to hear that. I think everything's going to be okay." She then giggled and added, "I also think a lot of phone calls and texts are going to be made tonight!" And we both laughed, knowing that was certainly true.

One of the best parts of moving to my friend's school was her assistant principal. As it turned out, he was the only administrator in the district who was a BCaBA (assistant BCBA). He understood autism. He respected Ms. Dawn's work. Both administrators participated themselves in Callum's daily life skills visits—saying hello, waiting his turn, sitting patiently in a lobby, before being rewarded by a spin in their desk chairs.

In fact, the whole school got in on it. The media specialist encouraged him daily to come and sit in his favorite rocking chair. The other children welcomed him as well and approached him on the playground. They looked out for him. Teachers from other classes so enjoyed his stimming they scoped out every Dollar General in the county for this one squishy toy he loved and bought them for him in mass.

And the first time he hugged the assistant principal, who could have doubled as a linebacker, that gentle giant of a man cried.

We had so many gains that the first year. After hearing Callum's story and realizing our speech acquisition window end was looming, they worked out a nontraditional setting for him for one year, with the end goal being full inclusion into a classroom. But in the beginning, we knew he wasn't ready for that. He needed intensive 1:1 attention and practice with learning self-control, how to request, and school procedures.

So, they went to the pull-out resource teacher and asked if she minded giving up a corner of her room. Any other veteran teacher would have. But not her. She welcomed Ms. Dawn, understood the plan, got on board with the BCBA (who she knew from when they'd taught together years earlier), and even helped her create a magical corner of her room with a "Callum's Growth Tree"—fairy lights, therapy toys, and a sensory play area. They even put blue and green filters over the fluorescent lights, because they'd heard that fluorescent lights could irritate autistic children.

In a sense, he had his own classroom. We were able to start over. To reintroduce him to appropriate school behaviors using nothing but positivity and rewards. The resource teacher had small groups of students who filtered in and out all day. So Callum was able to gradually acclimate to typical school noises, had table time modeled for him by slightly older students, and eventually joined in as he was able. This led to classroom visits and a slow, nontraumatic reintroduction to the school experience as it should be.

Within six weeks of the start of school, the IEP team had to hold *another* meeting—this time for the happy purpose of updating his goals *because he'd met all of them for the whole year already*. And suddenly, an IEP team previously tense and hesitant came alive with laughter, stories of success, ideas therapists had picked up at conferences, plans for new goals, etc. And I knew then it was going to be okay.

We met more than once that year to update his IEP because of how fast he was learning. He rarely melted down. He could sit and attend a lesson for more than thirty minutes before a sensory break. He learned to greet others, wait patiently, walk and not bolt toward danger, follow classroom and lunch procedures, and he began interacting somewhat with other students. He learned his letters and numbers, and colors. And he started to participate in circle time to the extent he was able. My child went from banging his head on the sidewalk and repeating IEP goals to receiving the student of the year award for the whole school.

The administration worked with the ESE department to create a pilot autism program at his school for the following year. The principal invited me to provide autism training to the entire staff, who, bless their hearts, stood in a line after to chat and ask questions. That April, many classrooms put up autism awareness decor.

That led to the superintendent inviting me to provide the same training to principals, followed by assistant principals, followed by reading coaches, and then offering it to all administrators who wanted the training for their own staffs. I was even invited to train school resource officers.

Later that year, when Callum had to walk up onstage for his award, two preschool classes joined him every afternoon in the cafeteria for a brief practice so he'd be familiar with a stage and audience and not be overwhelmed on Awards Day. He pulled it off perfectly, with a proud smile I've never forgotten.

And the next year, Callum was placed in a classroom where he continued to thrive.

What those administrators did was seek to truly understand his needs, think "outside the box" about the appropriate placement for him, trust an expert to help guide his curriculum that year, and foster a school community that welcomed him, and where all played a part in expanding his world. It wasn't a typical setup. It isn't the correct placement for every autistic child. But it allowed us to back up, start over, and get it right for him. Looking back seven years later, I know that reset to be what made the difference.

I learned much that year about what to do, what not to do, and what's a waste of time. Did the district make mistakes? Yes. Did I make mistakes? Yes. Would I do things any differently now? Probably. But was it worth it? Oh my stars, yes.

Callum is usually easy to take places, shows pretty good manners, and can ask for simple things he wants. That right there will give him living options in adulthood he wouldn't necessarily get if he'd continued on that trajectory of self-harm and constant meltdowns. No, I wouldn't change it. I did the best I could, and his life is better for it.

But I remain haunted by the children who don't have someone to champion them. For there is no question my son got more than students with similar disabilities. I know I'm the squeaky wheel that got the grease, a privileged squeaky wheel at that.

It shouldn't be that way.

But I can tell you those professionals who throw their hearts into the profession don't want it that way, either. They don't. Even at the highest levels of administration, their job is really about rationing resources.

No, it shouldn't be that way. But it is. So, I made sure my son's needs were met. And I advocated as best I could for the other students' needs to be addressed as well.

But all actions have consequences. And I would soon learn what they would be.

Chapter 22

When Victory Is Not a Victory: On What Badass Parent Advocacy *Really* Is

f you thought I was going to tell you a story where I become Kickass Autism Mom Who Makes the Educational Evildoers Rue the Day, you'd be mistaken. That's not because I haven't felt like becoming that mom. Oh, I have. I've sat on the phone with sympathetic friends while I plotted what I would do and say and how *I'd show them* [insert whomever]. My friends have joked for years that I have an airtight internal filter—that I somehow find a way to choose the right words rather than the first that come to mind. Most of the time, I'd agree it's true but blame it on genetics. In my lineage, I have five attorneys. I also have an English professor for a mother. So, I come from people who choose their words carefully.

What I learned from them was to be deliberate and cautious with my words, always weighing the cost-benefit. In the early days, I tired of convincing some district staff that I knew what I was talking about with regard to autism. There'd been some condescension in some meetings (though most were polite and respectful) and in some conversations.

I'd once patiently endured a school administrator confidently inform me that no, we couldn't accommodate my request to allow Callum to wait in the library during afternoon pickup because my three-year-old's sensory disorder was overwhelming him in the afternoon with screaming kids and buses. Why? Because it would be inconvenient. And didn't I know that autistic children have sensory issues? It's common and nothing to worry about. They just have to get used to it.

Yes, when my three-year-old son is bashing his head on the concrete and coming home and crying daily, it's something to worry about. It means he's in pain. He's suffering. He's overwhelmed. Those are all justifications for concern. And I was nothing but nice (niceness being a terminal condition for me) about it, giving her room to come up with another solution I liked less. I believe the superintendent ultimately intervened in the school pickup changes that created the chaos, and I remember indulging a tiny smirk. When your child has been harmed in some way, wanting a moment of satisfaction is understandable. And it sure is tempting to give in to.

If you have a gift for snark and a justifiable cause with the law backing you? Well, you can get pretty confident. And confidence is good. But your self-confidence isn't the goal here. Getting your child a free and appropriate education is.

If you cause the entire IEP team to hate and fear you, then you will reap the results of that in every by-the-book-but-uninspired lesson, a complete inability to just reach out and tell the teacher something (because they will no longer communicate without the whole team present), their emotional disconnects with your child, and people who aren't excited to tell you about the latest thing they heard about and how they thought it would be great for your child, and . . .

If they fear you, they will fear your child. They will fear allowing your child to play fun communication games outside in the sunshine, because what if they trip and fall? They'll fear being accused of not communicating one busy Friday with their usual paragraph update of the week. So, they'll make a form they can copy and place check marks to CYA on account of you. There won't be any more paragraphs. There won't be cute little stories. When you're wary of people, you don't want to take cute snapshots of their kids learning something new to send to them. And the bond you need to develop a successful parent-school relationship never forms.

That bond is everything.

I'm not saying that sometimes you don't have to swoop down and de-clare *something needs to change 'round here*. I'm not suggesting suffering abuse. Absolutely not. Call the superintendent. Call the police. Call the newspapers and TV stations. Raise hell the likes of which they've never seen. School-based abuse of children with disabilities occurs. No playing nice required.

But what I am trying to say—gently—is that if you're known as the Kickass Autism Mom Who Makes the Educational Evildoers Rue the Day—over *every little thing*—you might want to consider if you're achieving the heart of what your child needs or whether you are "showing them you don't play around." I've seen those parents in online forums bragging about how they told that IEP team about themselves, which I know sometimes needs to be done. But I think we must be careful how much we infuse our own identity into a situation that needs resolution rather than drama.

It isn't necessary to be a badass in volume or tone for them to respect your concerns and to understand that you have the knowledge to ensure compliance. You can do that with good questions and calm observations. You can do that by coming prepared with a Binder of Epic Proportions showing you've long been invested in the process. You still might need to "fight" for what you believe your child needs. But most of that can be ac-complished with a basic education in advocating for your special education student and data. And you should always remember that in the event you actually do go to court rather than arbitration, all of your actions—written, spoken, posted on social media, emailed, etc.—could be Exhibit A for the school district. Don't give them evidence you won't want others looking at a year down the line. As my father would have remarked, "People would win more often in court if they didn't screw themselves over leading up to it." Far better for those looking over those records to see polite, respectful communications/complaints and written follow-ups than to hear about the time you lost it in the front office and *told the principal to go screw herself*.

Over the years both as a teacher and as an autism advocate, I've known those parents. They may be lovely, delightful people in any other situ-ation. But in showing their ass rather than preparedness, they're giving in to instant over delayed gratification, the problem being that the other side will scramble to dot i's and cross t's in such a way as to protect themselves from litigation. Their primary goal will then become litigation avoidance, and your child's needs will come second. I can practically hear some passionate parents yelling, "Not getting sued *means* they're meeting my child's needs!"

No. No, it doesn't. They are not one and the same. Schools are required to provide a free and appropriate education, not the best education money can buy. Go to court with only that argument in your arsenal, and you'll lose.

Other than administrative, I've sat at that table filling several roles over the years: teacher, parent, litigant, and specialist. And I've learned a few things over time, the most important being that the special education parent-school relationship is an investment worthy of time, courtesy, communication, and just a little bit of grace on your part. What you want is to establish respectful ties with everyone in that room. You want everyone to feel good about that IEP, to realize the benefit to the student, and to get a little excited about the possibilities. You want *buy-in*, not wariness.

Now, I'm friends with parents who strongly disagree with me on this. I love and won't judge them. You do you and all that jazz. But after twenty-five years in education and over a decade as a special education parent, what I know to be true is that having the adults who care for your child seven or more hours per day afraid of you both is a Pyrrhic victory—the cost isn't worth the win. Don't make assumptions and threaten from go. Don't bring up lawyers. (Lawyers prefer to introduce themselves anyway.) Don't threaten anyone's job.

Your best move is to learn as much as they know about federal education laws, your child's rights, evidence-based "best practices" for your child's needs, how IEP goals should be written and measured, and the significance of various evaluations and assessments. Learn about the parent information centers in every state, reach out, and get some free training on how to advocate for your child.

Arrive dressed like you would for an interview, because you're going to be facing down a table of people in suits and professional dress with fancy letters behind their names. And that *will be* intimidating, no matter how nice they are. Give yourself that boost of confidence.

Take notes. If you are denied a requested service, politely request that denial *in writing*. (It will have to include a reason based on data—data they may or may not be able to support.) I recommend you get a printed copy of everything shown and discussed and save it in a binder chronologically rather than by category. Chronology tells a story. And it's the story of your child's growth and regression you may need to tell in order to make an argument for accommodations and/or services. If you organize by school years, you also won't need to continually upsize your binder and reorganize tabs. Include emails (print them!), prior notification letters, private evaluations, private therapy notes, etc., with the most recent documentation added in order. Bring your binder with you. Also bring a discussion agenda of your own concerns, with enough copies for all.

As a parent and IEP team member, you may contribute to the IEP goals. Learn how they're written. Google IEP goals related to what you wish to address for ideas. Immerse yourself into that team. After all, you're on it. And according to US courts, *your* attendance matters most. Everyone else in attendance could theoretically be replaced by someone else in the district. But not you. So, own it. But own it armed with knowledge and prepared to ask important questions. Believe me, they'll make note of your preparation, and it will always be in the back of their minds.

Will you have to fight a school? Maybe. Probably not. But maybe. So, learn what you need to learn *now*. An IEP itself should not be where you begin your education.

But whatever you do, don't introduce yourself as their adversary the minute you walk into the meeting. That's not badass parent advocacy. It may feel good when you're mad, but it isn't going to get you what you want: in loco parentis—for those people to do for your child *what they would do for their own*.

By all means, put a smile on your face and your best foot forward. When the adrenaline is flowing, winning battles may be invigorating. But you might lose the war. And then *everyone* loses, because there are never winners in war. Don't declare it prematurely.

Chapter 23

Inclusivity vs. Tribe:
On "Full Inclusion" in Our Schools

One weekend night a few years ago, Callum attended the first birthday party he'd been invited to by a classmate. All the other kids (mostly older) attending the party were fully verbal and had established friendships. No, he didn't fit in exactly. But the birthday boy's family were welcoming to all. And when he arrived, every single one of those classmates turned and exclaimed, "Hey, Callum!" before giving him fist bumps. He got to "play" party table games with Daddy and the other kids and won a bunch of candy. He had pizza. He stood during the birthday song. He sang the last word in each line. He was thanked enthusiastically for his gift. He ate a giant wedge of strawberry cake and got some more fist bumps and a genuine "Good night, Callum! We're glad you came." It was a success.

This sounds like an anecdote supporting full inclusion—where there are no "special ed" classes and where all the regular ed students welcome and accept the disabled ones. Where intellectually disabled students are educated right next to gifted ones. I'll admit, that sounds amazing and beautiful.

But the federal government reneged on its promise to fully fund IDEA.

That means there aren't enough trained adults in each classroom with appropriate AAC and educators who understand an appropriately modified curriculum—because we haven't trained them to do that very well unless they are special education majors. Now, you can propose to train them, but buy-in is something entirely different. New procedures and re-quired documentation are time-consuming. And there are still people teaching today who don't *believe* in ADHD, autism, or dyslexia.

But "inclusion" is favorite lingo in regular ed these days. And school districts, because it saves a lot of dollars (when not done appropriately), are enthusiastically adopting it as *stated* best practice. Besides, they had that one training, remember? So now, they're "doing full inclusion" more often.

But that doesn't mean there will be another person or two to assist in actually realizing that goal.

What there *will* be is a classroom filled with kids who have a huge edge over the "inclusion kid." Possibly, there's an aide assigned, but she's had to fill in for Mrs. Jones this week, who had a baby. Just put them up front in the seating chart and don't let them fail, okay? Nothing below 60 percent.

It is not possible to provide 1:1 assistance, small-group enrichment, and whole-class instruction and still remain in compliance with every stu-dent's IEP *with only one teacher.* It's not. And *any* "inclusion plan" a school district confidently touts as a "best practice" that doesn't involve new hires and the reassignment of former self-contained ESE teachers to be co-teachers is most decidedly *not* inclusion.

It's throwing children with disabilities to the wolves.

If that district hasn't invested in elaborate plans to teach about accep-tance and inclusion, then they weren't ever serious anyway. Now you have kids not learning, bored, attempting to compensate, and probably suffer-ing poor relationships with peers. And yet leaders wonder why all the vet-eran teachers are jumping ship and faculties are now made up of mostly four years of experience and under.

It sickens the soul to be assigned the impossible.

To watch a child with needs that aren't being met because you can't be in ten places at once is heartbreaking for the average teacher. Then there are those who are furious, "didn't sign on for this," and are determined to *prove* it can't work, all while obviously resenting the innocent student who had nothing to do with this fiasco.

Am I anti-inclusion? Of course not. For most children—both neurodivergent and neurotypical—it's been proven to increase learning and socialization. That's inclusion how it is supposed to be carried out and how it is supposed to be adequately funded to ensure it's *actually happening*. I'm not against inclusion at all. What I am is anti–false representation to save money at any cost—because we can now call it something else while providing no services to take the place of what was taken.

We can start a passionate debate here about inclusive education and how awful or wonderful it is that Callum now attends an exclusively special ed school. Do I feel a little like I caved? Sometimes. Do I know I could've strong-armed his neighborhood school into complying with full inclusion? Yes. But I'll tell you right now why some parents agree to self-contained classes or special ed schools.

Because of moments like that birthday party. Moments when other children are welcoming because there's zero pressure not to be. Moments when a newly teenage boy can proudly open gifts of cologne, gift cards, and trendy clothes alongside equally desired gifts of toy cars and dinosaurs—with no embarrassment about his enthusiasms. Moments when no one is the odd person out because everyone in attendance understands the state of Otherness. Moments when everyone can relax, smile, and just be.

I know how an ideal, inclusive world is *supposed* to be. But I also know it doesn't exist yet. And unless you have spent time in an exclusively special-needs school, then you cannot understand what the students and families get from them. They get the same thing that everyone who shares an identity or common experience gets from spending time in the company of others like themselves. It's why there are Girl Scouts, support groups, clubs, and Facebook groups.

It's how we human beings form our tribes.

Yes, I want inclusive education—under adequately funded, trained, and staffed circumstances. But I would be lying if I said we didn't experience something at that party that felt good and right. Like a hug. Like home.

And I feel all sorts of conflicted about that.

Chapter 24

Check Engine Light:
On the Effects of Stress on the Body

I n the past few years, some clever people have created online autism simulations. Autism simulations attempt to sensitize neurotypical people to
what those with autism experience daily. When you play an online autism simulation video, you're immediately bombarded with confusing
sensory input—loud and discordant sound, bright lights, and camera
movements that cause vestibular discomfort. Voices and background
noise become one, and the busy world suddenly becomes an unpleasant
place in which to be. And all you want is for that to stop.

But it's just a video. Two minutes of noise and visual chaos, and you're
done. I've watched them. And, while I appreciate what the creators aim to
accomplish with them, I've always understood that the lived experience
is far more than can be conveyed on video. I hadn't yet *lived* the pain of
sensory overload. The annoyance. The dislike. The tendency to get jumpy
and uncomfortable, yes. I have those traits, as did my father. But I hadn't
felt *pain*. Not even emotional pain, because I have autonomy and know I
can leave. Knowing you can leave—to escape if you choose to—is no small
thing. Sit and think about that sometime.

In 2014, a few weeks after we came to an agreement in arbitration, after Callum began an intensive summer program with his 1:1 para, Ms.
Dawn, and various compensatory therapies, he began to experience a
burst of learning and a growing ability to communicate simple things.

Quite naturally, the bad meltdowns (like putting his head through a glass cabinet panel) all but disappeared. Occasionally, we still had meltdowns, but their severity (for him and for us) was greatly reduced.

Although my advocate and friends were in the "make the district reimburse you for what this cost" camp, I always knew the assumed threat that I would seek monetary compensation was in my favor. But it wasn't ever part of my plan.

Because I was one of them. It's a small city in a rural county. We don't all know one another, but we all have friends in common, and you can't go anywhere without seeing someone you know. I love my city, but I don't blame our natives for moving to the anonymity of large cities. Small-town Southern politics are not unlike the way they're represented in ID network shows. Living in a place where you could make charts of the various scandals and how they're interwoven into other scandals is a tad dicey at times.

The local school system is, at the time of this writing, the largest employer in the county. And they have tight relationships with law enforcement who know all the Child Protective Services investigators who know all the folks at the courthouse and state attorney's office. And so on and so forth, and all I'm saying about many of these people I genuinely like is *we can't keep any secrets*. If you work in the school district, you know stuff. I still know stuff four years after taking a job in the private sector, mainly because I still know people in the district.

On a personal level, I like 99 percent of them. I respect the work most of them do. But I lament the decisions some have made—either forced by state and financial considerations or just ones they came up with and I disagree with. Even though I have a T-shirt that says BE CAREFUL OR YOU'LL END UP IN MY BOOK, I don't *really* mean it. I don't wish harm or retribution to people in troubling ethical quandaries (that threaten their continued livelihood and family's well-being). I wish I could inspire in them courage, but our souls are all walking at different paces on our paths. So is mine, and I hope some of those folks remember that my soul is embedded with my child's in a way they can't understand. He requires a different level of protection and a level of hypervigilance no one but the parent of a significantly developmentally delayed child can comprehend.

But it *can* be stressful. While I support welcoming and appreciating neurodiversity, to deny that it is so severe in some individuals as to be completely disabling and even dangerous for themselves and others is to perpetuate an absurd lie. It's awful to see a distressed, nonverbal twenty-five-year-old man wearing diapers and a helmet to protect himself from head-banging. As an autism specialist, I wonder what was done with him as a preschooler. Was he ever taught functional communication? Could he possibly have had more freedoms and a life more than he has now if someone had invested in those therapies back then? Is it still possible?

No, some autism stories aren't happy, miraculous, funny, or inspirational. They just are. And some of those days, you can almost feel the stress coming out of your pores. When you live in a round-the-clock state of fight-or-flight mode, your body *will* take note, even if you don't.

During that year of our due process case, little signs of stress began to show. Only I didn't take them for the warning signs they were. I was getting sick often, one case of bronchitis at a time. My immune system didn't seem to be working. I was waking early and unable to return to sleep. I'd had to buy all new clothes because I'd lost weight without trying. I'd had a major screw-up at work (that fortunately was fixable). Plagued by anxiety attacks, I even bailed at the last minute on an interview with Shannon Penrod from the show Autism Live—when she'd been so nice to interview me previously. And in the most terrifying sign of all, my focus and attention span were so bad I blew right through a red light—with both Bronwyn and Callum in the car. Fortunately, no other cars were coming, but that could have gone quite differently.

TWO or three weeks after we reached an agreement with the district in arbitration, I got my mother set back up in her home following months of rehab, and I got Callum settled into a new school, my husband planned a surprise birthday dinner celebration for me with friends. It was a fun evening, desperately needed, and I have lots of smiling photos to remember it.

I've never smiled quite the same since.

The next morning, I put on makeup, helped get the kids ready for school, and laughed about something my husband said as I walked out the door. Within a minute I was pulling into my regular parking space (as I lived within a mile of the school), got out of my car, and attempted to smile at a coworker.

That's when I realized half of my face wasn't working. I walked inside, looked in a mirror, and quickly decided I was having a stroke. I'd seen my father have two different kinds, and it's what killed him the second time. So my colleagues stayed with me and kept me calm while we waited for my husband to arrive. He has a nursing background, so he did some kind of quick assessment on me before deciding to just drive to the ER. After getting bumped to first place in triage (the only perk to facial paralysis) and a CT scan, it was determined that I had simply come down with Bell's palsy, a form of facial paralysis resulting from viral damage to the facial nerves. Relieved that it wasn't something life-limiting, I dutifully filled the prescriptions for antivirals and steroids and arranged a follow-up with the neurologist. And I returned to work and attempted to feign a positive attitude about my now-jarring facial expression.

As it turns out, I had a pretty severe case of Bell's palsy, as in near-total facial paralysis on one side. Within a day, my face became *overly* sensitive. The slightest touch of a fingertip was painful. A fan blowing on my face somehow gave me a headache. Because my left eye wouldn't close properly and I couldn't squint, bright light became problematic. I could barely see upon stepping outdoors, and bright indoor lighting was disturbing to me. My eyes blinking at different times blurred my vision. I had to tape my eye shut to prevent it from drying out at night.

But the worst was yet to come. Within two days, the Bell's palsy had worsened. And, because I had complete facial paralysis, the muscles in the ear that normally dampen sound ceased to work. The condition is officially called hyperacusis, but I called it Superman Hearing. Suddenly, I could hear *everything*—the filter on the fish tank, the ceiling fan in the other room, the pop in my husband's jaw as he ate. But it wasn't simply a matter of hearing everything. The problem was that it was all at the same volume or as loud as an explosion. So, everything became too much. I nearly went into a panic at work. The school bells were painful to me. A pencil dropping onto a desk made me jump. I had to ask everyone to lower their voices, and I couldn't tolerate radio or TV. I donned headphones and tried not to cry. But my voice amplified inside my head with the headphones on, so I couldn't tolerate speaking with others. All I wanted was to curl up in a ball in bed in the dark and wish the world away. Because the world? It *hurt* me.

And—although I'd *comprehended* the sensory integration issues impacting my son, I now looked at him with new eyes. I now knew how hard many outings really were for him.

And because of that, he is even more amazing to me. Amazing in that he walks through life experiencing these things (though I'm certain it's probably not exactly the same) every day. Whereas I shut down within a couple of days and hid out during the worst of it, he isn't given that option. He's twelve years old, and the world attacks his senses. When I'm alone with my thoughts and consider that, it steals my breath. And when he curls up in a ball and hides out from the world for a few minutes, I find myself understanding in a way I couldn't have before.

Did Bell's palsy make me autistic? Of course not. Do I now have a complete understanding of the autistic experience? Nope—not even close. Because Bell's palsy did not affect my ability to communicate. It didn't alter how I perceive others. It didn't change the way I process new information. I still think in words and not pictures.

But Bell's palsy did act as a tour guide of sorts. Like the Ghost of Christmas Present, it took me to a place I'd never been and gave me some experiences I wouldn't have understood on my own. It gave me a physical experience merely reading about couldn't provide me. It allowed me to see my son and his reactions to the world with another lens. It isn't often that we get to live as others before returning to our own lives. But when we do, we are changed—forever reminded that our own perceptions are just that, perceptions. When you realize that your perceptions aren't necessarily facts, then all manner of truths and possibilities open for you.

More importantly, I was given an unforgettable lesson in the importance of self-care. I can't say I've mastered it, but I now have a complete understanding about how the mind and body are connected. Stress doesn't stay bottled inside your mind. Whether you know it or not, it bleeds out into your body. And if you don't stop for a moment to address what's in your head, sooner or later it will demand your attention physically.

So, despite the residual paralysis, pain, hearing, and vision issues I still experience, I understand this lesson to have been both painful and a gift.

Of course, the most valuable lessons in life usually are.

Backseat Drivers and Other Perils

The eyes of others our prisons; their thoughts our cages.

–Virginia Woolf

Chapter 25

There's Still Time:
On Missed Invitations and Opportunities

n the early days, when a high-needs autistic child is still cute and the developmental gaps between your child and others not so wide yet, friends and loved ones will rally around you.

> *"We love her just as she is."*
> *"Of course he's welcome!"*
> *"I don't mind the meltdowns. Just tell me how I can help."*

And they mean it. They do. When a developmentally delayed child is small and cute and easily portable, full inclusion in your community seems possible by both strangers and those who love you. When you're just figuring out what life with a disabled child is going to look like, all those assurances of welcome feel like a lifeline. They feel like hope that we're all going to be okay.

But high-needs nonverbal autism doesn't resemble the glamorized autism of Hollywood. Yes, family and friends likely *know* about autism. But they know about the autism of their Facebook feeds—the kind of autism where an autistic girl sings the national anthem to uproarious applause. Or the autism portrayed on TV where a young Aspie solves the crime via clues tapped in Morse code *and* Sanskrit. They are, of course, all too willing to invite the young Sheldon Cooper they envision you raising to bake cookies for Santa or attend a pool party.

Yes, the savant manifestation of autism exists all right, and it's fascinating. History is filled with neurodivergent brilliance benefitting mankind. But that's not the norm. Savants are a minority of the autistic population. Autistic people with average intelligence outnumber them. And those with intellectual disabilities requiring moderate to high levels of assistance outnumber both.

What those who love, and like, you don't know is they've likely made promises they ultimately aren't willing to keep. That's because over time little voices and meltdowns grow louder. Little bodies grow bigger. Odd behaviors become more uncomfortable on the receiving end. Personal space becomes more important. And toileting delays are more psychologically difficult for others to witness or assist with as a child nears adolescence and sometimes beyond. In the presence of these realities of higher-needs autism and in the absence of the Hollywood variety, invitations begin to decline. Sometimes, people already know that a situation wouldn't be ideal for Callum, so they don't even ask. But it still hurts to not be invited.

What hurts more, however, are people who are supposed to love your child not making an effort to include them. They'll tell themselves they don't know "how to handle them" or "what they like." But that's a poor excuse to exclude someone. Inexperience and uncertainty I understand. Not sucking it up, asking for assistance, and getting to know them anyway? That's professing love rather than evidencing it.

This is an old post but one I've gotten good feedback on from readers who shared it with people in their lives who needed to hear it. Of all the responses I've ever gotten over the years, my favorite is still the mom who shared it with family who were so taken aback, they resolved to change their relationship with her child then. And they did.

There's Still Time

Once upon a time there was an autistic child. He wasn't "easy." He didn't talk like the other children in the family. He didn't play the same games. He wasn't interested in going to the same places—hot festivals, toy stores, and noisy restaurants. His family loved him, but he often wasn't included. He wasn't invited for sleepovers. He didn't get the same special outings as his siblings or cousins. Initially, he didn't notice. But as he grew older, he did. When they came by to pick up his siblings, he wanted to go, too. When everyone left without him, he stood at the window and watched them drive away. But they believed his parents understood—that he was too much to handle.

But he wasn't. He was a joy. The outings he enjoyed were simple— rides in the car, trips to the grocery store, splashing in the pool, playing in the mud, swinging in the park. But, for whatever reason, he was never invited to do any of those things—the things he could do and enjoy—and kept being passed over for the children in the family who, presumably, were more fun to spend time with.

He continued to learn, develop, and grow. Eventually, he knew. He knew he was different. But what he didn't know was what the family had assumed he would understand— that he was loved equally. That's because love isn't what's declared. Love is what's done. It's easily identified in any language—or lack thereof. And when dispensed unequally— and obviously—it denies both the receiver and the giver.

He knows. You know. And there's still time to do it differently.

Chapter 26

Your Friend's "Small Business": On What You Don't Owe People

We all know them. Some of us *are* them. And it's no secret, because those people do much of their business on social media. Sometimes, it's all they post about. Or you're going to get invited to their Facebook group. They're selling all sorts of things: scented wax, clothing, jewelry, handbags, kitchenware, you name it. That's fine. You buy something from time to time because you love them.

But some of them are selling items purporting to improve health. I'm not going to make an outrageous claim that *all* those products are snake oil. They might be perfectly good but overpriced vitamins and oils you're buying. (I say overpriced because multilevel marketing, or MLM, relies on multiple, tiered sellers—the company and the "consultants" who must *both* profit. Theoretically. Statistically, that's not the case.)

Essential oils are not in themselves bad or good. Many of them have been used throughout history for different purposes. Lemon has long been noted for easing nausea—especially in pregnancy. Eucalyptus has been used for years to ease stuffy noses. Clove oil will knock out severe dental pain almost instantly. I'm not claiming that plants and oils have no benefits. I am absolutely saying that none of them "cure" autism.

Why? Because precisely none of them can rewire brains.

Stop and think about that for a minute. Think about claims your otherwise wonderful friend has made. If any person within shouting distance complains of a hangnail, they'll exclaim, "I've got an oil for that!" Then they instruct you to rub it on the bottom of your feet for GERD (gastro-esophageal reflux disease) or something. Later, in the "informational call" or "party," somebody will share an anecdotal tale of being cured of *cancer*. And, sure enough, then they pull out the story of the parent who claims they "recovered" their child from autism.

Now I don't at all mind friends who tell me lavender, orange, lemon, or peppermint can soothe anxiety in autism. Because I already know that. I melt scented wax cubes all the time to create a relaxing atmosphere for myself. But they create a relaxing atmosphere for *everyone*, not merely autists. And relaxation has always been known to help anxiety and sleep. True enough. Worth exploring.

But they will not cure autism. Not even a little bit.

Neither will the magical grape juice sourced only via goat conveyance from the side of a mountain in Peru following a spiritual purification ceremony. Nor will vitamins and supplements. No, scientists haven't been "keeping" these miraculous cures from us. The truth about real scientists working on human medicine is that they're there because they have a personal interest. I've been blessed to meet many scientists who've become friends over the years. My best friend Beverly is a doctor. She worked in breast cancer research and now in a leading breast cancer center because she's passionate about finding a cure for it. I've known her all my life and can state with certainty no pharmaceutical company could buy her silence.

Many people became scientists, researchers, and medical professionals *because* someone they loved was affected by some disease or condition. (That was the case with her.) Not only would they not *want* to hide a cure, but how could anyone believe a secret like that even *could* be held? The man who invented insulin gave the patent away free because he believed that the right to health is universal. We allowed something inexpensive and easily manufactured to be adopted by others for profit. But the scientist himself gave it as his gift to the world. I've been fortunate to personally meet and know many scientists and their enthusiasts over the past decade. Not one of them would remain silent while lives were being permanently altered or lost.

Do you remember telling a friend about your crush in middle school? The sex of your baby before the gender reveal? A church member you're getting divorced? Then you can appreciate the planning and buy-in required to keep thousands of people quiet about a cure for autism that impacts one in fifty-four people. Most of us know far more than fifty-four people. Which means all of those thousands of people would be successfully hiding a "cure" and never mentioning it to any affected friends and family. That's not even beginning to calculate the scientists personally impacted by cancer. This conspiracy seems improbable to me.

Mark my words. If somebody selling something tells you there's a cure for cancer, epilepsy, autism, ADHD, and more and that scientists and doctors are hiding it for profit, sit down and do some math on the probability of that undertaking even being feasible. It gives "I could tell you but then I'd have to kill you" all new meaning.

Now, you and I know there's no autism cure. But you know and love some people right now who *are* eventually going to reach out to you about their "small business" and your autistic child. For the record, I find it just as improbable they're all evil, too. In fact, I know several, and they definitely aren't. But they've bought into their products. And they may love you and want the best for you and your child and push those products. As frustrating and awkward as those exchanges can be, they're mostly well-intentioned.

They'll PM you and say things like:

> *"Omg, you have to hear about this! This mother recovered her child with vetiver oil!"*
> *"Did you know these parents were able to take their child off of toxic medications with chemicals and he sleeps through the night now?"*

For your fact-checking pleasure, please be assured this former librarian has verified the following: *Everything you touch is a chemical.* Including water, essential oils, and mystical grape juice. Just because something is natural (poison ivy, for example) doesn't make it a "natural treatment" for eye conditions. Don't get suckered into "chemical free" and "all natural" claims. Nothing is chemical free. Chemicals are *matter*. All substances—including the air you're breathing—are included. Lava is natural. Helicopters are not. But I know which one I want arriving at my house during a volcanic eruption.

But some of them will push a little too hard and reveal a dark side you didn't know about. I've also received PMs like:

> *"Okay, but if you later decide you want to try to help his autism, let me know!"*

Yes, I sat and blinked at that one for a minute. There are some lines you're going to experience that leave you wide-eyed and wondering how you wish to react.

All of these and worse have gone to my private messages. Every "treatment." All the "cures." All the "alternative" and "holistic" therapies. With no research data to back them up. Merely claims by the PR team hired to create their websites. And they're pretty free to do it. It's perfectly okay to have twenty friends fill out a form raving about your products before claiming "data" showed improvement in 97 percent of those taking the product (who are sitting in your living room).

All due to its "synergistic" effects, of course.

At first, you might be willing to try anything. That's a mistake born of love. But know that there are bad people out there who will sell anything. And there are bighearted, wonderful people they recruit to sell it to *you*. Those good people don't always understand the difference between science-like information on a product website and an actual, *carefully* designed scientific study *with results that can be replicated*. They don't know about peer review and double-blind studies and what those terms mean for the conclusions they profess. So, they're true believers. Who might just be your mom's best friend, your boss, or even a fellow parent of an autistic child.

That's going to create some potentially awkward situations when you must say no without offending them. Granted, you might be the sort to not mind offending people in the name of truth. But if it's your boss's wife, you might wish to reconsider. How you say no, in my opinion, is entirely up to you. They put you in this position, and *you are not obligated to take on every possible unpleasant exchange.*

If lying is easier and doesn't affect your employee evaluation, say you already use the products and your bestie is your consultant. (The consultant honor code will probably end the discussion.) Change the subject immediately before they start the consultant downline tree discussion of people you might both know.

Or, say your child had an anaphylactic reaction to a product, and their doctor forbade it. They won't touch that. That was discussed in the informational meeting.

Or go ahead and educate them, which is very tempting and more common in the early days following diagnosis, when you might have the psychological energy. Later, you'll probably decide that's shaving time off your life you can't get back and stop bothering. I used to do more of the former but now live happier doing the latter. "Bless your heart" is often needed in those situations. I know my life has been better since I stopped feeling responsible for correcting *every* misconception. These days, it's really just the ones I feel like.

You have no obligation to buy snake oil. "Trying everything" sounds nice, but I'm going to assume you'd draw the line at arsenic, right? "Everything" hasn't earned a place in your medicine cabinet, so why would you give it to a child based on questionable "studies" mentioned by a loan officer trying to make a little cash on the side? None of those products will alter your child's neurology. So, however you choose to extricate yourself from those offers is perfectly okay and justifiable. Your job is to protect your child from predators—including predators of hope and money.

Besides, how do you think your friend would take it if you offered an oil to change their child from being who they are? Autism is not cancer. It doesn't benefit from "treatment." Some of its related issues benefit from therapies and medications to keep some problematic issues under control (insomnia and anxiety, for example). But you can't *cure* it. You'd have to remove the brain, miraculously find a way to move all the neurological connections to standard configurations, and put the brain back without doing any damage whatsoever. I'm not claiming I had straight As in science, but I can confidently state this isn't something medical science can do.

And know that even if you could do that, *your child would no longer exist*. You cannot separate the self and the brain. They're woven together with our perceptions, experiences, and biology. If I could snap my fingers and enable him to better communicate and understand? Sure. But I would never trade him for another Callum. Just as any parent wouldn't trade their child. To do so would be a primal betrayal.

I'm now going to issue you, your child, and anyone who lives with you an autism card. You now get to play it when doing so makes anything at all easier. That includes long lines at Disney, early boarding, and making up whatever is necessary to end unpleasant exchanges without causing yourself greater headache. You don't have to be a badass. Escape at your first opportunity.

Because the saying that you cannot please everyone is true. I'm going to say it again. *You can't please everyone.* If you struggle with this concept (as I have my whole life), you're in for some clarity. When people ask me the most important thing I've learned, I always answer the same way: I now know the difference between what constitutes an actual crisis and what does not. Upsetting a friendly acquaintance who is trying to reach her sales goal is not.

Autism is not a crisis. Your child is not diseased.

The lack of services, lack of parental support, lack of appropriate education, lack of AAC, lack of sufficient therapies, and lack of a sufficient number of warm and engaging adult living options is the crisis.

And the only cure that's needed here is for the hearts of those who make our laws and for all of us who elect them.

Chapter 27

Dear Friend Hesitant to Interact with My Autistic Child: On Those Afraid of Your Child

know my child makes you nervous. It's okay. Really. I still love you.

Knowing you to be the good and kind person you are, I see that the lack of interaction with him isn't deliberate. You are simply afraid, not of him but of doing something to upset him. I've had this same fear of being around other people's kids with disabilities in the past, so I get it. I do. But it makes me sad that you may be holding out and miss getting to know my sweet boy. Because he's worth knowing.

One truism about children with disabilities it's important to remember is that they are first and foremost *children*. But I know that many folks, you included, see my child and see his differences first. And I can't blame you. Callum *is* undeniably different.

But, really, he is just a boy, twelve years old. And, though he is autistic and differs from typical children, it doesn't change the part of him that is a child. Those of us who have, love, or work with disabled children get this. But as my child has grown and his needs have become more evident, I've noticed well-intentioned family, friends, and acquaintances struggle with how to interact with my son.

When my friends meet him and aren't sure how to engage him, it usually goes something like this:

"Will he get upset if I . . . ?"

"Is he doing this because . . ."

"But he is so _____! Are you sure he's autistic?"

I know you aren't avoiding him because you find him repugnant. You're simply hesitant. You don't know where to begin. You probably feel guilty about it. And you may feel that stress come over you when you see him, wanting to interact with him like you would any other child but fearful of saying or doing the wrong thing and setting off an epic meltdown.

(It probably doesn't help that you once saw *Rain Man*.)

So you hold back, unsure of what to do. I know you want a cheat sheet—a kind of map to guide you in interacting with him. And that's where I can't help you. Because getting a clear snapshot of a child with autism is a tricky thing. Hence, all the specialists.

I've used my multiple lenses analogy before, as it makes the most sense to me. Often, I try to figure out what is going on with my son and find myself asking, "Which is at play here? Autism? Being a twelve-year-old boy? Or just *Callum*?" I drove myself crazy doing that, trying to break him down into parts in my quest to figure out how to best help him. And finally, it hit me that I cannot analyze him in terms of one or another. *For he is all three.* He is at once a twelve-year-old boy, an autistic person, and himself—Callum.

It's like trying to take a picture with an DSLR (digital single-lens reflex) camera. Typically, you can simply point and shoot and get a pretty good shot.

But, if you are in dim lighting or have a great deal of movement or distance, you have to use specific settings and special lenses to filter and enhance the image.

Trying to figure out what motivates a nonverbal child can be complex. To get a picture of that, you need three (or more) lenses. First, you need the original lens itself to take a simple standard picture. Then you need a second lens that filters for various disabilities. (You might need several such lenses, depending on how many diagnoses the child has.) Finally, you need a lens that enhances that child as an individual because, like everyone else, autistic people have their own temperaments, interests, and fears. So, to get an accurate picture of a child with autism, you have to take a picture with all three (or more) lenses simultaneously. For if you remove one of the lenses, the image does not reflect the actual child.

The problem is that some of the lenses we need still haven't been invented.

What do I say to a friend who honestly wants to get to know my son but is hesitant about doing so? It's really simple. *Just ask me about him*. I'm all too happy to help you connect with him. I'll tell you all about him. Then, feel free to ask me what he likes, how you might best make a favorable impression, and what might upset him.

And, then, just go for it. Visit wearing comfortable clothes and be prepared for an atypical exchange. Take an interest in what he is doing and attempt to join him. He'll notice you. Pretty soon, he will likely begin interacting with you to some degree. And, if you let him warm up to you, you might even get to roughhouse and giggle with him. He'll love you, I promise. And, if you are unwittingly doing something that might not be the best way of engaging him, I'll be there to suggest another. Soon, he may sit right next to you. He will recognize you in the future and maybe smile when you walk in the door. You will have made a friend who will melt your heart.

And *then* you will have a clear picture of my child, a child like every other—yet not.

A child who loves, laughs, snuggles, fears, and delights as much as any other. He may do all those things differently. But he *does* do them in his own way. And knowing him and forging a relationship with him will enrich you both.

For not only is *he* worth you knowing, but I also happen to think *you* are worth him knowing.

Chapter 28

Kinds of Friends:
On the Inevitability of Changed Relationships

t's said an apology means nothing unless it is followed by action—to never again do what you did. But what if you can't help but do it again? Some apologies can't come with that promise. Some apologies just come from acknowledging unpleasant truth—not from being able to do much about it.

This will be true of some of your friendships.

It doesn't make those people less loved, but when lives diverge, we spend more time apart. Distance often means *distance.* I have friends with lives that don't intersect in any significant way with autism. They have their own lives, their own problems, and their own passions.

Sometimes, they just don't know what to say or do. Sometimes, they aren't as good of a friend as you thought. Some of it is invariably due to you not being the friend you once were.

A hard truth about parenting a child with a profound disability is that you're not ever going to be that friend again. You will not be as available. Your priorities have changed. They haven't necessarily become more noble, but they've changed. This means *you've* changed, and the dynamics of your friendships may have as well. You might just be doing well to keep your head above water while your friend needs more companionship or more frequent contact.

And your needs concerning the precious little free time you get may be vastly different than before.

Some of your friends will be so cool with that reality, you'll marvel at their awesomeness all the time. Those friends feel like oxygen. They're just happy when they see you.

But others will be pretty practical in their approach to your friendship. They'll "love ya to death" and miss you but stop reaching out as much until rarely becomes never. Some don't know how to ask, "How can I best be a friend to you?" Or maybe they weren't that invested in you all along, and that level of friendship is more than they were ever prepared to offer. (That happens in all kinds of relationships.)

A reality of parenting a high-needs child is that people you once couldn't imagine living without become just that. Of course, you still like each other's social media and love to see them when you can. But their seeming indifference to the massive changes in your life stings a little. And maybe they'd argue it's reciprocated. They wouldn't be completely wrong.

But your new reality is awkward to them, and their instincts are to keep things light. Eventually it's so light it just floats away.

You will have friends come and go.

It can be a painful realization in the early days. But there are two kinds of friends in this world: the kind who say, "Let me know what I can do to help!" and the kind who just *show up.* If you don't know the difference yet, be assured you'll get the opportunity. Life will ensure that.

And people *will* surprise you. The lifelong bestie you got matching tattoos with in college evolves into an acquaintance whereas another friend becomes your rock.

And some friends will be hurt. And that's hard because you love them. You know they love you. But they can't understand the amount of effort it takes to keep treading water. They haven't heard from you in a while, and it has meaning for them you never intended, but they still *felt.*

They equate time with love and don't understand that time now rules your life with an iron fist. They don't know how many times you've sworn to yourself you'll call or make lunch plans the next day. They don't know you've been up all night. Again. And they may never understand that there are times when the best you can do is to curl up in your shell and take cover.

So you apologize to them because their happiness and problems do matter to you. And if they called right now and needed a kidney, you'd be first in line. But it might take that kidney to get you there.

Because there will come a point when a teenager can no longer suffice as a caregiver. If your older child or adult child is not yet independently toileting, appropriate care will be more expensive and harder to come by in some areas than others. The patient's needs will be both nursing (hygiene) and possibly behavioral (limited communication). Insurance doesn't cover it. Unfortunately, most states don't offer respite care services for parents of minor children unless they're terminally ill. And you can ask only so much of teenagers and friends with no nursing experience. We all have our limits on what we can comfortably handle.

As your child grows, it gets harder to make time with friends or even talk on the phone. And if you're waiting for the plumber to come over for the third time this week following your child's sudden fascination with flushing nonflushable items, you might not find your friend's pressing problem as pressing as they do. You might even forget that worries are relative and judge theirs less worthy of concern. That can impact a friendship over time.

Even when you can make time with others, there's the sobering knowledge (if your child is nonverbal) that they can't tell you what happened while you were gone. They can't say, "She hurt me." The list of those you trust with your child gets shorter as their needs become more complex. Leaving them in the care of others is never carefree.

You try to maintain those connections. If you're single, that might not even be possible to do child-free. If you're partnered, you can trade for some alone or friend time, but your partner needs it, too. Then what of your relationship? Arranging care so the two of you can be alone for an evening or a romantic weekend can be difficult and expensive. When you get the rare opportunity to get away, you feel almost duty-bound to spend it as a couple. You want to nurture relationships with those you love, but it can come down to painful choices in priorities.

That's a harsh reality. Because you cannot define yourself by parental status or relationship alone.

If you do, you'll lose yourself.

Worse yet, you might forget how to talk about anything else—making visits with you is perhaps not the fun time your friends imagine. You *will* change in ways they might not like or be able to identify with. Hopefully, they're the kind of friends who'll love you through your evolution. The *you you were before* is still there; it's just sharing space now with the *you ever since.* And self-neglect, isolation, constant hypervigilance, and sleep loss can make you lose your own social skills.

Hear me well: *try anyway.* For your own mental health. For your partner. For the friends who love you. For your child, so they have a parent not quite so on edge. They might not like you to leave, but they'll probably enjoy you more when you return.

Don't forget how to laugh, how to embrace life. Make a point to keep up with the lives of those you love. Ask about *their* children, careers, and interests. Get out of your own head for a while and be *their* friend. It goes both ways. And it's not easy to remember to do. You won't always succeed. But you can't stop trying.

Because in worrying nonstop about your child's ability to access their world, you might forget how to access that world *yourself*—and all the people in it, too.

Which is problematic when *you're* your child's tour guide to that world.

Chapter 29

Let Them: On Accepting Help

The aspect of autism that is perhaps the most challenging to convey to others is an autistic child or autistic adult's need for sameness. When you are deluged by sensory overwhelm, social confusion, or an inability to communicate, not liking surprises is understandable. The ability to track and perceive the passage of time can be a challenge for them, so knowing ahead of time what will happen, who's going to participate, what will be expected, what might be different, etc., matters. It's a way of feeling somewhat in control in a chaotic world. When sameness becomes differentness unexpectedly, it can trigger any number of unpleasant reactions and fear. How that manifests is sometimes startling for those who want to help but are terrified that they won't know what to do. I can't begin to tell you the number of people who've said, "I wish I could do something" before trailing off. But when you have a disabled child, you get good at learning who actually means it and who is inwardly praying you won't take them up on it.

It's not ill will or a lack of love necessarily. And it's not hard to understand why a nervous friend doesn't want to be the one to accidentally send a child into fits of screaming. I get it.

That's what makes it so hard to find care you can confidently leave your child with. Will they get the medicine right? Will they remember the *exact* way I told them to make the chicken nuggets? Will they kindly and not resentfully assist him with personal care? How will they understand what he wants to stream next as he melts down in frustration?

It's not easy. So, you can get accustomed to just counting on yourself and not necessarily even mentioning something that would help or make a difference. You just don't go on that trip to the amusement park that overwhelms your child. You don't pressure wash the siding because you can't care for your child at the same time. You don't get those jeans hemmed. Or the oil changed. Something.

You learn to count on yourself.

There are "contests" that weave themselves all over the online disability community. In one such "contest," parents of disabled children make a web page and tell their stories of what a costly adapted tricycle would mean for their family. If their account is compelling enough, they have enough friends, and those friends join in gaining "votes," they can win. Of course, the vote tallies go up and down by the minute. So, the hopeful parents enjoy a roller coaster of emotions as they gain and fall behind. Because get this: *There's only one bike.* In all of America. And the families who "competed" but didn't win won't get anything.

Perhaps I'm being judgmental, but these folks have had to fight for years. Why should they have to compete in a competition requiring so much effort—simply for their child to get a chance to enjoy the feeling of the wind blowing through their hair like every other child?

I knew a family who entered the contest one year. After weeks of duking it out with other families, theirs came in second place. It was a bummer for half our county. Somebody quickly suggested a GoFundMe, and the child's sweet mother nixed the idea—saying that wasn't the sort of thing she wanted her friends' and family's money going to, and that they weren't in need compared to others who have less.

Although her son and mine have very different diagnoses and require different levels of care, both are considered severely disabled. Both will require lifetime care. Neither of them will ever be out on their own riding bicycles. I knew in a moment what that trike meant to her family: a chance for the four of them to go out together and enjoy a beautiful day in the sunshine. I knew she wanted him to feel the wind blowing through his hair.

But I also knew why she said no.

You get used to saying no. Because yes can bring about judgment and increased scrutiny. If I admit I need some help around the house, will they go back and tell others what a mess my house is? If I ask for help with transporting my child to a doctor's appointment, and he melts down, will they judge how I handle it? If I beg for a couple of hours of "me" time, will they feel uncomfortable helping my child with his personal needs? If I allow my community to help raise funds for something big, will I be judged later if they see me replace an aging car?

It's easier to keep quiet and expect nothing than to risk the look of judgment or pity on someone's face when they offer help. It doesn't help you. But somehow, it hurts less. It doesn't knock at the door of self-doubt, and it doesn't bring shame. I get it. I've experienced it firsthand. So I know why your instincts might be to go inward.

But it's *not* easier. It just *feels* easier at the moment, like the instant gratification of procrastinating something important. There's brief relief in saying no. But it makes all the days after that much harder.

There's a rule well known when flying in airplanes. If your oxygen masks drop from above, you are supposed to attach your *own* mask first and *then* your child's. That's not because your life is more valuable. It's because if you lose consciousness while trying to attend to your child first, neither of you gets the oxygen.

If you continue to deprive yourself of air, there *will* be effects. And not just for you.

Do you buy a pricey piece of equipment that will deprive your family of other things in order to afford it? Probably not. And maybe you wouldn't dream of asking for money from others under normal circumstances. But parenting some children with disabilities in a world where we live and work so detached from one another isn't "normal circumstances." Oh, disability is normal. It's always existed. But if the care needed exceeds the resources—which include more than financial—then *it's okay to accept that help.* Wouldn't you, under a friend's similar circumstances, contribute some help if you could?

People often don't know what to suggest for help. If they ask, give them ideas. Perhaps it's an occasional freezable dinner for *those* days. Maybe they could take a sibling for a special outing that doesn't need to be sensory-friendly. Or run the dog to the vet—not easy if you are pushing equipment or keeping a safe hold on a child prone to "bolting" into traffic. Or come to *you* to visit, where your child is safest and most comfortable, and enjoy some adult conversation—for some of us, *any* conversation. We love our children. But some situations are more challenging to navigate with a vulnerable child in tow. Some tasks are harder to accomplish. (Ask me about the time the dog ran the leash around me in the vet's parking lot, trapping me and landing me on my posterior, while I held tight to Callum's hand not too far from a busy four-lane road.)

On some days, an angel on earth popping up from nowhere saying, "Give me two loads of dirty laundry. I'll be back," is what your spirit needs to refill again. For when we are isolated from others, it's like taking the sun away from plants. They try to live; they stretch. They grow. But not strong enough. And without enough light—enough love, laughter, and hugs—we do the same before we succumb to weakness. We need our communities. Our communities could use some getting off their couches and *doing* good things in their own towns instead of fundraising to send the church teenagers off on expensive mission trips. When what would have *really* helped that remote village was the cash.

We are too cut off from one another. And we're managing more with fewer hands. It's no wonder our crisis in mental health.

Being strong is commendable, and I know a little something about needing to show strength—forcing yourself to look the world in the eye.

But as a fellow parent of a disabled child, I also know better than most the actual financial costs of having a child with so many needs. I know how expensive physical therapy, occupational therapy, speech therapy, adaptive strollers, medication, bedding, specialized care, and more really are. An average family—no matter how responsible and self-sufficient—cannot possibly pay for it all.

As parents of disabled children, we get used to doing a lot of fighting for our kids. One of the ways we fight for them is to help prepare a place for them in their own communities—to open their neighbors' eyes to their needs and desire to be like everybody else. The irony is that we're not always so good at asking for and receiving help.

So, I'm going to make a plea to you from the extraordinary brother- and sisterhood of parents of children with disabilities and say: *let them.* Let your friends and community help you on this one. Allow them to buy your child that bike. Accept organized weekly dinners. Let them offer to pick up some laundry and return it. Let them give freely from their hearts and love *you.* If a friend offers to learn more about your child to provide you both with a break from each other, take them up on it.

Because our children don't belong to only us. They aren't just our responsibility. They belong to their communities, too. And, if we genuinely believe that it takes a village, then we must step back and let the village get to know them and love them, too.

Traffic Jams and Good Samaritans

If I had a penny for every strange look I've gotten from strangers on the street, I'd have about 10 to 15 dollars, which is a lot when you're dealing with pennies.

—Andy Samberg

Chapter 30

Dear Shopper: On Judgment by Strangers

For the love of God, would somebody make that brat shut the f**k up?!"
Standing in the center of the courtyard of the European Village in Palm Coast, Florida, following an unsuccessful dinner and autistic meltdown in which we'd had to leave early, the man's shout from somewhere nearby stopped all conversation. Everyone turned to stare.

It had been a new restaurant for us with unfamiliar foods, and Callum's good mood had quickly soured. "Shoes on! Car! Shoes on!" Yes, he was ready to go.

But when we walked out into the courtyard, he saw a large fountain . . . with a pool. Only it wasn't the kind of pool you're supposed to swim in. That social norm escaped Callum entirely, and he began to insist, "Pool! Pool!" We tried to walk him over to it and allow him to run his fingers through the water to satisfy him, but it didn't. Instead, he started trying to pull his clothes off in the middle of the courtyard. Because he doesn't have the language to comprehend the nuances of pool versus fountain, we weren't making any headway calming him down. He had already melted down inside the restaurant, and the only thing that would end this drama was leaving. So, Sean picked up a shrieking Callum, still chirping, "Pool! Pool!" And we started to make our way out of the courtyard, when the man shouted.

Most people who met our eyes were kind and smiled. Some even glared in the general direction of the man. But the part of that long humiliating walk out to the parking lot that I heard for days?

It was the sound of others clapping.

MOST people are kind. Really. After all, it takes only a moment for observant folks to notice "otherness" in a child—even a child whose disability is "invisible." So when Callum is flapping, verbally stimming, or fixating on his ever-present and ever-spinning ball, most people catch on quickly that he's autistic. Usually, they'll smile. Sometimes, they'll ask questions. As a veteran teacher, I never mind the honest questions. Else how are people to learn, right? A few will stop and tell you about their grandchild or neighbor who is autistic. And I've met some lovely strangers over the years.

But we've encountered other strangers, too. The ones who stare in judgment, clearly waiting for us to snatch up and spank our son. The ones who pick up their things and move to other seats. The ones who accidentally on purpose sigh and comment just loud enough for us to get the gist. These are invariably the folks who subscribe to the oft-shared on social media, "There wasn't any 'autism' when I was a kid. Somebody just cut down a switch, and suddenly we weren't 'autistic' anymore!"

I've met those people everywhere. In doctors' offices. In grocery stores. At parties and barbecues. If you're super unlucky, it's even family. But, most disturbingly, I've met them while conducting autism awareness training for schools. There are many people out there who don't believe in invisible disabilities until they are personally touched by them. And their patience for them is limited.

When Callum was little, I'd panic, duck my head, and escape as soon as possible. These days, I'm better able to handle it. (That's not to say I don't quickly scramble out the door of, say, a theater performance if he isn't handling it well. We do try to be mindful of others and teach and observe good manners.) And that's because I've learned that successful outings and experiences take practice. If we're trying something new, we often take two cars. If we need to step out for a moment before attempting to reenter, we do. If the full experience just isn't in the cards that day, we go home. We do our best to be considerate, but sometimes strangers will just have to deal. If Callum is sick and I need to pick up a prescription, there's a chance others will have to experience some autism awareness that day. And when they do, I've learned the best cure for the attitude that ails them is to look them directly in the eye with a neutral expression. Either they'll chicken out and leave us alone or they'll keep staring. Then I'll speak up and silence them with a smile and dose of kill-them-with-kindness best performed by Southern women—making sure to speak only loud enough that those nearby will all then stare at the starer and judge them accordingly. Those aren't among shining moments in my human journey, but they're certainly among the more satisfying ones. Thicker skin and all that.

When Callum was younger, I had one such encounter in the grocery store. It led to a blog post that practically wrote itself and was popular with readers. One of my readers had the clever idea to print a few to carry in her purse for just such an occasion. So I did the same. Unfortunately, I've had to pass out a few over the years to rude passersby offering unhelpful suggestions to improve my parenting skills. And I didn't stick around to watch them read it. I have no idea their reaction, and I've mostly learned not to care.

I've learned that perceptions are rarely changed by sharing facts and figures. It's always human interactions that make a difference. But I like to think somewhere out there somebody read it and opened their heart just a little. I choose to believe people can do better.

Dear Shopper,

Yes, I know. I'm aware that my child is screaming. Not just a regular scream, but an ear-piercing, sanity-shattering screech. Even if I wasn't seeing and hearing it, I would know by the expression on your face.

Clearly, you have raised your children better than me.

That's what you were wanting to say, right? There certainly can't be any other purpose to you stopping in your tracks to stare or elbow your companion or, better yet—give knowing looks to other shoppers passing by.

I have no doubt that you have lovely, well-behaved children. Grown, tax-paying, law-abiding citizens who would never have dreamed of screaming like this in public when they were children. Judging by your expression and utter exasperation, you've never hesitated to let them know who was boss.

And I know that you did your best with your children, that you loved them, and want all children to have a solid upbringing in which to start their lives. You are, in all probability, a good person. You probably don't mean any harm.

This is what complicates what I want to say to you. Because, despite my anger toward you, I happen to have been raised well, too. I don't want to be ugly, even though right now I feel like it.

Because I know some of that anger is misdirected. It's misdirected because I, too, have stood in judgment of someone like me. I, along with almost everyone, have stood in public and watched a scene like this one play out and thought to myself, "Clearly, that woman has no control over her own children. When I have children, mine will never behave like that." I, like most people, wasn't quite as obvious about it as you. I didn't stare or make comments that could be heard. But I was every bit as decided. So, some of my anger is really directed toward Human Nature, which refuses to be put in its place.

The nice thing about human nature, however, is that it can be overridden. And all it takes is but one experience, a single human interaction, to the contrary of your own firmly held convictions. Then presto whammo—you are a new and hopefully improved person.

Let me introduce you to my child. Like you, I marveled at the miracle of life upon becoming his mother. Like you, I rocked, burped, and inhaled his sweet baby scent and thanked God over and over for the gift of him. Like you, I had dreams for my child. Yet, there your path and my path diverged somewhat.

My precious child is profoundly autistic. Yes, I've seen Rain Man, *and, no, my son is not likely going to be a great card counter. Autism encompasses a broad spectrum of abilities. And, like you and me, every autistic child who has it is different from the next. Yet, they do often share some similar traits—sensory overload and meltdowns are one of them.*

Everyone has what I think of as an internal alarm system. Most of us have ours in good working order. But some people with autism have hair-trigger alarm systems. Theirs can go off with what seems to average folks like little to no provocation. But there IS always provocation. Neurotypical people simply aren't as sensitive to seeing and hearing the triggers, and inevitably that's exactly preceding when the alarm goes off.

And when it does, it can be loud. *Everyone in the vicinity wants nothing more than to have it turned off, including the people who love them. So when you see me "placating" my child and "giving in" to his tantrum, I'm really just desperately looking around for the alarm key or trying to remember the correct code to turn off that blaring alarm. It isn't his fault. And, no matter how upsetting it is for you, I assure you it is that much more alarming for him.*

I'm sorry you haven't had quite as pleasant of a shopping trip as you had anticipated. It hasn't been so enjoyable for me, either. The problem is, I must feed my family, deposit my paycheck, and pick up prescriptions—just like you. And, unfortunately, no one arrived at my house today to watch my child so that his unusual behavior wouldn't upset anyone in public. So, I must leave the house and so must my child. Because I have to teach him about the world. And I have to let him practice controlling his alarm system. So that he can go out into the world successfully, too.

With so many advances in early detection and communication interventions, many of us will be able to see our dreams come true for our unique children. And for some of us, those dreams will have to be reenvisioned. We may need to redefine happiness and success. For life is like that. We constantly must reevaluate our expectations of ourselves, our families, and sometimes even shoppers in the grocery store.

I'm hoping that your single human interaction with me has given you an opportunity to do better. For, with 1 in 54 children being diagnosed with autism, you'll have more opportunities to make a positive impact in the life of someone like me. All it would take would be a smile, a pat on the back, or a "Bless your heart, honey, hang in there" to refill a stressed-out parent's reserve of patience and calm. You could be the bright spot in our day. And, then, if you want, you are welcome to ask all the questions you want. Your curiosity doesn't offend me. Most of us aren't the least bit upset to talk about our kids—any more than you are. If anything, it's an opportunity to educate and dispel myths.

And, maybe, just maybe, you'll be standing there when the alarm gets turned off. Maybe you'll get to see what every mother wants the world to see—the unique personality of her child, in our case hidden behind a mask of fear, anger, and frustration.

Who knows? Maybe I'll get to see the one hidden behind yours.

Chapter 31

Holiday Inns, Movie Theaters, and Waiting Rooms: On the Kindness of Strangers

One truth about having a child with an obvious disability is the discovery that there are more jerks in the world than you might have previously estimated—especially if that child is impacted by their senses and prone to meltdowns—or, you know, just makes noise people aren't used to. The sudden clarity of the preponderance of unpleasant people can be jarring and depressing. It can make you not want to go out into the world with your child but remain home, safe in your little bubble.

I went through that for a time. Confrontation isn't easy for me, and my skin just didn't seem to be thickening fast enough.

But I'll tell you another truth about having disabled children. There are also beautiful, kind people in this world, and they far outnumber the jerks. Their numbers, intuition, and goodness will surprise you. They'll announce themselves in different ways: a long look followed by a simple kindness, a voice speaking up on your child's behalf to one of the jerks mentioned above, a smile and pat on the shoulder by a mother or grandmother who knows and understands, or a direct interaction with your child without expectation but enjoyment for whatever way they can respond. Somehow, those folks have a way of being present right when you and your family need it most.

But you must go out into the world to meet them.

When you do, a little of your faith in your fellow humans will be restored.

ON our first road trip to Cartersville, Georgia, we stayed at a Holiday Inn Express for most of a week. At the desk, we asked how full they were. They weren't. So we explained Callum's stimmy enthusiasm and asked if it would be possible to get a room on the ground floor away from other guests. They happily obliged.

The following day, we went to breakfast. In the dining room was a giant fish tank filled with colorful saltwater fish. Callum was enchanted, staring, flapping, and squealing his delight. He was small—not yet three—but the staff and other guests seemed to love his enjoyment of the fish. For the next couple of days, we had to take several walks to visit the tank.

On around the third or fourth morning, we went down for breakfast, only to discover our favorite table by the fish tank was taken. Callum began whining, crying, reaching out, and calling, "Fi! Fi! (Fish)."

And then he had a complete meltdown.

The staff helped us make a to-go breakfast bag, and we returned to our room instead. But, apparently, the staff got sad about it. The servers enjoyed watching Callum in front of the fish tank each morning and spoke to the manager without us knowing.

The following day, with a bit of trepidation, we went downstairs again for breakfast, only to discover a RESERVED sign on our table. We looked at it, looked at each other, and were just about to grab and go when a staff member came out and said, "Oh, no! This table is reserved for him for the rest of your stay. We want that baby to be able to see the fishies."

And I still have the video of his chirpy delight.

I remember taking Callum to our local theater for one of his first movies. We were nervous and prepared to hop up and leave. It wasn't a "sensory-friendly" showing, and we didn't want to be the cause of other people not being able to hear or enjoy the movie when they'd paid to do so. But Ms. Amanda, who then owned and ran our theater, overheard our contingency plans (we'd taken two cars) and immediately told us if we felt the need to go early, they'd give us free passes to return later and finish the movie. (She also told us to let them know if anyone dared to be mean.) And then she waited patiently for our boy to take his time looking through the glass at candy before going through the process of confirming his selection by getting down on his level and waiting for each shake and then finally a nod of his head.

And then Ms. Amanda turned around and opened a cabinet and pulled something out to give us—a glow stick! She snapped and activated it before telling us that she'd heard some kids like Callum didn't like the dark and found it scary, so she'd picked some up to see if it helped her most sensitive customers.

People like that don't know what that kind of welcome means—how it fills the depleted reserves of a parent constantly wary of unexpected cruelties.

About halfway through, the candy ran out. Callum is severely language-impaired and doesn't understand the plot of a movie, so when song and dance numbers end, he can get a little wiggly. Sean decided to try walking to the concession stand to get another snack. Callum took them through another careful selection process. But when Sean pulled out his wallet to pay, Amanda put up a hand to block him and insisted that whatever helped "our little buddy" get through a movie successfully was on the house and shooed them back to Bronwyn and me. Well, the walk and extra treat *did* get us through that movie successfully.

At another point in the movie, Callum—who carries a little rubber bounce ball at all times that he twirl-stims with his fingers—dropped his ball in the darkness (something he rarely does), which, of course, proceeded to roll down the slanting floor. Sean was ducked down low, trying to search as unobtrusively as possible, as Callum must have that ball, or everyone would've soon known his displeasure. Suddenly, a smiling face appeared from a woman who'd seen where the ball had gone and gotten up to retrieve it. We thanked her and apologized for the interruption. She just smiled again and informed us it was her pleasure, that she was an ESE teacher and she understood why that ball was crucial.

Yes, the best people have a way of popping up in unexpected places—and at just the right time.

We emerged from that movie theater feeling like we'd conquered Everest. Callum was happily flapping and jumping about, and we hugged Amanda on our way out. We've been to many more movies since. We got the same kind of treatment. Only once did we ever have to take her up on free return tickets. And once, as the most thoughtful gift, she gave us a Family Night Out certificate for movies and snacks on the house. A simple gesture, but that understanding and compassion encouraged an anxious me to keep trying new experiences with Callum. I did, and many of those new experiences turned out fine, too.

And so it was that simple human kindness expanded my son's world.

ONE of the places you become quite accustomed to as a parent of a high-needs autistic child is the pediatric therapy waiting room. If ever there was a judgment-free zone, that's the place. You meet all kinds of parents and children. Children with challenges like those of your own child. Children with both fewer and greater challenges. You chat with others about feeding, therapies, speech successes, meltdowns, insurance, and more. Some of those conversations are empathetic, some of them are funny, and some aren't conversations at all—consisting only of knowing looks that linger a moment but speak more than words could anyway. Then, when the therapists come out to brag about a child's success that day, everybody smiles. Every patient walking out has an instant fan club consisting of complete strangers.

And there's a lot of collective wisdom in those waiting rooms from people whose worlds and lifestyles have changed dramatically, people whose perspectives are different than before from the new lenses they were given, too.

On one visit, I remember an older gentleman watching the lobby TV while waiting for a child. He'd observed me struggling with a grumpy Callum on arrival, a minor meltdown, and finally my collapse once our beloved speech therapist Ms. Sarabeth came out to rescue me and take him back. I remember I closed my eyes and leaned my head back to take some deep breaths.

And then I heard a scratchy old voice. The older gentleman had stood to greet the child he'd been waiting for. He looked at me, smiled kindly, and said, "Nothin' to do but love 'em as they are. You just keep lovin' him, and it's gonna be okay, Mama. It's all gonna be okay." Then he picked up his cane, took the child's hand, and walked out.

I then heard a faint echo of a Bible verse I was required to memorize at my private church school . . . Proverbs 15:23: "and a word spoken in due season, how good it is!"

Chapter 32

"God Chose You" and Other Platitudes:
On Rejecting Harmful Mindsets

Platitude:
a statement that denies by implication what it explicitly affirms.
—Edward Abbey

S omebody somewhere reading this is going to get their feelings hurt, no matter how gently I try to convey this. They may even have said some of these things to me in the past and are now cringing.

I don't want that. But this is something parents of children with disabilities hear, and sometimes the sentiment can mess with your head— especially if you are a person of faith. Because they often attach it to biblical verses you've been taught all your life to believe. And now, they're telling you that the God of your faith deliberately disabled your child for some unrevealed purpose.

It's always an innocent exchange. Somebody who provides a service in your home. A stranger in a store. Your high school French teacher you bump into at dinner. They encounter your child and either try to interact and are confused, so you explain. Or they notice unusual behavior and figure it out for themselves. But it goes like this:

"You know, don't you, that God only gives special children to special people to raise?"—while reaching for your forearm and looking deeply into your eyes. They want you to know they mean it. They want to say something nice, and they're trying to be good people. Kindness *is* the intention.

However, although kindness is the literal interpretation of many of these platitudes, often something unspoken echoes behind them. In this case, I'm sure most people who say such things aren't even aware of it. But it's there. It hangs unsaid in the air and follows the parent home, to work, to bed. And it's one of those things you find yourself thinking about at three a.m. when you wake early and your fears have you all alone as a captive audience.

If you are a believer, then perhaps that's an idea that previously was a comfort to you. That everything happens for a reason. That God is using all of your experiences to further His divine purpose. It's a popular refrain of Christians in particular. Having been raised in a church school in the Bible Belt, I grew up hearing that idea in everything. Every win. Every loss. Every accident. Every misfortune. Every death. The idea is that God is in everything and knows "all the plans" for you. I still remember that verse I dutifully memorized from the book of Jeremiah.

It's a comforting idea that everything happens for a reason. If there's a reason, you might (a) be optimistic it will lead to a good ending and (b) feel less alone/afraid. But when your child is melting down, banging their head in frustration over something not effectively communicated or some sensory assault, the idea that the ultimate loving father—God—deliberately chose high-needs disability for your child is unsettling. You wouldn't have done that to your child intentionally, and God is supposed to love them even more than you, right? So why would God use an innocent child to achieve some purpose He certainly could have accomplished in some other way that didn't hurt *your* baby?

There are times when you haven't slept in nights, and your child is suffering from encopresis, but the constant cleaning up of that is so ceaseless as to leave you a shell of yourself. That happens for some parents. And it's precisely on those days that some well-intentioned person serves up that idea of spiritual comfort.

Another you hear frequently is, "God bless you. I couldn't do what you do." Again, at first it sounds like a compliment. But what are they really saying? What do they mean when they say they couldn't "do" this? Do they mean they literally wouldn't care for their own disabled child? In those instances, I always respond the same way.

"Of course you would. As would any parent who loves their child. And if you wouldn't, I wouldn't like you very much."

That usually shuts them down. People think they're complimenting you, but they're not. What they're really saying is that my reality as the parent of an autistic child must be so awful, they can't imagine living it. Which is a hell of a thing to walk up to someone and say about their child and family.

Thus far, I've resisted the urge to retort that I'm sure I couldn't do what their family does, either, and walk away, leaving them wondering. But that's been a close thing.

I'm no saint. My son, like all children, is a source of joy for us. We love him, and we *like* him even more. He makes us laugh every day. Of course, some hard stuff accompanies his differences. But it's not a grand sacrifice. It's parenting, which I signed up for willingly. And if you enter parenting without knowing that life—and children—come with a lot of fine print, then you shouldn't become one.

If you want to show kindness to the parent of a disabled child in public, try a warm smile. If their child is in a meltdown, offer to help them grab the last few items on their list or help them get the groceries to the car. If they're looking anxious in a restaurant because their child is getting a little loud with echolalia, smile and either offer help or ignore it. If they try to apologize, be kind. Tell them what a good mom/dad you think they are. Tell them their child is beautiful, cute, or clever. Wait patiently if the parents encourage the child to interact with you and interact back if prompted by the child.

But for the love of God—literally—please don't tell them that the God they may pray to and seek comfort from deliberately gave their child any situation or condition that might be life-altering or life-limiting.

On days that seem like the world is out to get you, you don't need to hear that the Supreme Being affixed a target to your back.

Off-Roading

Tell me, what is it you plan to do with your one wild
and precious life?

—Mary Oliver, "The Summer Day"

Chapter 33

Good with Words:
On the Legacy I Can't Leave My Nonverbal Son

There's a long list of things I don't do well.

I have no athletic talent whatsoever. When balls fly in my direction, my first instinct is to duck. As a little girl, my mother signed me up for dance. My first memory is the instructor coming over to explain that the goal when tap dancing wasn't to swing my leg back and forth in the air. The shoe was supposed to lightly tap the ground.

In gymnastics, all the other little girls were cartwheeling about the room. But holding my arms over my head and encouraged to launch, I never could bring myself to trust the ground. Like those annoying team-building exercises when you're supposed to fall back into someone else's arms, I caught myself every time.

When we used to run the football field for the Presidential Physical Fitness Test, I walked. Proper push-ups have evaded me my whole life. And despite the popular wisdom that one doesn't forget how to ride a bike, I proved that untrue by cycling right into a mailbox when I got on a bicycle for the first time in decades.

I can't sing. Well, I *can* sing. But most would agree I *shouldn't*.

Interstates terrify me. There are simply too many cars doing too many things and way too fast. So, in situations with fast lane changes, I become overwhelmed, panic, and my hands tighten on the wheel so hard my knuckles turn white. My anxiety is so heightened that—even though I'm a good driver in any other place—I avoid driving on the interstate as I fear my own fear will cause an accident.

Fitted sheet folding eludes me. I can't whistle or snap my left fingers. If blow-drying my own hair, the brush gets caught in my hair. Every single time.

And when the physical science professor at the community college posted grades in the hallway, I nearly skipped out the door with delight over my "D" in the course and a "C" in lab because I knew they were good enough to transfer to the university along with my AA degree.

But as a young girl, I discovered an affinity for manipulating words. When asked to write simple rhyming poetry in school, the lines popped into my head immediately. Not only the rhyme but the rhythm itself. It just flowed with little thought. In high school, I remembered right before the bell that I had a sonnet in iambic pentameter due in AP English the next period. So, in the five minutes between classes, as I was walking down the hall, I wrote the entire poem—and got an A.

True or false tests make me nervous. But give me an essay question and I breathe a sigh of relief and rub my hands together.

Pretty much anything to do with words has always been my playground. I loved reading aloud in school and later as a teacher to my class. As a child, I read a book a day—loving popular '80s series Dark Forces, Twilight (not the sparkly vampire variety), and Sweet Valley High.

Later, I delved into the classics, enchanted by Mark Twain, Toni Morrison, and William Faulkner. Tongue twisters, word games, crossword puzzles, calligraphy, typing, foreign language, linguistics, and logic (math—with *words!*) all came easily.

I was the student other students asked to proof their papers. Friends asked me to write résumés, letters of application, and valedictory speeches. Principals requested brochures, websites, grants, social media, and help with mission statements. And obituaries have become the final gift several families have asked me to write for loved ones.

––––––––

WORDS have always come easily to me, likely inherited from my father and mother. And though I never expected to pass down any physical talents or beauty, I assumed that a love of language and reading were gifts I would give my own children one day. I envisioned them curled up in my lap as I introduced them to Dr. Seuss, Shel Silverstein, and Harry Potter. Words would be my legacy.

But as the years have passed, I slowly realized I couldn't give them to my son. He simply isn't wired for them. And although I've had enough time for some introspection and perspective on the loss of dreams we assign to others, I will not lie and say the loss of mine didn't hurt. I wanted to give him what has always given me joy. But he is not capable of receiving them.

Once I moved past that loss, reality set in. Harry Potter, though delightful, isn't needed for happiness. It certainly isn't required for survival.

But some words are—words like "no," "want," "hurt," and "afraid."

For someone whose entire life has been dedicated to words—via teaching, being a librarian, writing, and speaking—I have been unable to give my son the words he needs to fully express himself. To clarify his wishes. To defend himself from those who would neglect or harm him.

Yes, I know that doesn't make me a failure. It doesn't make Callum less worthy. But it makes me ache—ache in a way that only the parent of an entirely dependent, defenseless child can understand. It's like a nursing mother whose breasts ache with milk but who can't reach her child. It's the only thing I would ask from the genie in a bottle. No riches. No eternal life. Just enough words for my son so that I can one day die in peace.

SO, in blogging and advocacy, I tried to make up for the words I couldn't infuse into him. My posts, tweets, and essays were an attempt to speak for him. To explain him to a world I knew didn't understand. To put the Big Bad World on notice that this child is fiercely loved and protected. I tried to paint a word portrait of the beauty of his life. A demand he not be deemed expendable.

I *wanted* local social media friends to fall in love with him, knowing that it would be locals caring for him one day. There's no question I set out to make him known in our city—to establish him as someone accompanied by a world of hurt for anyone who wronged him. So that, one day, when the inevitable predator came searching for his next victim, he'd take a long look at my son and, in self-preservation, decide, "Not that one."

For unlike the fairy tales I once yearned to share with him, monsters actually do walk in the light.

In some ways, it worked. Callum has thousands of followers who love to cheer his successes and laugh at his Callum-esque antics. Locally, strangers will walk up in a store and ask, "Isn't that the boy from the newspaper? I follow your posts!"

But in the end, it's still just me trying to give him the words I've always loved. If not one way, then another.

In the early days, I used to say I was his voice. That I spoke for him, like a translator. Many parents, well-intentioned and with children like mine, claim to do the same. What they mean is understandable. You don't want your child's best interests not represented.

But speaking for your child's best interests and being their voice are *not* the same thing. It took me a while to understand that. Believing myself to be his voice is presumptive and disrespectful to him. For unlike the artificial intelligence collective in *Star Trek*, we are *not* Borg.

He is a human being with thoughts, feelings, reactions, and perspectives that are his own. The problem is they aren't destined to be revealed. He's old enough now that we can be realistic with our predictions of future communication. Could we be wrong? Of course. Do I hope we're wrong? Most definitely. But statistically, the evidence increasingly indicates that how he expresses himself will always be limited. That whatever observations, associations, and fascinations he carries will not likely be revealed in this life. To claim I can do that for him is a lie.

Instead, I'm charged with advocating for my son to be given the most access possible to his world. For he is a citizen of it, too. That includes insisting he is given every opportunity to communicate to the extent he is capable. To demand an education that will best prepare him for his individual capacity for independence. To speak for his health needs, psychological well-being, and physical safety. And to stare down injustices that take the form of unequal access to all the joys of living—playing, traveling, new experiences, eating out, theme parks, movies, friendship and love (in whatever way he wishes to express those), and the opportunity to pursue his personal interests. That's what my voice is for.

But it does not and never will take the place of his.

To not understand that is to compromise his dignity—the dignity that all human beings deserve by birth,

This one was taken on a joyful afternoon following more than a year of him not being able to tolerate water on his face or clothes. A Florida sunshower began as we got out of the car, and he started squealing with joy. We played in the rain for an hour and got soaked while he flapped away. It was a happy day.

no matter their neurology. Not recognizing that may begin with good intentions, but it's a slippery slope that can lead to the long human history of not considering the developmentally disabled as equal. We cannot allow productivity alone to be the value measurement of human life. Because one day, if we are lucky to grow old, our own productivity will slow. And the devaluing of one life will always lead to the devaluing of others.

THAT comes with great responsibility. I do not, simply by having birthed Callum, own his story. I own mine only. But since our stories overlap, enhance, and violate one another all at once, I must be a good editor. My self-advocate friend Audra once described my blog as "carefully edited"— something she approved of. And she's correct. It is.

I set rules for myself. Pretty much anything was open when Callum was a toddler and preschooler. Potty training and temper tantrums are how we all begin. But along the way, I saw and read many photos and posts from other parents of disabled children. And I was *horrified*.

Yes, families need to know about the sometimes-harsh realities involving toileting, tummy troubles, social skills disasters, and bullying that often occur when parenting autistic children.

But would any neurotypical twelve-year-old son want me to discuss his toileting and puberty online? Doubtful. It would embarrass him and make me a terrible mother he would need years of therapy to process.

Well, then I owe my developmentally disabled twelve-year-old son that same dignity. It's complicated because the nature of his severe autism is such that I have questions the average parent can't help me with. Moreover, some issues aren't merely his own but intersect with every member of our family. Because we all have needs, too—emotions, frustrations, exhaustion, and guilt. All rolled into a confusing jumble of love, fear, determination, and sometimes unflattering human nature.

So, I must constantly balance what I'm trying to accomplish in my little corner of the advocacy world with Callum's dignity, the needs of the rest of the family, and my own. All with the unsettling understanding that his disability is such that I will likely never be able to ask his permission. I hope that the person he is and the nonexistent person he would have been without those disabilities would share my values and know and understand that I did the best I could. That he would approve of what I tried to do and forgive the inevitable times when I failed. I have to forgive myself for the times I needed to use words involving him to express myself—my own truths and experiences in our interwoven stories. The scale dips and sways over and again.

Parents, your words and representation matter. They can be gifts; they can do good. They can help clear your child's path in this world. But they can be selfish, too. If they are used solely to garner pity, then you need to ask yourself who you're really speaking for. And even in our weakest moments, we must not forget to respect and honor the actual voices we may never get to hear.

Chapter 34

When He Isn't Cute Anymore: On the Days I've Been Dreading

've had the title above in my head for a decade, knowing I'd eventually write it. Because as the severity of his disability became more evident over time, I knew the free passes enthusiastically given to him by strangers when he was young and adorable would begin to taper off one not-so-distant day. The people who knew him when he was small won't find him a threat or off-putting when he's an adult.

But if we are fortunate, we grow old. And I remember my granny explaining the sadness of no one being around anymore who remembered her when she was young. So there will come a day for Callum when he lives with those who won't remember him young, either.

Right now, life is pretty good for him. His beloved 1:1 aide Ms. Dawn has been with him for as long as he remembers. As my dear friend Jackie pointed out, she's almost a second mother to him. He attends a public school for special-education students. Although there is an "autism class" in his age group, he's in a mixed-grade class for students with intellectual disabilities.

Some proponents of full inclusion have been surprised to hear that. But for Callum, that placement is perfect. And for him, it might as well be full inclusion. Most of the students in the class are verbal, can read and write to varying degrees, and can follow classroom and school procedures. Academically, intellectually, socially, and developmentally, they are all "ahead" of him. But they are who I want him to emulate. Not because he'll look less autistic, but because I want him to know about good manners. About how you're supposed to do certain things in the world—eat in a cafeteria, follow class rules, wait your turn, take a walk, etc. And peers will do more to help with that than adults ever could.

The difference between this class and forcing full inclusion at his neighborhood regular ed school is that these classmates have zero judgment and the utmost patience for him. Many of them began in traditional schools and transferred in later. They know what it feels like to be perceived as dumb. If he doesn't line up, they say, "Come on, Callum!" If they're working in small groups, different students volunteer to help him. His work is heavily modified (though related), and they get a chance to be considered the smart one. He loves being around other kids, and his classmates love him. He's sweet, and they're protective of him. It works for us. He's happy.

But after twenty-one, that's all gone. There are day programs, and our local chapter of The Arc is fantastic and run by an administrator, Kari, with the utmost respect for the dignity of their program clients and residents. But those attendants will see a likely six-foot-tall man with facial hair. Who maybe still needs assistance with personal care. Who perhaps has a meltdown on their watch—screaming, whining, stomping. And *that* certainly won't be cute to them.

There's a reason why baby animals are cute. Mother Nature is crafty that way. Little bodies, big eyes, and vulnerability. We mammals are suckers for it (if we're not, you know, eating some other mammal's baby). But it's what helps your toddler not get tossed out in the yard after scribbling on your grandmother's quilt with a red Sharpie. Cuteness is an evolutionary defense mechanism indeed.

At age twelve, Callum's cheeks are still baby smooth. He has big, dark eyes with those impossibly long eyelashes only young boys seem to have. His voice is still a sweet, chirpy little high pitch. His giggles and pleas to be tickled or play "This Little Piggy Went to Market" are endearing, and he expertly wields that cuteness to get his way—especially when charming ladies. He snuggles, gazes into your eyes, and loves being loved on.

And with a developmental age of just under two, that makes sense. For his developmental age, it's appropriate.

But when he's a man, it won't be cute anymore. It will be perceived as weird at best and possibly threatening at worst. And inappropriate for the caregivers working with him to dole out. There will, by necessity, be rules about that sort of thing. Callum, sadly, will have to learn the rules, too. We live in a "stand your ground" state. There are stories across the country of adults with disabilities—often autism, hearing impairments, or mental illness—who have been shot and killed due to the shooter misunderstanding their actions and the victim being unable to explain. To not teach Callum to avoid touching strangers could get him *killed*. To teach him to communicate sufficiently so that a meltdown doesn't become frightening to someone "in reasonable fear for their life" *is paramount*.

I've admitted to friends that I know we're lucky. If there were a Level 3 autism jackpot, we hit it. He's a naturally happy soul—with a gentle temperament so reminiscent of my daddy that it takes my breath some days. Days that he smiles at me with my father's eyes and lifts my hand to his back, signaling he'd like his back scratched. Daddy loved that, too. He's delighted to go places and loves long drives, porch swings, and things that bounce. He's cooperative and interacts to the extent he is able while learning. And he giggles and lights up a room with his smiles.

Now, I'm not claiming he can't be a pill. All twelve-year-olds can. But it's pretty much explainable—sensory overload, sleep loss, or confusion over a change in routine. With careful planning, he's relatively easy. And "easy" and "sweet" disabled adults are obviously less likely to be injured in a takedown. So it's hardly surprising a caregiver might form closer bonds with them than those who bite, attack, and scream. People tend to love Callum, find him adorable, and shower him with, "I love him so much! Give that sweet boy anything he wants!" (an idea sneaky, chocolate-loving boys can get behind). I was sent home a note once from a pediatric therapy center we visited that said, "We love him and argued about who gets him." Yes, that makes me smile. I love that people love him. That'll make life easier for him than for others.

What haunts me is wondering what temperament a person working with my son possesses. Direct care attendants are paid very little. No formal education is required to work with developmentally disabled adults. If you're making minimum wage, have no experience working with that population, have little knowledge of their diagnoses and needs, and perhaps have a temper, how might you react to a grown man refusing to eat and angrily upending a plate of food? Might you scream at him, causing sensory overload? Try to force him to clean it up? Grab him roughly? Worse? What if that resident is Callum, having an awful day and needing a little understanding?

I'm going to die. I don't have an immediate expectation for doing so, but life does surprise. Regardless of when, a day will come when there is no more me to protect him. No one to ensure his needs are met. I can dictate in a will what I want, but financial considerations and the reality of changes in plans give me pause. I need to live forever. But I can't.

Who will give him the love he needs? It's not likely he'll progress developmentally beyond a couple more years. Although his mind, emotions, and understanding might be that of a four-year-old, he's genetically likely to be over six feet tall. Right now, he doesn't understand to keep his hands off people he likes. He still crawls on laps and comes running into our room in the middle of the night. We're working on keeping hands to ourselves with strangers right now. For Callum, it's affection—an acknowledgment that he likes you. But for a young woman he walks up to one day and rubs her arm, it might be interpreted as a violation. That's terrifying. Because there are cases in which that very thing has happened. At the same time, it seems cruel to deny someone with the mind of a preschooler physical affection. One day Mama and Daddy won't be there to cuddle. Will he always ache for that? Will he keep looking out the window, wondering what's taking us so long to return? When he isn't cute anymore, who will love him?

Part of me wishes he could stay little forever. But he's twelve now. Pretty soon, he'll grow that facial hair, and his voice will deepen. He'll be big. And strong. He might still be the sweetest thing ever, but he will be a man. He'll want independence at times. He'll want to go where he wants and when. He'll see other young men driving cars and making out with girls. He'll have all the same hormones racing through him that they have. Only he'll have none of the social understanding. And no ability to protect himself from harm. He's as equally unconcerned with oncoming vehicles as he is with public nudity.

The no-fear-of-danger stuff is always scary. But what's more frightening is danger coming to Callum in the form of an abuser. That's the nightmare of every parent of a severely developmentally delayed child. That the predators we read about almost daily in the news will one day find our children when we are long gone. That's what keeps me up when I wake too early from Callum running in to sleep beside us. He's too old for it. At least in physical age. And we keep swearing we're going to teach him to stay in his own bed.

But then I look at him in the light from the window. That sweet face tucked against my shoulder. At peace in the absolute certainty he is loved. And snuggled up to his whole world—who he has no understanding will one day die. For him, we just won't have returned. *Ever.* Will he feel betrayed and abandoned? I don't know.

And that's why I give in.

Because I want him to soak it up all he can while we're here. To let the feeling of being loved overflow his days so that when we're gone, some remains.

When he isn't cute anymore, I want him to remember our arms.

Chapter 35

Doing Feels Better: On Defeating Helplessness and Moving Toward Advocacy

I n December 2014, when Bronwyn was seven and Callum was five, we drove them over an hour away to a nearby city searching for a "Sensitive Santa" experience. Visiting Santa hadn't been a terribly rewarding experience for us as a family thus far. On the checklists for sensory trauma and potentially disastrous results, taking an autistic child to meet Santa ticks a lot of marks:

- Loud, busy locations
- Bright, fluorescent lighting
- Long waits
- Strange, new experiences
- Interaction with an unfamiliar, possibly terrifying person in a red suit
- Bored photographers who take only one shot you pay $25 for by which to immortalize your misery

We were hopeful, however, as we'd heard about Sensitive Santa events. They're designed for children with disabilities and are supposed to have features such as individual appointments, soothing lighting, some privacy, a Santa trained to not push a child past their comfort zone, etc.

So, when I heard one was being offered, I signed us up, envisioning this ideal experience where we'd get a photo memory often elusive to parents of autistic children—smiles, peppermint sticks, and the wonder of Christmas magic.

We arrived at the shopping mall early on a Sunday morning when it was still closed to the public. Organizers set up an entrance for families to enter by appointment. It was quiet, and Callum was in a good mood. Then we turned the corner in search of Sensitive Santa.

That's when we saw the line. The line families *got to stand in by appointment*. A teenager was alone, running the whole operation with no organizers present. Stressed, autistic children were standing in line with their nervous parents and whining already. We signed a clipboard check-in left at a table near the entrance to the line and took our place.

That's when the choo-choo train that children can ride on a track around the mall started up, along with its endless loop of ice cream truck–style Christmas tunes. Santa just sat there on his Santa throne, never budging to help take a nice picture for any child. If a crying, sensory overloaded child approached, Santa looked over at their parents with a "What do you want me to do here?" expression. Children were unceremoniously dumped on his lap or allowed to sit in a chair next to him. And a single photo was taken—*quickly*. Callum whined, wouldn't interact with Santa when it was our turn, and it took forever to get him to sit anywhere near the large furry man in red.

Despite this being an event hosted for special-needs families, they still charged $25 for the photo.

We left, not irritated so much as sad. Callum didn't give two hoots about Santa, so I wasn't sad for him. But Bronwyn had been excited. She had a list. Yet so much effort had to be put into arranging them for even one potentially workable shot that Santa had forgotten to ask her what *she* wanted for Christmas. I had to assure her there was time to write a letter to him and let him know.

Sean was pissed off in the way of all fathers dragged to malls for miserable experiences. Bronwyn was crying. Callum was whining because Bronwyn was crying. And I, flabbergasted, complained the entire way home about the incompetence of the event organizers. Other than opening the mall early, precisely nothing had been different or sensitive about that experience. But they still got our $25 for a crappy picture we wouldn't be displaying.

I remember thinking, *"Somebody ought to do better."*

A couple of months later, I bumped into a different Julie, a school psychologist friend and a fellow church member. I don't remember how it came up, but I told her somebody could put together something special with the right place and team. We got to brainstorming in that conversation, and soon I hit on the idea of doing a Sensitive Santa event at our church's parish hall. The parish hall, a charming old nineteenth-century house, had a cozy, carpeted, and furnished room with couches and a fireplace. Usually, it was used for church brides on their wedding days or for small group discussions and confirmation classes. But at Christmas, that room is lovely. The church ladies decorate the mantle and put up a tree next to a big wingback armchair.

Thinking of that wide, carpeted floor, the soft lighting, the French doors that could be closed for privacy, a nearby kitchen and bathrooms, and all the tables in the hall—with a playground just outside the back door—the idea began to take shape. While talking about the Sensitive Santa experience out loud, Julie and I realized how uniquely suited we were to be doing something like this—right at our own church. Not only did we have the perfect facilities; among our little church's small membership also happened to be a lot of teachers, administrators, and even the superintendent. What if we could do this "in partnership" with the school district and the ESE department (which Julie was a member of)? She suddenly remembered that an ESE department colleague, Kori, had once been a wedding photographer who had gotten training in "special-needs photography." And she was fluent in American Sign Language (ASL). We remembered her former teacher's aide Petra also had experience in ESE and spoke Spanish. By partnering with the ESE department, perhaps we could sweet-talk the superintendent into offering "comp time" (tickets used for free personal time to leave school early) for ESE employees who volunteered to staff it.

And we happened to know two perfect Santas—one a gentle grandpa with a snow-white beard and years of experience playing our church's Santa and another who'd been a Santa to our local special education school for many years. We got that look two women with a great idea get when conspiring. Julie went to talk to Father Bob and Kori. I made an appointment for us with the superintendent. When we got enthusiastic yeses from all, Julie, Kori, and I got to planning in earnest. The ESE department got into the spirit, recommending specific families for the department to reach out to first before sending them my way to get registered. One or two of the staff had Santa elf costumes.

We organized our event into individual appointments of fifteen minutes each. Families were first recruited by district ESE employees and staff (due to FERPA—Family Educational Rights and Privacy Act—privacy laws). Our guiding principle was that our event wasn't for children with disabilities capable of enjoying a regular Santa experience. Just because a child has Down syndrome or is blind doesn't make them incapable of going to a mall. Lots of kids with disabilities can handle malls fine.

The first invitations were chosen carefully. We also took some to a local pediatric therapy clinic and asked them to follow the same guidelines when passing them out. Families contacted me. I took as much information as I could about successfully engaging with their child and whether they would be bringing siblings, who were always welcome. (That part was *never* in doubt.)

We also encouraged the family to dress for a family picture if they liked. After editing them with love, Kori donated all the images and signed off on all photo rights. After that, they could print or use them as they liked.

Businesses had donated refreshments, food for volunteers, toys, paper products, ink, etc. Volunteers got a quick autism training. We recruited some teen "elves" to help families get out of their cars, up the ramp, etc. Kind, quiet teachers welcomed families who showed up early to enjoy cookies, hot chocolate, etc., and ushered families to tables with coloring books and a friendly face to engage with them. And we helped many a frazzled-looking parent wipe the kiddos down and comb their hair while hugging them and telling them to stop apologizing.

Two high school students (including Kayley, an advocate for a nearby summer camp for children with cancer and a survivor herself) took on the technical aspects of trading picture cards with the photographer and printing out at least one photo per family with others uploaded later that night to our Facebook page (or emailed privately).

And magic happened. Nervous, stimmy, and even crying children walked in with parents whose expressions I knew were those of parents used to leaving quickly. When one such boy came in, Kori put down her camera and took him on a little sensory tour of the kitchen, letting him reach up to touch the hanging pots, see all the things, and have a cookie. Then they went back to the room, where he promptly rolled around on the couch and floor. Santa put no pressure on him whatsoever. Eventually, he got curious and came up to him. Soon, they were engaging in the child's way—touching Santa's beard and face. And Santa just smiled.

His mother walked out of that room crying. It was her son's first ever picture with Santa.

Throughout that day and in all the years following, these families throw their arms around us and thank us for being a safe space for them. These families have become like families to us. Some of our Sensitive Santa children have since died. We know the meaning of these photos and this experience for their families. Our team always says Sensitive Santa is the happiest weekend of the year. And it's true.

Helping to organize this event taught me something that's been a guiding principle for me ever since. *Doing feels better.*

I've listened to many a parent over the years lamenting that "they" should do something to help families like ours. "There ought to be" this. "Somebody needs to do" that. So they post it to social media, and fuss about it at support group meetings, and tell everyone within earshot what "they" ought to do. And then they wait around, hoping for years that'll happen. To me, leaving it there is not a good feeling. It's a helpless one. It's

also a pointless one. Nothing good in this world has ever happened because somebody *wished* it would.

There is no "they."

But there is "we." There's definitely "I." That's a potential beginning
for anything we might dream of for children and families like our own.

I'll tell you what I learned from my own sense of helplessness and
yearning for "them" to do whatever. And that's that waiting leads to more
helplessness. If you or your child needs it, it's almost certain another family needs it, too. Going out and recruiting others to help you figure out how
to do it feels a hell of a lot better than helplessness—because helplessness
leads to anger and resentment, not solutions. Necessity really is the mother
of invention.

I've carried this realization past Sensitive Santa. I've pestered law enforcement until somebody listened, and a team was formed. In partnership with the sheriff's office and the school district, we put together a
nonprofit that provides tracking technology for children and adults prone
to autistic elopement or wandering due to dementia, intellectual disability, etc.

There wasn't a local online support group for families of disabled children and adults. So, I took the liberty of making one. We now have over
three hundred families in our region who can share resources, events,
etc., and have spread to other areas of Florida.

The grocery store was hard for us as Callum got bigger. I read about a
company called Caroline's Cart that made a grocery cart with a large
enough seat for an adult to face whoever was doing the pushing. We didn't
have any here, so I asked our grocery stores via letter and persistent personal introductions to managers while shopping. Our two main grocery
stores now have these carts available.

Our district hadn't ever provided autism awareness training for staff,
so I asked the superintendent for that to happen. She invited me to present
for all the principals, followed by all the assistant principals. That led to
other schools requesting it. And the teachers in those meetings got excited
to hear about an autism endorsement for teachers.

I didn't do anything heroic. I didn't write hateful letters to the editor.

I merely asked and asked again. In terms of advocacy, I didn't know what I was doing. But soon, other people joined me. They called and asked, too. And invariably, they knew somebody who could help. Good people got excited and joined in, too. Beautiful things happened.

One day, in the wee hours of the morning, I received a phone call from 911 asking if I knew where Callum was. Blinking in sleepy confusion, I realized he had crawled in sometime in the middle of the night and was right next to me. A citizen noticed a little boy in the median of a state highway sometime after four a.m. A deputy responded and, because of training, thought to lift the pants leg of the boy's pajamas. Sure enough, he was one of our Project Lighthouse kids. After a brief description, I knew who he was without even having to look up a number, and he was reunited with his shocked and terrified mother, Amanda, who was sound asleep. (Jayden is a wicked-clever little Houdini.)

I hung up the phone and had a moment to reflect on every call, presentation, meeting, form, and more. They had been worth it a thousand times over in just that one morning with that one child. Everything.

But here's my point: "They" didn't do it. *We did.*

So, once you get past the diagnosis and start of therapy years and reach a point of wanting more, consider playing a part in making that happen. You'd be surprised how many people are out there waiting for someone else to take the first step but will happily take the second beside you and invite others. Be that someone. Because "they" really will come—in the form of you and friends you make along the way. And in helping make the world a little better for your family, you'll make it a little better for others, too. That's empowerment and community. It trumps helplessness any day.

Trust me. *Doing feels better.* Now, get out there and find something to do.

Other Passengers

To paraphrase Oedipus, Hamlet, Lear, and all those guys,
"I wish I had known this some time ago."

—Roger Zelazny, *Sign of the Unicorn*

Chapter 36

I Should Have Known: On Autism and Girls

When Bronwyn was about six years old, Sean sold his car to a classmate from the college. When she and her husband came over to take a look at it, she brought their daughter inside to visit and enjoy the air-conditioning. Their little girl, a bit younger, was disabled, without the ability to speak or walk. But she could sit up, and she smiled at us and made happy sounds. Bronwyn walked over and sat down in front of her, holding a doll, and asked if she wanted to go play in her room. The mother kindly explained that her daughter couldn't walk or talk. After Bronwyn innocently asked why, the mother answered her honestly: "We don't know. Like your brother, that's just who she is."

Bronwyn then asked if she'd like to play dolls sitting right there. And the mother responded that her daughter wasn't able to hold the dolls just yet. Bronwyn looked at the little girl closely for a moment before leaning in and whispering, "Stay here. I'll be right back." Then she ran off to her room before scampering back, carrying almost all her dolls in tow. She proceeded to sit back down in front of the little girl, laying the dolls out around them.

And then she stole my breath by lifting the dolls to the other child's eye level and dancing them about—delighting the excited little girl while she gently talked to her and told her stories of the dolls' adventures. I was entranced by my daughter's intuitive kindness at such a tender age, as was the child's tearful mother.

I didn't yet realize that Bronwyn's intuition ran deeper, her compassion fueled by an innate understanding that I didn't yet understand.

Do you remember the big reveal in *The Sixth Sense*? In a flashback montage, Bruce Willis, the therapist, retroactively notices what he had not before, seeing the same experiences but suddenly through a new lens. He thought he was helping. Turns out he's got the problem. And he was stuck.

In our family, the only kind of autism we had known (or rather, realized we'd known) was the higher-needs variety—the kind with severe communication difficulties, impaired judgment, and, in my son's case, intellectual disability. It *seemed* as though lightning had struck the same place *three* times.

But the womenfolk got to talking. My aunt brought up similar characteristics those of us born into the family carried. It was her opinion that my grandfather had traits. My stepmother and I saw exactly what she was talking about. Then she brought up my dad and some of his eccentricities. My dad was beloved by many, but anyone who knew him well would remember some instance of him being referred to as "peculiar." Daddy knew, and even laughed about it. She and my aunt also noted I was a "bit of a character, too." We noted these similarities and thought them amusing, but I didn't give them more thought than that.

Fast-forward some years and an autism diagnosis for my son.

One afternoon, a school-district electrician did some work in my library. We got to chatting, as Southerners do, and sorted out the people we had in common. He knew my dad and had done some work for him at my grandparents' beach house. When I made a dry joke about how that must have been an experience—remembering just how "particular" my grandfather could be—he started chuckling about how my daddy warned him that Grandpa was just that. He allowed it was one of the more exasperating experiences he'd had as an electrician.

Knowing what I know now, I'd absolutely describe my grandfather as having what was once called Asperger's and is now labeled Level 1 or mild/low-needs autism. I've been told he was a top-notch warehouse manager, and even though he wasn't all that well liked, management knew to put him in charge when it needed fixing. He saw the big picture down to its details instantly and knew how to make things efficient.

But he struggled to maintain long-term friendships, was considered somewhat ornery, and offended gift-givers with inappropriate reactions. Big decisions caused him great anxiety and he'd get to "studying up" on a thing to the point of obsessing so much it never got done. My grandparents lived in that beach house nearly twenty years while he studied up on who to have install air-conditioning *in a house they built with vents installed*. He had a sophisticated onion storage system and detailed notebooks full of years' worth of winning Lotto numbers. (I now rest my case.)

But the electrician's visit that day got me thinking back and remembering. And I began to see my family with new eyes.

My father and I had some unusual things in common. I shared with him a great dislike of loud establishments. I'll sit and wait for a table for twenty minutes to avoid being seated in the bar area. The clanging and noises are overwhelming, and I struggle to pay attention to whom I'm with—eyes darting everywhere and forcing myself to make eye contact. My father hated certain restaurants, all due to sound. Although he was an intelligent, witty, and wise person, my granny said he didn't speak until he was three years old. And it was a family joke that he was never looking at the camera in family photos.

I'm particular about my sheets and practically remake my bed every night, feeling for specks of sand (you try living in Florida and judge me). For years now, when I do my evening bed ritual, Sean pokes fun of me by knocking on the headboard three times and repeating, "Penny? Penny? Penny?" like Sheldon Cooper. I can't stand clothing around my neck, nor could my dad. He insisted on certain necklines for all his shirts. Sensitivity to scents and often detecting them before others noticed was something else we shared. We both had "enthusiasms"—subjects we immersed ourselves in—and told people about them often, whether willing or hostage. His were World War II naval history, Sherlock Holmes, stud poker, and political theory. He read volumes of books on the subjects, studied them carefully, took notes he tucked between the pages, and always steered conversations back toward those topics—seemingly oblivious to my thirteen-year-old stepbrother Tyler's eyes glazing over on Taco Tuesday night. But being who he was, he'd just belly laugh at the groaning and teasing.

From Jack the Ripper to the construction of the Chicago World's Fair to antique reference book collecting, I'm the same. I loathe crowds and can be a little verbose talking about my favorite topics. I saw us as quirky people with dry senses of humor. And I figured some DNA was involved as well. But neither my father nor I was *disabled* by these "quirks" I'd now call traits. We *noticed* them. People close to us saw them. But they didn't negatively impact our lives. While it may be true that we share some traits with our children, *that's* the difference between autism and not.

So, when Bronwyn was little and began showing "quirks" herself, I just saw . . . my side of the family coming through. She was smiling, cooing, crawling, walking, talking, and doing all the developmental milestones, *it seemed*. But, on the other hand, she was slightly klutzy, really opinionated about her socks, and developed into a highly selective eater early.

But so was I. My dad introduced Gold Toe socks to me because I couldn't stand the seam, nor he. So, when Bronwyn began to fuss and cry and pulled off her shoes to get at her socks, I knew why. In my mind, she was flying through developmental tasks, ABCs, 123s, and the like. To me, she just had the family quirks.

Because I was an only child and wanted Bronwyn to have siblings, we planned Callum to follow close in age. Sure enough, she was two and a half months from walking when we found out I was pregnant, and my yakking began again. Just as it had with her. For the whole nine months.

She was just twenty months old when he was born, and my attention was divided in half. By the time Callum began to show signs, I was hyperfocused on him and thought her high intellect and vocabulary meant all was well. That became the lens I viewed her from—smart, funny, quirky, sweet, and fussy, but neurotypical. So, though I loved her just as much—sang to and rocked her nightly—autism took over my life.

I didn't see the needs she had, hidden below the surface.

So, I didn't know to begin intervention with her as well.

WE'VE often teased Bronwyn about her birth. Like most babies, she was born screaming. But unlike most babies, she just kept going. Through me hemorrhaging, getting fixed up and cleaned, footprints, swaddling, and being held, she kept screaming. She was still mad for nearly an hour before she finally exhausted herself.

She didn't take to nursing well. Hating to be on her back, she struggled against positioning (we tried them all) and fought against latching. It always took Sean's help, and I think she and I both cried each time for nearly two weeks. We supplemented some, and eventually, she figured it out. But it was rough early days.

In the hospital, we had already learned she didn't like being on her back. Now, they'll tell you that babies who don't want to be on their backs must be placed on their backs anyway and will adjust. Bronwyn did not adjust. We tried sleep positioners, but she screamed until picked back up and put to someone's chest. Exhausted, we put cushions behind our backs, under our arms, etc., sat up with a pillow behind our head, and took turns having her sleep against our chests every two hours. It's not recommended or approved of by any medical organization. But we had to sleep. And that's how we accomplished it for months.

Finally, a nurse told us about a breathing tracker we could put under the crib mattress that would go off if the baby stopped breathing. We tested it with weights several times, and it worked. And she could soon roll over by herself anyway. I thought she was just a very opinionated baby. But, since then, I've spoken to many parents whose autistic children did not like being placed on their backs as babies. No, it's not a "trait." However, there are many little things common to autistic people that aren't described in diagnostic manuals.

I'd once read somebody's opinion that the problem with children today is that they're so overloaded with salt and sugar that they can't appreciate flavors. So, having been a picky eater my whole life, I decided I didn't want to do that to her. We were *so* good. Her first food beyond cereal was mashed avocado. We then introduced green beans, carrots—all the vegetables.

Finally, we brought in fruits. She ate everything. We moved on to spaghetti, mac and cheese, chicken, and all the things kids typically love.

But around three, she began to eliminate foods. If something she liked as baby food was now cooked at home and had texture, it was a no. Certain brands were nos. She began to pick at the cheese on pizza, pulling off bits that didn't look right. She soon stopped eating cheese altogether. It didn't upset her stomach. But she was suddenly revolted by cheese and wouldn't eat anything it had touched. Remembering that my stepbrother Tyler doesn't like cheese, either, I didn't realize it was a problem. In hindsight, Tyler didn't *like* cheese—but he wasn't phobic about handling it. She is.

She would go on streaks when she wanted the same food around the clock for weeks, before refusing to ever eat it again. And she was getting so skinny we had to supplement with nutritional shakes. It wasn't long before her entire diet consisted of:

- Chicken nuggets from specific chains
- French fries
- Plain white rice (Mahatma only)
- Tomato soup (one brand only)
- Broccoli
- Tomatoes and some fruits
- Steak (only her dad makes it right)
- Calamari
- Ketchup and soy sauce
- Snack food, some cereals, and candy

No, this list is not the end of the world. But Bronwyn struggles to eat at restaurants, school, and other people's homes. Being fourteen, she's hyperaware of other people watching and doesn't want others to draw attention to it. So, she prefers to eat alone. However, the scent of other people's food can literally make her sick. Therefore, overnights must always be carefully planned. And you can imagine how fun road trips can be with her wanting to eat at only one restaurant chain.

But it wasn't just sensory-related issues I noticed. When Bronwyn was three or four, Debbie, a visiting OT from Early Steps working with Callum, played with them both on the floor. Debbie liked natural settings and situations for therapy and would make use of sibling interest whenever she could. But after the session, Debbie told me she noticed something. While horse playing, she saw that Bronwyn couldn't turn her head in some positions without falling over. It looked like Bronwyn had some proprioception (an understanding of your body and where it's positioned) issues that I might want to mention to her doctor and have evaluated.

I asked my sister-in-law Julie, also an OT, who told me she thought she had seen the same but wasn't sure. By comparison to her brother's issues, it didn't seem like a big deal. We did follow up, but we thought proprioceptive issues might have meant just klutziness, figured the OT would be beneficial for any child, took her to therapy, and didn't sweat it too much.

By four, the issues of attention and hyperactivity were being reported at school. But Bronwyn was sweet, respectful, funny, and excelling in learning tasks, so we tried behavioral things to help her as we weren't too keen on starting stimulants at such a young age.

In kindergarten, we heard a lot more of it. Academically, she was doing great—reading, writing, etc.—but she was starting to not finish tasks in class due to being distracted, usually by some object, pen, or pencil she was fidgeting with. Since Sean has ADHD (and I didn't yet know how common autism is misdiagnosed in girls as ADHD), we figured she just took after him.

It began to affect her self-esteem by

I knew by the time I took this picture. Here she was, quirky hair and purple scarf, enjoying the smell and feel of grass on a breezy summer day in the mountains.

first grade when she would get behavior cards pulled, so we decided to try some Ritalin. On the very first day of taking it, she came home with a note from her teacher that said, "She was a different child today." Well, conventional ADHD wisdom tells you if it's ADHD, you'll see an immediate difference with meds. So, we added another diagnosis to our family and went on.

It was second grade when things took a turn. Bronwyn had been attending the same little local private school I'd gone to myself. Since it was still teaching phonics, that's how I wanted her to learn to read—not whatever perpetually new thing the county adopted after sending somebody off to a convention.

We started receiving complaints of "bad behaviors" and the teacher sent her off to the principal, which was utterly absurd, as none of those behaviors involved other children, anger, stealing, or disrespect. The referral would read, "Was twirling pencil" or "Wouldn't stop wiggling in seat" or "Constant tapping."

Then a friend and fellow parent of a child in the same class pulled my husband aside and told him he'd seen this teacher not only be unkind to his own child and others, but it was no secret that she didn't like Bronwyn. Worse yet, she hadn't just moved Bronwyn's seat; she had moved it away from *all* the other children. And then the part that broke my heart: she used Bronwyn as an example to the class of how not to act. So, the other children began to see her as "bad," too, and began rejecting her. Then, to make things worse, the teacher banned her and her best friend from even playing together *during recess*. So, after a day spent sitting away from the other children and being teased by the teacher's pets for being wiggly, her teacher didn't think a lonely seven-year-old deserved to spend time with her friend.

Now, for a seasoned teacher to withdraw her child from school in the spring to enroll her at another school is something one doesn't see often. But that's just what we did. We took her to a public elementary school with a bang-up principal and staff who understood ADHD, and my child came home happy the first day. She's never been "in trouble" since.

But other issues began to come up. Bronwyn's handwriting is awkward and slow. She had excellent recall of math facts (drilled in private school) but now faced word problems with multiple steps and a whole different way of doing math. Once several steps became part of the activity, Bronwyn was less likely to finish it on time. Often confused about the directions, she was embarrassed and wouldn't speak up to ask for clarification about what to do. She began to fear math due to the multiple steps required and was convinced she couldn't do it—despite math being a strength for her in lower grades. Her backpack and desk were always in disarray. She stopped making straight As.

Socially, in upper elementary school, she was a little awkward. I thought it was self-esteem issues following the bullying trauma of second grade, but this was a class of sweet kids. None of them were doing that. No one was being unkind.

But her "quirks" began to impact relationships with other students. She didn't seem to understand that she had to lead into conversations about favorite subjects and not just walk up and start talking out of the blue if she wanted to talk about something. She cared more about her own little worlds of imagination, elaborate characters and costumes, and story lines. She created these miniature stage sets that wrapped around her room and could not be touched lest she completely freak out. She even carried little mini projects for her stage sets to school to work on.

The other children were *polite*, and she innocently called them all her friends. But she didn't have many good friends at school. (She did have a good friend outside of school.) There were no invites to sleepovers or calls for playdates from classmates. When her grandma or aunt visited during lunch, they noticed sometimes she played by herself, trying to get near groups but not quite knowing how to be like them.

Not coordinated enough to catch on to gymnastics or cheerleading, she didn't share the same outside activities as the other kids. She wasn't a pariah, her teachers assured me, but Bronwyn felt the annoyance of others. She noticed it. Looking back, I realize how even though she was smiling, her eyes were constantly scanning the room nervously. The funny thing is, she always wanted to go to school. You'd think not. But she did.

Her teachers over the next three school years were excellent. I talked to them all about social and academic concerns. They loved her and helped as best they could. They also noticed little things, but we tried to chalk it up to her being a late July baby, younger than the others, the artsy type, and we were optimistic she'd find herself and her tribe.

But by fourth grade, I began thinking there was more than ADHD going on here. I mentioned it a couple of times to others, but it wasn't taken too seriously. It wasn't until Sarabeth, Callum's private speech therapist, let Bronwyn come back during a visit, leading to a discussion, that it was suggested to me we have a language evaluation. Sarabeth had noticed some things, too, and wanted to test her. Bronwyn had already been referred for OT and gifted, but we'd never done a language evaluation by a speech-language pathologist.

Sure enough, when it came back, we discovered a massive gap between her social-pragmatic age and her vocabulary. Her vocabulary was age eighteen. Her social pragmatic language (the social use of language) was age six. Of course, Sarabeth explained that finding. But by then, I knew what it meant. By now, I'd added an autism endorsement to my teacher certification. I'd started doing professional development for teachers and admins on autism.

That twelve-year gap in her social communication skills versus her vocabulary was significant and signaled another learning disability—usually in conjunction with autism. All that time. All those signs. *And I had missed it.*

Only now, my sweet girl had racked up signs such as food aversions, social difficulties, executive functioning issues, sleep issues, repetitive behaviors, and anxiety. All diagnosed in a family with three cases of high-needs classic autism, that grandfather of mine, plus whatever you want to call the traits my dad and I shared. Combined with the fact that girls are often misdiagnosed with ADHD first and are often diagnosed later as a result . . . and, of course, I went there. But nobody but Sarabeth and her aunt Julie saw it but me.

I was even told by more than one person that maybe I was "seeing autism everywhere."

Yes, the realization stung. For years, I told my readers not to distrust their instincts, but I had. So, we didn't get a head start on teaching her ways to work around her learning differences.

Sixth grade was rough. I saw how Bronwyn's struggles with writing, note-taking, and organization were affecting her self-esteem. When I realized she wouldn't survive in math class like this, I pulled her from that subject to do virtual learning to save the grade. It worked. But by that time, the math damage was done. She hates it now.

Worse yet, time was lost. Had I realized the organizational issues Bronwyn had and accommodations she really needed, she'd have had them sooner—and not be trying to figure it all out now that the content had gotten harder.

I finally took her to a mental-health practice, made my case, and we ordered up testing. Soon, she gained a couple of other diagnoses: ARFID (Avoidant Restrictive Food Intake Disorder), a food phobia, and a processing delay (her IQ is high, but she has a lag in processing). The neuropsychologist didn't diagnose her with autism but noted all the individual diagnoses she had by then in a list: ADHD, anxiety, depression, ARFID, a phobia, social pragmatic communication disorder, and a specific learning disability.

When we met with the psychiatrist, he looked at it, asked me questions about my family, and said he would have preferred a different assessment than the one given. (I didn't know why at the time, but I researched why later.) The doctor said he'd "seen this sort of thing before in autistic girls" and stated, "If it walks like a duck, quacks like a duck, and has a duck for a brother, I'd say it's probably a duck." But before he could order the test he preferred, he transferred out of the practice, and I had to start again with the new doctor. I was beginning to lose hope.

Dr. Henschke proved to be an outstanding psychiatrist. She *listened* to me, looked at the history, and asked about the impact on her schooling. I showed her the assessment done and the research that showed wasn't the gold standard for a child with Bronwyn's characteristics. However, she was already familiar with that and with the subject of autism in girls as well. Her concern had been that Bronwyn's autism was mild and worried it might negatively impact her school placement—which she knew to be in an academic magnet.

But she listened when I explained how an OHI (other health impaired) ESE classification comes up in teacher portals. It worried me because I knew perfectly well that some might not bother to look further, and none of her teachers would know what social pragmatic communication disorder meant. They'd see: ADHD, processing disorder, ARFID, anxiety, social pragmatic communication disorder, proprioceptive delay, and sensory processing disorder and not have a clue that all that together was really autism. "Mild" autism, if you will, but autism.

But if that code said "ASD" (autism spectrum disorder), they'd see it immediately. And even if they didn't know a whole lot more about autism, it was far more likely they'd understand that than her current list of associated conditions.

I told Dr. Henschke that Bronwyn had asked me once, "What's wrong with me?" I wasn't at all sure how to answer that. But I suspected, and I wanted to introduce her to "her tribe"—a whole community the world over who experience what she experiences, are proud to be themselves, and will help her understand who she is. I wanted her to learn to advocate for herself—and for her to be able to do that, we needed to give it a name.

Dr. Henschke looked at me for a moment, nodded her head, agreed that all that made sense, and gave Bronwyn a long-overdue diagnosis of autism. I nearly cried.

I wasn't crazy. (Again.) I wasn't "seeing autism." On the contrary, I *recognized* autism both as a professional with formal training *and* as her mother. But I had allowed self-doubt and the ignorance of others to delay getting her the help she needed. I will always regret that.

One day when she reads this, I want her to know that I couldn't sleep the night before that appointment. I kept launching my speech to the doctor in my head—what to say, which studies to bring. I drove bleary-eyed, wearing red as a confidence color, and I listened to that courage playlist I have when I must fight. (Because there really aren't any mountains high enough, are there?) And if I couldn't get through to Dr. Henschke, I was going to drive Bronwyn several hours away to a specialist with a background in girls with autism.

I didn't end up needing all that because Dr. Henschke is a great doctor.

She listens and respects our priorities for care. She's willing to look at what you bring and prints out things she wants you to read, too. She understands my fear of addictive substances (family history of that). And she's careful and methodical in trying increases or decreases of meds. I've always thought doctors have three speeds regarding their testing and prescribing: too aggressive, too hesitant, and in between. I like them in the middle. So, I immediately made her Callum's doctor, too.

And a few months later, with a resulting bit of sleep in me, I scheduled an appointment with her as well. We all three have the same psychiatrist, which I highly recommend. When you do it that way, it's so much easier for them to know what's wrong with all of you immediately. Of course, she laughs when I tell her this.

Seriously, find a doctor you love. Your mental health *is* your physical health. You'll understand that a bit better later. Take care of it now.

IF you have an autistic child, you may have considered your other children, too. But hear me when I say this: *autism in girls can fool you.*

Females do have a brain-based communication advantage. Does that mean all autistic girls will use spoken language? No. Some of them have changes in their brain wiring too profound to allow that. (They may or may not communicate in some other way, however.) But most have a slight edge. It's thought to be a reason why girls are so underdiagnosed, often not even until adulthood. Their interests may align more with their peers, but it might seem a little obsessive to you—like they're probably taking it way farther than the other kids. So maybe the other little girls don't respond well because it's odd. Remember, at this age, likely no one has explained *why and what* to help the other kids understand, accept, and welcome. Autistic girls may become intensely fixated on a new trend, making lists, interrupting unrelated conversations with facts about the new topic of interest, and working for hours on an elaborate project that cannot be moved. They may have a lot of anxiety and hence struggle to make decisions. It can also mean a lot of anime, cosplay, gaming, and homemade slime recipes.

But they *will* eventually find their tribes. Bronwyn has (and they're a lot like her). This is especially true if you can get them into schools with solid arts or STEM programs. The finding of the tribes is no small thing. Once they identify with one, they try on all its hats, searching for the right look. And they're always aware they're not quite as good as the others at picking up the latest thing, dance, or style.

Since starting my blog, I've befriended autistic women online—many I've known nearly a decade or have even met in person. They had been the only other ones agreeing and gently suggesting long ago that Bronwyn was on the spectrum. I always agreed, to an extent, but was adamant she didn't fit the technical triad required (she does actually) and that no one would diagnose her. I'd need the foremost specialist on autism in females or something.

Turns out, I didn't—just a good, competent, compassionate doctor who keeps up with changes and medical research. We'll move forward from here, doing everything we can to love, support, and encourage Bronwyn to be her best self—more importantly, her happiest self. We've got some skills to learn, but they're doable. And many of them she's learning herself now that she's maturing. She's going to be okay. We've got some work in learning ways to get around what she struggles with, but she's smart. She's observant. And hopefully, with time, she'll learn to advocate for herself, understand herself, and learn to use her talents to her advantage. I have faith in her. Bronwyn has this persistent way of seeing the kindest and most moral way to think about a thing. She's an old soul, as they say.

But being "mild" also makes others less likely to understand her actions, reactions, or odd no-actions (freezing, crying, etc.). Callum is fortunate in that way. At a glance, you can tell he's "different." Not so with her. You'd have to spend some time with her to see it. That can make people less compassionate about her invisible needs.

With low-needs autism (Level 1) or Asperger's, they risk being misunderstood and disliked, even by teachers. This is why so many adolescents with autism struggle. They either aren't diagnosed and are therefore judged as if they weren't autistic—or they are diagnosed, and no one does anything to help those around them understand and adjust accordingly.

Girls with autism often spend so much time "passing" and worrying about "passing" that they can't focus. The hypervigilance required is simply too much.

At the time of this writing, the world is still battling COVID-19. Students across the nation have had to adjust to new ways of learning remotely, and it has been hard for Bronwyn. In the resulting political turmoil over vaccines and mask mandates, she has suddenly become more aware of our world. She's forming her own conclusions on right/wrong, justice/injustice, cool/not cool (or whatever it is they call it now). For the most part, I like many of her conclusions and find them well-considered, compassionate, logical, and practical. She has this arid sense of humor and can be a total goof. I love her approach to fear. She argues to herself, "If I don't try, I don't stand a chance." And then she goes and gets a part in the school play! Or bleaches her hair cotton candy pink. She's brave. I love that about her. She doesn't get that fearlessness from me. But her heart is even bigger. I've never once seen her even wish someone else harm. I've certainly never noticed her exclude anyone. The truth is I more than love her. I happen to *like* her a whole lot. And if, at some point, she wants to tell her own autism story or otherwise, she can. This one ends with me merely liking her just as she is and loving her unconditionally.

However, Bronwyn is fourteen, with an understanding Callum will never have. So, of course, I asked how she felt about my sharing this part of our collective story. I would never want to embarrass her in any way, so it was up to her. But I also didn't want to spend a decade writing about our autism family's story and then leave out a significant update that could perhaps save some girl years of unnecessary struggling before being identified.

Bronwyn separately arrived at the same conclusion and said yes.

And then utterly stunned me when she said, "I trust you."

The next story is hers.

Chapter 37

Two Sides of the Same Coin:
On Mild vs. Severe Autism

There's a great debate in the autism world about the changes to diagnostic criteria in the *DSM-5* (*Diagnostic and Statistical Manual of Mental Disorders*, fifth edition) a few years ago. When they put all autism under one umbrella and removed the diagnosis of "Asperger's," that didn't go over well with two groups. Autists who proudly proclaim it as an identity and resent the change. And parents of severely autistic children—who feel their children's many needs are being swept under the rug by those who are able to advocate for themselves. Some of those families have even formed a new nonprofit, the National Council on Severe Autism. Among their goals are to support policy, programs, and resources for impacted families.

However, their formation and writings haven't gone over as well with autistic self-advocates. Many autistic people view the NCSA as an organization promoting autism as tragedy. Being autistic, they don't like that perception and feel it contributes to a lack of dignity and respect for autists, ensures their isolation rather than inclusion, and promotes thinking that leads to parental murder-suicides of autistic children and adults. In addition, they argue that doctors don't undiagnose other conditions simply because some patients fare worse.

I've sat back quietly and observed this controversy, completely understanding the concerns of the autistic community (and finding them valid) but also knowing the NCSA isn't wrong about there not being enough to support the higher-needs end of the autism spectrum. I live that reality, and I know it to be true. There's a segment of the autism population working, mowing their lawns, raising families—and, yes, I'd agree the needs of low-needs autists are different than my son's. Still, I've read some of the parent-group statements and positions and cringe at the wording.

That said, I do believe reasonable people ought to acknowledge that there can be two truths existing side by side. First, we *do* need to address the needs of the profoundly developmentally disabled. *And* we simultaneously need to stop presenting our children and families as tragedies.

Because self-advocate autists aren't ignorant. Of course they're aware some in their community are profoundly disabled and require lifetime care. I'm sure as human beings, they realize issues like sleep loss, self-harm, and communication struggles are stressful for families. But if you keep clicking on news stories about autistic children killed by parents, you find a lot of neurotypicals' reactions are: "How sad. I feel for that mother." The injustice to the autistic child is seemingly irrelevant. Quite naturally, that outrages them.

Both sides seem to have an inability to publicly express compassion for each other's perspectives and emotions.

And even though I do find it difficult sometimes to find a "safe" way of describing an autistic person's needs—in a way guaranteed to not offend or marginalize someone—I disagree that "Asperger's" isn't autism. I think Levels 1, 2, and 3 *are* more accurate. But I live with *both* a Level 1 and a Level 3. So that's allowed me to think all of this over with new eyes.

What I now understand my son and daughter to be is flip sides of the same coin. They appear different. But they're made of similar traits to varying degrees.

Both have: sensory issues, meltdowns, OT-related developmental delays, proprioceptive issues, social deficits, communication issues, repetitive behaviors (stimming), impulsivity, difficulty with executive functioning, food aversions, sleep deficits, difficulty imitating others, an inability to follow a point, fine motor problems, and anxiety. The fact that one of them manifests most of those more intensely doesn't negate the experiences of the other. And, in some ways, it's more complicated for Bronwyn. People don't have high expectations for Callum; they just enjoy and accept him. They don't try to attribute other motivations to his issues.

But Aspie types are often treated as if their difficulties are deliberate or the result of "bringing it on themselves." So, they may be able to "pass" as neurotypical, but people are continually annoyed with them. And since Bronwyn is very bright, she analyzes and absorbs that in ways Callum doesn't. Although the average person might feel more compassion for Callum, my daughter is currently the one struggling more. Callum is happy. She's having to learn ways to "get around" issues that give her trouble: taking notes, being more flexible, multistep projects, inferencing (big on state exams), organization, and more. She'll get it. But it makes being fourteen a lot more challenging. Because in the ways that count, she *is* a typical fourteen-year-old. She spends hours on various devices talking to friends, playing games together, avoiding activities with parents, rolling eyes, testing her snark, giggling, shrieking, and trying out different identities and looks. Autism is an inseparable part of her, but it's not the only ingredient. Personality and temperament count for most of what makes a person.

So, even though I prefer the convenience of the term "Asperger's" (for description purposes) and even like its affectionate moniker, "Aspie," I don't agree that they're different conditions but merely different manifestations based on individual circuitry. While many of their needs are similar—sensory, routines—others are quite different.

And I agree that Hollywood productions are so busy glamorizing autism and making it "cool" that they're ignoring segments of our community that need almost total support. Representation matters—which is why so many of us cried when *Sesame Street* introduced the first autistic Muppet, Julia. By overlooking the representation of those with high-needs autism, the realities of families and institutions supporting them are deemphasized to the masses—in favor of fictional detectives whose cases are solved by a genius autistic child.

That plays a part in ignoring the need to plan better for their futures. And, yes, we're being somewhat cruel in the refusal to acknowledge that raising a profoundly disabled child can be *hard*. Hard on the body, hard on mental health, and hard on the wallet—in its most severe forms. Instead of rolling our eyes at that truth, it seems clear that supporting these families with more services translates to helping high-needs autists more as well.

But in asking for that, it doesn't mean that we as parents get a free pass to present other human beings as tragedies. As lives not worth living unless they're "cured" and crosses to bear while we vlog ourselves crying over our misfortunes. Or as burdens we "humblebrag" about carrying while declaring ourselves "warrior parents" to the world. Now I'll be sure to fight for my son to have what he needs to prepare for his future. But I'm a mother and advocate, not a *warrior*.

Autism is part of who my children are. And I am *never* declaring war on my children.

Recalibrating

If you don't know where you're going,
any road'll take you there.

—George Harrison

Chapter 38

He Proved Me Wrong:
On Presuming Competence

Until he began to approach upper elementary school, I still hoped that one day Callum would become fully conversational and self-supporting in adulthood. As frustrated as I was that nobody could predict his future skills, it's probably a good thing I didn't know then what I know now. Because he's old enough now for us to make reasonable predictions about his future.

Despite using picture exchange and single spoken words, Callum does not appear to have the cognitive ability to develop grammar.

Some might roll their eyes over the necessity of grammar. But without it, all we have are names for things. And that's not enough. For what do we do with the things? Do we get to keep them, or do they belong to someone else? When can we access them? And for how long? Where are they? And why do they sometimes stop working?

The mere naming of something doesn't suffice. And that's where we are now. Callum's receptive language is stronger than his expressive. But he's also learned to compensate by noticing tone, gestures, routines, etc. How much he understands is a mystery. But ultimately, he doesn't understand enough to care for himself.

Even though my hopes when I wrote this piece years ago were for spoken language and a life he's not quite wired for, it doesn't change the message. We don't know what he knows. And we likely never will.

But it doesn't suggest there's a total absence of understanding. And it doesn't mean we can't figure out other ways to help him comprehend. For example, he can't say which slot the forks go in or why, but he can put them away in the right place with enough practice. He can get one if requested. And if he heard me angrily saying "fork" repeatedly as I wash his hands, the table, the seat, and the floor, he can deduce I'm unhappy with him and perhaps even feel bad about his own difficulty using forks. The same kind of fork he watches classmates successfully use every day.

Does that permeate? I don't know. But it *might*. And if it does, it's vital that what permeates doesn't damage his self-esteem.

So, yes. *Presume competence.* It costs nothing. It safeguards dignity and self-worth, and it's what you would want to be done for you if something like, say, a stroke was to strip *you* of language and grammar—but leave your mind active and alert.

And even though we still aren't having conversations, exactly, and probably never will, everything else below is still valid. Callum sees himself and what he can do in my eyes and in the eyes of those of Team Callum. Because of that, he learns to do more and more for himself.

Of course, that's true for all of us, isn't it?

He Proved Me Wrong

One of the phrases you hear a lot in the autism world is "Always presume competence." If you aren't familiar with the expression, it's a simple concept. Autism is a neurological difference in the brain affecting perception and expression. Yet, some people assume that it must necessarily coincide with an intellectual disability. This is just as incorrect as believing everyone with autism is a genius, another autism myth. Autism exists in persons with widely different intellectual abilities, from the intellectually disabled to the average Joe to geniuses. So, because we cannot currently assess the intelligence of the severely affected, we don't know what is happening in their minds. It might be that a brilliant person is hidden behind their autistic traits, and we simply don't know how to interact with them. And it could also be that an autistic person may be intellectually disabled and lack to varying degrees the ability to comprehend what is happening around him. But, in the absence of knowing with certainty, we must give them the benefit of the doubt. I would certainly hope that if I were in their shoes, the same would be done for me.

But "Always presume competence" can be a hard rule for neurotypicals to follow. That's not because we don't agree—at least in theory. But high-needs autistic people may not give a lot of signals that they understand something. They often don't appear to be listening or watching. And, when you ask them to do something based upon what they have seen or heard, many do not respond as we would expect them to. In the absence of any visual indicators demonstrating competence, it's easy to wonder whether understanding is happening at all. Because we neurotypicals find it difficult to grasp why someone who understands doesn't respond when it's in their best interest.

It's a lot like religion. You can be taught the tenets of your faith, and you can reason out your belief system in your head. But it is natural to question what we cannot see in the day-to-day grind of living—just as human beings have long pondered the existence of God. Likewise, we wonder if our severely autistic loved ones really comprehend all that is happening around them. Maybe you've never wondered. Perhaps you are like those people who've never doubted their faith. But, if you're like me, you have wondered, worried, and sometimes been haunted by the possibility that you are wrong—along with the possibility that you are right.

When I realized Callum was autistic, one of the first things my aunt, a mother of two grown autistic children, told me was never to talk about him while he's in the room and to always believe that he knows what's happening. She shared a story of her son recalling an event from years earlier that she had thought he hadn't noticed.

But he had, and with perfect recall of the conversational details. Because he didn't speak much verbally at the time or cooperate with what was requested of him, my aunt assumed he wasn't listening. Having known him at that age, I would have agreed with her. He didn't appear to be listening. At all. No, we shouldn't have assumed it, but unfortunately, it's too easy a mistake to make in the absence of evidence to the contrary.

Fast-forward several years, and now I have autistic children of my own. But even having heard her story, I questioned the truth of it regarding my own child. I'll admit, I was somewhat confident of my own ability to read him. I thought I would see the proverbial lightbulb go off, and then I would presume competence. But Callum, in the tradition of children everywhere, surprised and humbled me. Amid a "language explosion," Callum began to repeat words. Words I was afraid he wasn't comprehending at all.

My worries for him have eaten me alive inside and haunted me in the middle of the night. And they've impacted my perception of what he knows and what he can do. That's led me to an important realization: I must tame my fears. I have to keep in mind that fear is nothing but a good survival tool. Like every emotion, it has a purpose. It helps us run from danger to safety. But the only threat in assuming his understanding is the off chance I'm wrong and might feel disappointed. And my fear of disappointment is a selfish reason to give in to worry. Not disappointment in him, of course, but in the realization that he will not be able to direct his own life.

My father and I shared a philosophy: "Prepare for the worst, and you'll never be disappointed—only pleasantly surprised on occasion." Which is an excellent guideline when planning for hurricanes. Unfortunately, it isn't such a great directive when raising developmentally delayed children. For, like all children, they see themselves reflected in our eyes.

One day, Callum spoke his name for the first time. And I missed it. It sounded more like "Cam," so I didn't pick it out of his typical babble chatter until he said it a few more times—while waving at his own reflection in the rearview mirror. (Yeah, I know. Sometimes, I'm not so bright.) I remember turning and asking him what he'd said but really believing it to be nothing. So, he looked back to the mirror, waved at himself again, and said, "Callum," with the sweetest smile. I stopped breathing for just a moment, though I was thrilled that he finally spoke his own name. But what hit me was his determination to be seen and heard. He kept on until I got it—and then he confirmed it. Apparently, he was motivated to speak his name by seeing himself in the mirror. A reflection he liked.

So, now I must learn how to adjust the mirror in my eyes to reflect who he really is and who he can be. Because he is watching. He is listening. He is learning.

And when he looks at himself through me, I want him to like and be inspired by what he sees. For, if what he sees in my eyes is not faith in him, how will he learn faith in himself?

Chapter 39

It's Not How Hard You Tried:
On Nature and Nurture

I vomited throughout the day, every day, the entirety of both my pregnancies. It's called hyperemesis, and hardly anyone knew what it was until the Duchess of Cambridge made it famous. (Thanks, Kate!) But I was *sick*, so nauseated, I couldn't tolerate moving. I couldn't take smells. A few times when I couldn't keep down water, they had to put in IVs or hospitalize me. I lost twenty pounds with both pregnancies. During that time, the only thing that allowed me to work (if you could call it that in the condition I was in) was the antiemetic Zofran combined with Reglan.

Can you guess how many times I wondered if I "gave" my children autism? Want to take a stab at how many people have suggested it to me?

A few years ago, a young mother privately messaged me, wanting to know if I had nursed Callum. She was tearing herself up because her mother-in-law had suggested her son was autistic because she didn't breastfeed him. Already worried about her son's development and future, this woman blamed herself because of bottle feeding.

I nursed my babies, a beautiful experience I wouldn't trade for the world. I loved it. Note the following pronoun: I as in *me*. Not necessarily another parent.

Yet, both of my children have IEPs. My breast milk did not confer standard-issue neurology to them. Instead, it made them chubby and sweet and, by necessity, a little more attached to Mama. They're still autistic.

So, if you're beating up on yourself for not breastfeeding, stop. Didn't take those prenatal vitamins? Stop right now. *You did not harm your child.* They were autistic in the womb. It wasn't the lack of breastmilk. (As advocates against "mom-shaming" women who don't or can't breastfeed like to say, "Fed is best!") It wasn't because you didn't stay home with them. It wasn't because they watched *Yo Gabba Gabba!* before the age of two—no matter what your mother-in-law implied. You didn't "fail" them because you didn't know Floortime or love them enough—"love" taking the form of every suggestion given to parents of autistic children about how they caused their child's autism.

Did you or the other parent give your child autism? Well, there's probably a decent chance of it. It tends to run in families. And scientists have found a lot of associated genes. So, should you blame yourself for that? Hardly. Would you blame yourself for your child's dimples?

Many people throughout history are believed to have been autistic, based on records of their lives and descriptions by others. Many of them had children, who had their own children, who had even more offspring. Do you see my point here? We're finding autism in DNA because it's been passed down for thousands of years.

What-ifs abound in parenting a child with high-needs autism. There are lots of theories as to its cause. And umpteen zillion theories and techniques of how to facilitate speech, how to increase socialization, and how to replace problem behaviors, but you can't possibly do them all. As a parent, you try to make the best decisions in real time. Later, it's easy to second-guess yourself and question if you made the right choices in schools, medications, and therapies. Having had four diagnosed autistic family members and seeing them develop differently despite having similar therapies, I've realized that most of how an autistic person "functions" is simply determined by how they're wired. As parents, we can best help them navigate their world by taking that wiring into account and accepting it. This means we can stop torturing ourselves about what we could have done differently. It also means that although we do have to worry about best preparing them for their world, we aren't responsible for "fixing" them.

They aren't broken like bones; they are *whole*. But, yes, a different kind of whole.

It wasn't what you did, and it wasn't what you didn't do. It's not how hard you tried.

It's just who your child *is*.

Chapter 40

No Dead Bodies Required:
On Redefining *Hope*

While co-presenting in a panel session at the OCALI convention in 2017, I listened to a conversation between parents of autistic children. My co-presenters, Jerry and Joanne Turning, Jason Hague, and Jodi Collins, and I were relating our experiences as both parents of autistic, limited-verbal children as well as professionals who serve similar families. During Q&A time, Jerry and Joanne discussed how they love, enjoy, and accept their son as the person he is. When they were finished, a woman interrupted them with oversimplified advice to "just [insert unsolicited opinions], and he'll be fine," noting that her child is now married with a family of his own. She finished with, "You'll see. Don't give up hope."

Jerry and Joanne were a class act while struggling to not argue with the woman they clearly saw as well-intentioned. But I knew what that patience was likely costing them on the inside. I know what being on the receiving end of such advice really feels like.

When an autistic child is very young and diagnosis new, parents hear much unsolicited advice about not making assumptions about the future, holding high expectations, and holding out hope. In the early days, those sentiments can be reassuring and uplifting. Because you're still hoping for the most independent future possible for your child. At two or three years of age, the idea that a child might not have functional communication for life is overwhelming. There are still dreams of gainful employment, romantic relationships, and perhaps even college and grandchildren. You hear of those "successes," and you want your child to have full access to all the things everyone else's child will get to choose from in life. So, hope becomes a mantra, and soon we equate longing with love. As though the absence of that longing—"hope"—is somehow the absence of love. And that idea catches on and is soon repeated by everyone the parent encounters.

But children grow. And if you have a child whose developmental age doesn't keep pace with their physical age, eventually reality sets in, and you alter your plans. Yes, there are stories of children who didn't speak until twelve and who went on to lead fully independent lives. But the reason those stories make the news is that they are the exception. A child entering their second decade without functional communication, the ability to care for their basic needs, and showing consistent evidence of intellectual disability is going to be an adult in need of lifetime care. Is acknowledging that reality a manifestation of failed parental hope, thus a lack of love?

I have a dear friend who adores Callum. She sees all the beauty we see in him and is fascinated by his development, charming personality, and many eccentricities. But every time he makes a developmental gain or surprises us with a new skill, she marvels, "See? There's nothing wrong with his brain! He understands everything that's going on."

Only he *doesn't*. He doesn't understand everything that's going on. His brain is wired differently than other people on a profound level.

Yes, he can certainly learn and grow. Yes, he will continue to develop new skills. Yet as we approach his thirteenth year, our hopes for him have evolved.

But a funny thing happens when you begin to admit that to others. You can see it on their faces. It's as if they equate more realistic expectations for the future with giving up hope on your child.

"Oh, you don't know that! He could still go to college and raise a family."

"You'll see. He'll prove you wrong."

"Don't you know all autistic people are geniuses? It's just hidden inside. He understands everything."

"You just have to keep the faith. We'll put her on the prayer list and claim victory in His name!"

It's a hell of a position for a parent to put themselves in—that of trying to defend lowered expectations for their own child. Because some people do not want to hear the truth. Truth makes them uncomfortable, so they'll deny it even to the person the truth impacts directly. The problem with those denials is in leaving families unsupported in their new normals. We find ourselves not only adjusting for a future we hadn't planned for while having to convince others to accept it, too. That's too much. The burden of proof shouldn't rely on us. Because what exactly are they trying so hard to get us to deny? That the world's made up of every kind? Well, it *is*.

Yet friends and loved ones, particularly on social media, inundate us with this unrelenting insistence in having "hope."

If you have an autistic child, you've seen the news stories and viral social media shares I'm referring to. Friends tend to tag you in them or PM them to you. They're stories of autistic kids who didn't talk but do now, autistic children who enter college at ten, autistic children in competitions, and autistic adults who graduate from college. And you don't mind the stories because human beings persevering in the face of adversity is, of course, a beautiful thing.

But invariably, somewhere in the story is a quote that goes something like this: *"When experts told her that her son would never talk, never have friends, never graduate, she declared, 'Over my dead body.'"*

Those quotes are all sorts of inspirational—for some. But if you have a child whose disability is profound, those lines are felt like a slap.

Because some disabilities cannot be overcome.

They can be accepted, worked with, planned for, and accommodated, but no amount of parental love and determination can erase them.

Callum is not going to law school. He's simply not wired for that, and I can't rewire him. That I accept that and love him unconditionally does not reflect his having not been raised by someone willing to try harder.

Even knowing differently, that implication lands heavily in my heart every time.

We have a documented family history of autism. Enough so that we are participants in the SPARK study, the largest genetic study of autism in the world. (And one I'm delighted to endorse and direct you to in "Places to Go and Things to See.") Professionally, I've studied autism. I'm familiar with various studies of its possible causes. I understand the development of those with autism versus those without.

But if you think I haven't lain awake in the early hours of the morning, obsessing over what more I could have done—what I missed—to help my child live the best life possible, you'd be wrong. I have second-guessed myself a thousand times over in my heart, even when my mind attempts to reassure me that Callum is simply who he is and who he is was always going to be from the moment of conception.

When folks like me see those Facebook shares and hear friends and family continue to define hope for us, it can breed resentment. And it has nothing to do with resentment that somebody else's autistic child is doing well in life. On the contrary, many of those stories are beautiful. I'm genuinely happy for them. But how they are framed and sold to a public greedy for "inspiration porn" is over the top.

When the football team captain invites the autistic girl to the prom, I don't want her to lie awake later, wondering why there were news cameras present. Sit and think about that for a moment. It implies that the news media had to show up to celebrate somebody wanting to hang out with *her*.

Yet, parents are tagged daily by friends—on pretty images with empty platitudes and inspiration porn stories. In particular, they like the ones about parents who wouldn't give up hope. That's due to a pervasive belief that somehow accepting the limitations of a severe disability is "giving up" on a child.

My son has severe disabilities that place him in the "highest needs" category. He is considered functionally nonverbal (cannot communicate basic needs), high-needs autistic, and profoundly intellectually disabled with an IQ of under 50. He's old enough now and has had enough supports in place that we can make some realistic, informed predictions about future supports and transitional planning. Is it possible we'll be wrong? Sure. But all things considered, it's highly unlikely.

Precisely how is my acceptance of who he is "giving up" on him? The implication is he's somehow a failure if we do "give up" and he doesn't achieve what others believe is necessary for him to be a successful human being. Is he a failed soul should he not grow up to go to college or marry? Is he our failure if his brain simply isn't wired to do those things?

A paraplegic isn't a failure when they can't regenerate a healthy spine. Likewise, a person with Down syndrome isn't a failure because they failed to rid themselves of an extra chromosome. So then, why is my child a failure if his brain fails to form typical neurological connections? Where did anyone get the idea that all we have to do is "believe" to alter a person's physiology? Nobody suggests visible disabilities are failures. But they certainly do the invisible ones.

If others know or love someone who overcame early developmental challenges but went on to live a typical life, that's great. I'm delighted for them. It makes life easier if that's your path. But people would do us a kindness by ceasing to insinuate we aren't doing something right if it's not in the cards for our loved ones.

My son's future is ultimately not going to be the result of "just believing" in him. *I already believe in him.* I believe he is delightful. I believe his soul is beautiful. I believe he has dignity and value.

As for "giving up hope," that expression no longer has the same meaning for me. I've merely given up a delusion. And I happen to believe he's still worthy—just as he is.

So, am I giving up "hope"? You're damned right I am. I'm giving up hope of him being anyone other than the charming person he already is. I'm giving up "hope" in unrealistic dreams of futures he isn't going to have, and I'm replacing it with *genuine* hope for him to be the happiest Callum he can be. And I'm doing that with all the IEP goals, therapies, love, prayers, tenacity, and exposure to his world that I can pack into his formative years.

But in the end, he's going to be who he is meant to be. So, since it's good enough for me, it ought to be good enough for everyone else.

Because—over *my* dead body—will he be relegated as somehow less worthy for not doing the unexpected and unrealistic.

The presence of an autistic adult in the world who doesn't make the newspaper is not a statement of failure. Not of society, not of his family, and not of himself. And other than steadfastly insisting he be given every reasonable opportunity any other person must have to live, learn, and grow, no other declarations need be made—and no dead bodies required.

And no. I'm not going to give up hope for that.

Chapter 41

Pandemics, Hurricanes, and the Parts of Speech: On What He Doesn't Know

When I wrote the proposal for *The Scenic Route*, the tentative title of this as-yet-to-be-written chapter didn't have "pandemics" included.

We didn't yet know what our grandmothers and great-grandmothers knew about diseases and dark times like the COVID-19 pandemic—the days before smallpox and polio vaccines, antibiotics, and knowledge of Rh incompatibility. Of course, as adults, each of us has surely known someone who has died. But entire families being wiped out—grandchildren knowing it was them who gave it to Grandma before she died—this is new to us. Generation X and younger enjoyed years of never worrying about measles, mumps, and polio. We've been spoiled in that innocence.

We've all now learned more than we imagined about the randomness of devastation, the fragility of our security and fortunes, and the nature of human beings in times of national and global crisis. We know there are heroes. We know there are monsters.

My son, due to the level of his intellectual disability, does not. He doesn't know who is "safe." He doesn't comprehend the laws of physics applied against one ill-timed pedestrian. He understands many situations. He knows a lot of words, and he can often deduce what's going on. But unless he can touch it, abstract concepts are inaccessible for him. He does not understand days of the week or the passage of time, so "yes" is *right now* to Callum. Having a developmental age of not yet two, his difficulty in waiting is developmentally appropriate. Without being able to communicate "hurt," he can't understand "danger." He doesn't comprehend "broken." And I don't know that he'll ever understand "death." For Callum, it's all about how long you're going to make him wait for the device to charge, how long he'll have to wait for the power to come back on, how long we must wait to go back to our regular weekly restaurant breakfast routine with Daddy. And because I cannot explain *when* or *why* to a child who understands only *yes* and *no*, that's made weeks without power following hurricanes not merely sweaty, joyless affairs but miserable, hellish versions of *Groundhog Day*. Because try as I might, I cannot teach this boy certain concepts he must be able to conceive of—to *understand*.

I spent years trying to convince middle schoolers that the parts of speech actually matter. But even I had no idea just how much. Because when your brain is wired in such a way as to not understand the difference between *around, before, because, and, both* there will be concepts you simply won't be capable of grasping. We've taught Callum to look through pictures, menus, his AAC device, and his PECS (Picture Exchange Communication System) book, but he's twelve and still does not understand that he can have a grilled cheese *and* fries. He still thinks it's one or the other and will not choose a side dish. He wants the fries. But he wants the grilled cheese more, and he does not understand that *he can choose both*. He doesn't understand "and."

He knows the words for a lot of things. He recognizes patterns in human behavior. He problem solves. He plots. And if sufficiently motivated, he'll demonstrate stuff he's figured out. But what I finally realized—from a writer's perspective rather than a mother's—is that he's got the nouns and verbs; it's the other parts of speech he's not capable of absorbing. For that's what typical children do—they absorb the language around them. Only he doesn't—not all of it. But what he doesn't absorb is significant, because knowledge builds on other knowledge.

I'm not under any circumstances going to romanticize the COVID-19 pandemic. What beneficial things came out of it weren't worth what we lost. Still, it, too, was a detour—for all of us. And it's been a hell of a long one at that.

For Callum, initially it was great. His favorite thing in the world—being with Mama and Daddy—was in abundant supply. I don't know if there's ever been anyone so happy to be under quarantine (or hurricane watch) as Callum. And at least during the pandemic we had power, devices, hot water, etc.

But heaven-on-earth got a little boring for him. Unfortunately, we lost our sitter, too, during quarantine, which was not so fun when working full-time from home. Between that and trying to homeschool two autistic middle schoolers simultaneously, I won't lie. Callum had a lot of free time. And the most interesting thing happened: he began to seek variety in his entertainment. Callum, who prior to the pandemic played only *The Wizard of Oz* or *Willy Wonka*, began wondering *what else was there* and demanding to see it. He began requesting we spend long minutes scrolling through each and every streaming service, while he signaled to keep scrolling, never settling on one.

He became impatient with waiting for me to get off the phone with students, and sought to figure out the microwave, to see what happened if he pressed all the Keurig buttons, and began exploring our music playlists on our phones. With all that time and cut off from all the stresses of the world, his innate curiosity kicked in.

When not busy defending himself from or reacting to the outside world, he's a different person. That shouldn't be such a shocking concept, but if you know or love someone autistic, seeing the results can steal your breath.

Because every little thing they are dealing with is *that much*. Consider what we could do with every school campus tuned in to that—how much more our children could learn, grow, and wonder.

The pandemic gave me a glimpse of my son *not* stressed and suffering overwhelm. It gave clarity on the impact of sensory stressors on . . .

everything. And it made me rethink what skills might be most important for him and which ones don't really matter.

We've all learned a lot about what truly matters.

And with all due respect to adjectives and conjunctions, they don't.

What matters is how we handle ourselves when our navigational guides fail us, with what attitude we *choose* to explore the detours, and how we show grace to the other drivers on the road.

Chapter 42

If You Were "Cured" Tomorrow: On What I'd Never Ask For

"If there were a cure for autism, would you give it to your son?"

Standing in front of a room of teachers I had facilitated an autism training for, I'll admit the question startled me. I had just answered a question about the causes of autism (not vaccines!) and what research was being done when her hand went up. I think I blinked a lot.

It's not that the question is surprising really. If you pay attention to the news or social media, people are always running 5Ks, raising money, and hash-tagging phrases like #cure4autism or some such. In the online autism community, it's discussed often. Either parent bloggers are sharing their autism-related hardships of the day and pleading to the masses for a cure or autistic self-advocates are warning of the dangers of science finding one and eradicating autistic tendencies in everyone. Opinions about theoretical cures abound.

Prior to our brief and ill-advised detour into the world of "alternative autism treatments," my answer would have been an easy yes. But, having witnessed high-needs autism in my family, it terrified me to see it in my toddler. Moreover, I had not yet learned about all the autistic people the world over leading happy and rewarding lives—lives with value.

But several years had passed since. I had fallen more and more in love with the beautiful little soul my son is. *Flappiness Is* had taken off, and I met people all over the world. Families, autistic adults, advocates, and more. I learned what was possible for those with autism, and I learned how many #actuallyautistic people did not want the core of their selves "cured."

There are great works of art, literature, music, science, technology, and more that wouldn't have existed were it not for those on the autism spectrum. And some autists have done absolutely none of those things but are still people who would no longer be themselves if not for autism.

Yet, I've also had opportunities to meet the most severely affected autists, who accompany profound intellectual disabilities. Those who cannot communicate—human beings wearing helmets so as to not harm themselves, bashing their heads against walls. People who will never have any real choices—any true freedom—in directing their own lives. And families haunted by the reality that one day they would die and leave their vulnerable loved ones in the care of those who might harm them.

Some might be shocked that I can't give that easy yes anymore. Because other parents would. They'd gladly trade having a self-harming, violent, intellectually disabled child for one who could care for themselves one day. And maybe they'd judge me for not jumping at the chance for a cure. But for me, with one child on the severe end and another on the mild, where is the line? Giving my daughter an increased attention span for math might be an easy fix for something that troubles her. But she's a delightfully quirky, hilarious person whose way of looking at the world contributes to it. I would not want to cure her of herself. I like who she is already.

How autism is manifested in my son is quite different. While he can communicate some, he can't communicate effectively enough to avoid intense frustration. His intellectual disability is significant enough that he will likely never understand many basic concepts. Certainly, he will never live without full-time support. But autism is not something that can be separated from who he is. It's woven into all parts of him. And if I were to cure those parts, he would no longer be Callum.

If you asked me if I would cure pancreatic cancer, I'd instantly tell you yes. Because cancer kills. But curing cancer will not erase cancer patients. They would continue to exist as the people they were before becoming ill.

Autism is not the same. It's more like the deaf community being asked if they all want to be cured. I can assure you their answer is no. Deafness is woven into their language and culture in a way that the hearing world does not understand. Well, autistic advocates feel the same way. They have their own communities, sense of identity, and pride. And that's understandable to me.

So, I'd say that Temple Grandin's response to the issue of curing autism is best. She remarked, "In an ideal world, the scientist should find a method to prevent the most severe forms of autism but allow the milder forms to survive." Yet we're a long way from that ideal world. And slippery slopes come to mind. What will satisfy us? What other traits will we seek to eliminate from the human spectrum?

No, I didn't have a simple answer for the question of curing autism. But later that night my heart had an instinctive response to the thought of it. And this is what it said to my children:

If You Were "Cured" Tomorrow

If you were cured tomorrow, life would be easier for you.
You could eat without ritual, go anywhere without fear, and would
    understand everything being said—even when it isn't being said.
If you were cured tomorrow, people wouldn't stare. Your play would
    not be questioned and corrected. You wouldn't feel compelled
    to move and shout and seek in the ways that you do. Instead,
    you would sit in rooms where people talked to you instead of
    about you.
If you were cured tomorrow, I would ask you to explain so many
    things.
If you were cured tomorrow, you would gain better access to all those
    beautiful dreams we wished for you before we knew you.

But, if you were cured tomorrow, you would be a stranger to me.
Living a stranger's dream.
And I would never get to see you live the dreams you have for yourself.

*If you were cured tomorrow, my worries would be eased—but my
    heart would be broken.*

*Because I love you. You you. Not some hypothetical you. Not the you
    you might have been had you not turned out to be you.*

It's all very complicated. And it's all very simple.

If you were cured tomorrow, I'd miss you.

On Things You Should Know
Before Jumping into the Autism Community

AAC—Assistive and Augmentative Communication. Basically anything you devise to assist someone with a disability in communicating. It can be as simple as finger signs (leading up to ASL) or a laminated set of pictures representing favorite items and activities, leading up to emotions and observations. (Callum stopped progressing at PECS (Picture Exchange Communication System) Level 4B—attributes and descriptives. We've been stuck there for a while now. That may be where he remains. If so, that's okay. We'll keep looking for better technologies and ideas to teach him the most self-sufficiency possible for him. *That's* success.

#actuallyautistic—This is a popular hashtag on social media. It's often used in posts where the writer wants responses from autistic people only. Other times, it's a statement. But you can bet anyone using it will always want to know if you've ever asked someone autistic, listened to or read work by someone autistic, etc. This crowd is all "nothing about us without us." And how could anyone not see their point? You don't create a nonprofit to encourage women entrepreneurs and then make the entire board of directors men. For one, the optics are terrible, and two, you're actually missing a vital perspective there. You're depriving yourself of good information, which is ultimately depriving somebody you love of *your* having it.

Articulation (speech)—Speech therapists assess your child in two areas really: communication and articulation. One is the ability to share information with others. The other is how you sound when you do it. Some kids need attention in both. But at Level 3 (highest needs), *communication* will always take precedence. Ultimately, it matters little how well you articulate when you don't know what to communicate. Don't worry about a lisp at this time if they can't communicate, "Stomach hurts." If your child isn't speaking, articulation is unlikely to be the problem. *First things first.*

ASL—American Sign Language. Somebody is going to write me about this, but I've considered all the pros and cons, and I'm just not a proponent of teaching ASL as AAC for autism. There are three reasons for this:

- The deaf community is a culture within itself. Unless the autistic child being taught ASL is also deaf or a hearing child of deaf parents part of a wider deaf community, I don't see an advantage to teaching a child to communicate in a language they will likely be exposed to only rarely. If an autistic child orders a grilled cheese at Applebee's by sign language, what is the statistical probability the server signs fluently? Maybe. Most likely not. But every server on the planet knows what they mean when they show a picture of a grilled cheese sandwich. Coming right up! That's the goal.

- In the way of all assumptions, we forget that the way we think of something may not be the same for everyone else. Many people would be shocked to know that ASL isn't merely a word-by-word finger translation of English. It's a whole different language—with different grammar, word order, and a lot more individuality involved in how things are described. If your child ultimately ends up without the capacity to understand grammar, then those single signs won't be much different in terms of being easily understood. By pushing sign language, you've essentially assigned a child with a communication disability to learn two languages instead of one.

- While delayed motor skills and other occupational therapy (OT) issues aren't a requirement for a diagnosis of autism, it is noted that they often occur simultaneously. It isn't at all uncommon for autistic children to be learning to use a fork in OT or to be using an adaptive pencil grip in class. Finger signing can be very specific, and children with motor skill deficits may struggle with it.

Asperger's/Aspie—Officially, at least in the United States, this diagnosis no longer exists in medicine. (It still does elsewhere, confusing everyone unnecessarily.) If you or a loved one received this diagnosis, your doctor probably won't bother correcting your preference for the term. As it stands now, in the United States, there's only "autistic disorder," and it's described individually by assigning levels. Level 1's needs require the least amount of assistance. Level 2 needs a moderate amount. Level 3 needs constant assistance. So, if you were an Aspie, now you're probably a "Level 1 autistic disorder." Yeah, I know. I like "Aspie" better, too. It's warm and fuzzy, whereas a leveled disorder is not. The good news is that nobody reasonable really cares if you still use the term. I use it. I mean it either descriptively, proudly, or affectionately. I get the argument that it's the same thing, simply to what degree. I'll even agree that's true. I know some folks prefer the term because it carries less of a stigma. The fact is that if you say "Asperger's," people assume a degree of capability. If you say "autism," they're not so sure. Suddenly, a bunch of questions get asked, and things can get difficult. Saying "Asperger's" is easier. Saying "Level 1 Autistic Disorder" is technically correct. Do with that what you want.

Autdar—Not a real word. But used humorously or observantly by many in the autism community who get good at picking up autistic clues and find themselves mentally diagnosing random strangers.

Autism Speaks—I can't believe I'm going to write this. But I wouldn't be a very good Scenic Route tour guide if I didn't warn you that not everybody loves Autism Speaks. There is a big part of the autism community that shuns anything related to it. But there's no question they're top in visibility and reach. I guess this is the part where I have to go on record, huh? Well . . . first let me say this a perfectly comfortable fence to sit on, and I plan to continue sitting here a spell. The gist is that Autism Speaks was founded with the intent to cure autism, something not at all appreciated by the self-advocate community and by those who support the values of neurodiversity. At the time of its inception, very little was known, very little research was conducted, and there were few resources for frightened and overwhelmed parents. I'm not going to dispute good intentions as I can't conceive of anything but its founders loving their children. That said, the organization took too long to evolve. It certainly took too long to listen. And even when it was getting some excellent advice by such brilliant minds as John Elder Robison, it didn't officially reject its own history of supporting questionable research. New people are at the helm now. The mission has reportedly changed. There is zero question that Autism Speaks has done some amazing things for the autism community in terms of legislation, fundraising, and providing resources. I'm cautiously optimistic that they're listening and responding, because they have considerable power. If everyone's missions aligned, they'd be a hell of an addition to the team in terms of people on the ground and resources. That's my hope anyway. Just know that if you befriend self-advocates and speak up in support of Autism Speaks, you may find yourself unfriended. I realize Autism Speaks might not like me saying that, but they can't deny that the perception exists. I know they have some good people doing good things working for them. But I think they'd be well-advised to consider issuing a more complete mea culpa.

BCBA—A BCBA is a Board Certified Behavior Analyst. There aren't a lot of them out there—a combination of unreasonable fee caps for their services combined with the level of work they must do to even reach that certification—so it can be hard to locate those services in more rural regions. Lots of people can apply the basic principles of positive reinforcement. You don't have to be a BCBA to perform applied behavior analysis. You just have to be observant and take good records. (There are many excellent guides for parents and teachers.) But BCBAs themselves are uniquely and expertly trained with thousands of clinical hours. They've seen every struggle out there. The good ones know the problem is rarely the child. The problem is almost always the environment. And that's not a judgmental statement necessarily. You can't help it if the store's overhead lights are triggering. Or if you're having a hard time making administration understand that placing a loud child with Tourette's in the same room as a sensory-avoidant autistic student is perhaps not the wisest decision. The problem with BCBAs and teachers is that teachers often feel threatened by the idea that the child was triggered in some way rather than that the child is the problem. Autism could almost be defined as the state of being easily triggered. But behavior analysts aren't looking to attack; they're merely recognizing patterns and making actionable, measurable, positive plans for replacing that behavior. Teachers, if a BCBA shows up in your room, dance a jig and *listen to their observations*. It's the most constructive, objective criticism you'll ever get. Pick their brains while you've got them. I studied it some in grad school. It's a fascinating field of study. As it turns out, we really are kind of predictable. Practiced according to modern ethics and values, and behavior analysis is a proven and humane way to teach or unteach hard-to-communicate concepts. And I like the way the good BCBAs and BCaBAs masterfully and positively coax kids into learning new skills.

Functional communication—This is the very first goal with a nonverbal or limited verbal child. Imagine landing via parachute in the middle of a foreign country where no one speaks your language. You're thirsty, hungry, have to pee, need a hotel, and everyone keeps looking at you, guessing wrong, and not meeting your needs. Pretty soon, you'd get highly frustrated. Eventually, you'd probably resort to pantomime or pictures. Your child might not yet conceive that objects and activities have names, images, icons, etc. If that's the case, then they don't understand that you know those words/images and will respond to them when prompted. Functional Communication Training (FCT) is a therapy with just that goal in mind. To have that "light of understanding that shone upon [her] little pupil's mind and behold, all things are changed!" breakthrough, a young Annie Sullivan had fingerspelled W-A-T-E-R over and over into Helen Keller's hand as she pumped water over it. Will achieving functional communication ensure that your child goes to college? No. To a large degree, that's up to their wiring. But if the wiring is there, you can find ways to connect it. What functional communication will do is provide your child access to their fellow humans. Without communication—whether spoken, written, or via images or "talkers"—a child is in solitary confinement. We already find that inhumane for murderers. How, then, do we find it acceptable for children?

Functioning—Here's a word that will earn you some enemies, the objection being that we are more than a list of our deficits. There's really no way to describe a snowflake with one word, because snowflakes are unique. So are people. What's deemed "high functioning" seems to be interpreted as conversational—thus little need for assistance. I know a fantastic self-advocate who can speak authoritatively on issues related to autism but lives with her supportive parents and cannot walk city streets by herself with confidence. Yet, despite the need for supports, she is able to hold a position working with children. Some would label her "high functioning." But you can't define anyone's functioning. You can only describe it in various contexts, and then look at the whole picture in helping make decisions. Having said that, from a professional perspective, I recognize the need to be able to refer to certain subsets of our student populations—for planning, for grouping, social interactions, etc. Not many other terms exist. Whether you're a professional, a loved one, or an autist, just remember that labels are tickets and placeholders.

They don't describe very well, and they don't have to define. It's funny how many words we humans have, and yet so many things aren't named well.

IDEA—The Individuals with Disabilities Education Act. Federal law that mandates a free and appropriate education for children with disabilities (to include providing needed therapeutic services). You probably haven't read the IDEA, but it is readable and not too long. Get out your highlighter and page flags and learn it. After that, go look up "landmark special education decisions." That's the meat of what you need to start learning about. You don't need to be a lawyer. But you need to know the law. Just as "Ignorantia juris non excusat" doesn't work as a defense for crime, it most definitely doesn't work as a defense for not advocating for your child.

IEP—Individualized Education Plan. Parents, you have a say-so in your child's IEP. The school may have failed to present it to you that way, but you do. Your job is to go learn about IEPs, IEP procedures, and IEP goals. Waiting until they start kindergarten is too late. Today is too late. Get on it.

Neurodiversity/the Neurodiverse—These are the preferred term(s) for describing anyone whose neurology and thinking aren't developmentally "typical." This would include autism, Asperger's (outside the United States), ADHD, dyslexia, apraxia of speech, and more.

Neurotypical—Anybody who isn't neurodiverse.

Occupational Therapy—This therapy is not about jobs or occupations *necessarily*, although it can be. Occupational therapists help patients learn alternative ways of accomplishing skills needed in their individual lives. For some children, that might mean assistance with writing. For others, dressing or self-feeding. It varies, but it all comes down to helping people do things independently.

Physical Therapy—May or may not be needed, based on the physical coordination and development of the child. But it's common for autistic children to require assistance with activities such as climbing stairs (a patterning issue), balance, kicking, throwing, swinging, and riding a tricycle.

Recovered—All right, I'll say it. *There is no such thing.* You cannot reshape your child's brain and neurons. Because that's where it comes from. Go watch any presentation on autism and brains by Dr. Brenda Smith Myles, and walk out and tell me I'm wrong. She's got a lot of brain scans to show you. Combine those with any basic study of brain-based learning, and you'll suddenly understand why those with autism struggle with this or why they can't do that. Since we can't regrow either limbs or brains, autists must learn to work around their disability to the extent they are able. If they do an exceptional job of it because they're wired in such a way as to be able to compensate well *and* they are fortunate to have good teachers, therapists, friends, and family, they might be able to "pass" as not autistic. In that event, they might lose their diagnosis because it isn't evident then. But their wiring didn't change. Those who know them best will still see it when they rip off their masks. The problem, of course, is what it takes from them to fake it all day. It's no wonder autism and self-harm are so closely connected. In short, no. Your sister's best friend's aunt's star-level MLM product businesswoman can say whatever she's taught to say. But that grape juice did not "recover" your child or anybody else's.

Self-advocate—In the autism community, this means an #actuallyautistic person who advocates on behalf of themselves and others with autism. Like any other category of people, they're not all in agreement on all the controversial issues. There are nice ones. There are not nice ones. But I think it's important to listen to them. After all, they understand a part of your child you never will.

Sensory Integration Disorder—Almost all autistic people have it, and it looks different for all of them. It comes down to the autistic brain being unable to correctly process sensory input. Either they under-process and crave it. Or they overprocess it and are overwhelmed to the point of meltdowns or panic attacks. SID is the culprit behind most negatively perceived classroom behaviors. What autism specialists aim to do is help others understand that those negatively perceived behaviors are a student's ineffective attempts to communicate their distress about something. Our primary job is to teach them to communicate in any way possible so as to mitigate that distress.

Spectrum—First it was puzzle pieces. Now "spectrum" is becoming less popular as a conceptual representation. Critics believe it propagates the cookie-cutter concept of severity versus individuality (the aforementioned woman who does not cross the street alone). Autistic people rarely fit the spectrum model. They might have some traits you'd consider Level 3 but be able to do something else you'd associate more with a Level 1. There's a newer conceptual model of autistic differences I like better and will list in "Places to Go and Things to See."

Speech Therapy—Speech therapy addresses two things: language and articulation. A student or patient may need either or both. With autism, the SLP (speech-language pathologist) will typically focus on receptive and expressive communication, AAC, as well as helping them communicate appropriately in social situations. Articulation is about the movements of the mouth and tongue in making sound. Articulation therapy would be for issues like a lisp. Speech therapists also can assist with feeding and swallowing issues.

Speech vs. Communication—To the average person unaffected by disorders involving hearing, articulation, or intelligence, communication is either spoken or written. To imagine an existence without the ability to produce spoken or written language is so mind-blowing and tragic that they refuse the one speech therapy approach most likely to result in spoken and written communication! It's a myth that picture exchange, sign language, and other AAC reduce an autistic child's chances of becoming verbal. It's actually the opposite, although nothing is ever guaranteed. Callum has had it all and, at twelve, still uses verbal approximations of a limited number of words. Some he has mis-generalized, but they've become his vocabulary anyway. He simply isn't wired for more. His receptive language is much stronger than his expressive, but he isn't always motivated to display it upon request. Despite a significant and very real intellectual disability, he's quite smart about some things. See my point about the fallacy of labels regarding people? The research overwhelmingly shows early intervention, including AAC, to be beneficial in bringing about a best outcome for the individual child. When we began, he was beating his head on the floor. As he learned to communicate more, his outbursts lessened. He'd been communicating all along. We just hadn't been listening. Now, he happily goes places and chooses from menus and hangs with Daddy at the barber or car wash and is a happy child. Most of the time. And when he isn't, we relentlessly search for clues before chalking it up to something else entirely, which I address in Chapter 20, "What I'll Never Know: On Inexplicable Tears and Autism." Most of the time, we figure it out with his help, combinations of AAC, and whomever has more patience that day.

Stimming—Self-stimulation. I know. Sounds tawdry, doesn't it? But get your mind out of the gutter. That's not what we mean. Stimming is any repetitive behavior a person uses to self-soothe, regulate, or self-entertain. It often involves the senses such as scent, movement (touch), sound, or interesting visual . . . enthusiasms (watching out of their peripheral vision, for example). Callum stims with a ball, his voice, and by rocking while listening to music. Every person is different.

Vaccine injured—Whenever you encounter this expression in a post or thread or casual conversation, I want the words "Danger! Danger!" to echo in your mind before you extricate yourself as quickly as possible toward the nearest exit. You're going to see a bunch of overconfident people proudly share "the secret truth" revealed in standard vaccine inserts required by the FDA. Vaccine injury is indeed mentioned. And it does happen. Some people have such a violent allergic reaction to a substance that their airway is constricted, and they suffer brain damage from oxygen deprivation. That causes parts of their brains to not function properly. Many of those behaviors would be described and diagnosed as autistic. So any attorney worth their salt—and you better believe the FDA can afford some good attorneys—included the diagnosis in the tiny package insert that accompanies every drug in America, along with everything else that can accompany the severest of allergic drug reactions, including death. That is not at all the same thing as "the government admitting vaccines cause autism right there in the insert!" It's just not. If you don't believe me, ask a lawyer. They'll explain. I'm sorry for those who suffered the loss of children to an extreme allergic reaction. But there are far more parents mourning children who've unnecessarily died of preventable diseases. Would I choose thousands over dozens? It may be painful, but my answer is yes. How could it not be? Vaccinate your children. They were autistic in the womb, not because of the MMR.

Places to Go and Things to See:

On People to Follow, Organizations to Know, and Books to Read

WEBSITES

ADDITUDE: https://www.additudemag.com/

The Arc: https://thearc.org/

Asperger/Autism Network: https://www.aane.org/

Autcraft: https://www.autcraft.com/

Autism Live: https://autism-live.com/

Autistic Self Advocacy Network (ASAN): https://autisticadvocacy.org/

Autism Internet Modules: https://autisminternetmodules.org/

Autism Science Foundation: https://autismsciencefoundation.org/

Autism Society: https://www.autism-society.org/

Autism Speaks: https://www.autismspeaks.org/

Center for Parent Information and Resources: https://www.parentcenterhub.org/

Disability Scoop: https://www.disabilityscoop.com/

LessonPix: https://lessonpix.com/

National Autism Association: https://nationalautismassociation.org/

National Autism Center: https://www.nationalautismcenter.org/

Organization for Autism Research: https://researchautism.org/

Paws 4 Autism: https://www.paws4autism.org/

Picture Exchange Communication System (PECS): https://pecsusa.com/pecs/

Project Lifesaver: https://projectlifesaver.org/

Sibling Leadership Network: https://siblingleadership.org/

Simons Foundation Autism Research Initiative (SFARI): https://www.sfari.org/

SPARK: https://sparkforautism.org/

Special Olympics: https://www.specialolympics.org/

Spectrum News: https://www.spectrumnews.org/

The Spectrum Wheel: https://themighty.com/2020/03/autism-spectrum-wheel/

Surfers for Autism: https://surfersforautism.org/
Thinking Person's Guide to Autism: http://www.thinkingautismguide.com/
Wrightslaw: https://www.wrightslaw.com/

BOOKS

Aching Joy by Jason Hague
The Asperkid's (Secret) Book of Social Rules by Jennifer Cook O'Toole
Autism Adulthood, 2nd ed., by Susan Senator
Autism in Heels by Jennifer Cook O'Toole
Autism Spectrum Disorder by Chantal Sicile-Kira
Beyond the Wall, 2nd ed., by Stephen Shore
Blazing My Trail by Rachel B. Cohen-Rottenberg
Chicken Soup for the Soul for Parents Raising Kids on the Spectrum by Dr.
    Rebecca Landa, Mary Beth Marsden, Nancy Burrows, and Amy Newmark
The Hidden Curriculum by Dr. Brenda Smith Myles
High-Functioning Autism and Difficult Moments by Dr. Brenda Smith Myles
How to Be Human: An Autistic Man's Guide to Life by Jory Fleming
I Wish I Were Engulfed in Flames by Jeni Decker
Ketchup Is My Favorite Vegetable by Liane Kupferberg Carter
Letters to Sam by Daniel Gottlieb
Look Me in the Eye by John Elder Robison
Love That Boy by Ron Fournier
Making Peace with Autism by Susan Senator
Neurotribes by Steve Silberman
Raising Cubby by John Elder Robison
The Reason I Jump by Naoki Higashida
Ten Things Every Child with Autism Wishes You Knew by Ellen Notbohm
Thinking in Pictures by Temple Grandin
Thinking Person's Guide to Autism edited by Shannon Des Roches Rosa,
    Jennifer Byde Myers, Liz Ditz, Emily Willingham, and Carol Greenburg
A Thorn in My Pocket by Eustacia Cutler
Uniquely Human by Dr. Barry M. Prizant
Visual Supports for People with Autism by Marlene J. Cohen and Donna L. Sloan
We're Not Broken by Eric Garcia
*What I Wish I'd Known about Raising a Child with Autism: A Mom and a
    Psychologist Offer Heartfelt Guidance for the First Five Years* by Bobbi
    Sheahan and Kathy DeOrnellas
Wrightslaw: From Emotions to Advocacy by Pam Wright and Pete Wright

Acknowledgments

It astonishes me to be writing acknowledgments for this book. Not because I'm not enormously grateful to many, but because I never planned to write a book. As a daydreamy girl, a terrible poet, and an avid reader, I dreamed about it. But I figured I probably wouldn't, because what would I write about? Yet here we are. This life is something else.

First and foremost, this book wouldn't exist without my children. So, above everyone, I must thank them for giving me our story. From these two, I've learned more about compassion, respect, patience, tenacity, and courage than I could have ever imagined. They have been my greatest teachers in this life, and I am the luckiest mother in the world to call them mine. I love you and thank you, my babies. *Honest to goodness, I do* . . .

I would also like to thank all the lovely #ActuallyAutistic readers, writers, and self-advocate friends I've met along the way. Your insight and friendship has been immeasurable to my understanding, and I thank you—in particular, Chloe Rothschild, Rachel Cotton, Stacy Woodruff, Audra Parker, and Janni Ball. Thanks for pointing out what my eyes might have missed.

Thank you to my readers, who've shared their stories, suggestions, celebrations, and more over the years. Many of you have become dear friends over the years, and I adore y'all.

I won the author lottery when my editor, Sara Carder, "found" me online and believed I could do this. From go, I've relied on her wisdom and vision. My agent told me, "Sara is the *best* at what she does." And she didn't lie. Thank you for everything.

Speaking of agents, I need to thank Michelle Tessler of the Tessler Agency for taking on a writer clueless to the book publishing world and helping me to navigate this process. Not even once did she shake her head and say aloud, "How on earth do you not know this?!" Thank you for your guidance, encouragement, and bang-up representation.

I want to give a big shout-out to assistant editor Ashley Alliano for her always kind help with all the details and deadlines that accompany writing a book. And I'd like to thank the entire crew at TarcherPerigee for helping to transform a vision into a reality. You rock. And sorry about all those instances of "etc." Every time I use that abbreviation, I'll reconsider and think of you.

I read somewhere that writers fresh under contract do one of two things (I don't know if that's true): they either get insecure and clingy with need for reassurance, or they disappear into a hole during the book-writing process. I kind of dropped into a hole for two years. But I wasn't ever alone. I'd like to thank those friends and mentors who read drafts, allowed me to bounce ideas, or otherwise emotionally supported me: Rhona Scoville and the rest of the "Florida Mafia," Erica Rountree and my beloved Girls Night Out Gang, Dr. Sara Beth Hopton, Jennifer Sykes, Koleena Schmidt, Jamila Theobold, Jodi Collins, Kim Richards, Jeni Decker, Lydia Mayhood, Jason Hague, Jackie Carey, Ashley McCool, Liane Kupferberg Carter, and Christy Cothron.

Thank you to all past and present members of The Group That Cannot Be Named. You know who you are and how you've supported me. Man, I love you jerks. #FlushTheSporns!

For every professional who aided in my understanding, thank you. This includes Jennifer Middleswart, James Buchanan, Dr. Sarabeth Kirkland, Debbie Lennon, Robin Calhoun, Julie Porch, and all the therapists who've ever worked with my children.

If it weren't for Team Callum—Dawn Blankenship, Linda Becker, Myrt Hill, Maria Herrera, Rachel Fells, and all the wonderful school administration, teachers, and support staff—understanding how frazzled I've been, sending texts and extra reminders, ensuring I got school pictures, and forgiving me for forgetting Fall Festival, I wouldn't have made it. Thanks for taking care of my boy with such love during this time. It's meant everything.

Thanks to the kind staff at the Palatka Holiday Inn Express for taking care of me on all those weekend writing stays. And especially for the late checkouts. You're the best!

A very special thank-you is owed to my Millennial Therapist Extraordinaire, Justin Dement, and the best psychiatrist the whole world, Dr. Jacqueline Henschke. Just by doing the amazing work you do, you held this neurotic writer together for the past couple of years. I'm forever grateful. No, you may never relocate. I have spoken.

I'm indebted to my family (and Kayla Boyd!) for their support, childcare, chauffeuring, advice (even when I annoyingly don't follow it), and understanding while I've lived in this "hole." You kept me going.

To my mother, late father, uncle, and beloved teachers who worked to instill in me a love of reading and writing. Hey, it worked!

Daddy, I know you, Sheila, and Granny would be beaming. I sure wish I could've seen that.

None of this would have been possible if not for my husband, Sean, and for his own trust in allowing me to share our lives, for believing in me, for meals delivered to the bedroom, for disco funk dancing breaks in the kitchen, and for all those hours holding down the fort while I disappeared to write. And he still looks hot in a kilt. Thanks, Baby.

Last but not least, my eternal love and gratitude to Jenni Mayhood, Sandy Tilton, and Dr. Beverly Roseberry. You three already know what your love, support, and *showing up* has meant to me. I have a spare kidney and a shovel (to bury a body)—no questions asked—set aside should you ever need me. I love you.